Praise for *Through a Long Absence*

"In this meticulously researched and intricately imagined story, Joy Passanante honors—in the best possible way—the love her parents discovered in their youth, maintained through the long absence of war, and carried to the grave (and one imagines, beyond it). Elegiac and deeply loving in tone, this daughter's re-creation of her parents' lives also serves as a reminder of the toll war takes on the human souls of the survivors."

　　—Pam Houston, author of *Contents May Have Shifted*

"With skill and devotion, Joy Passanante follows the trail of her father's youth working for a bootlegger, his passionate courtship of her mother, and his years as a U.S. Army doctor overseas and under fire in World War II. Her book is a remarkable and moving tribute to family love and tradition."

　　—Alison Lurie, Pulitzer Prize winner

"With insight and compassion, Joy Passanante embarks on a journey to investigate one of the great and often unsettling mysteries of life—who were our parents before we came into their lives?"

　　—John Sayles, novelist and filmmaker

"*Through a Long Absence* is bursting at the seams with the real stuff of life. War, love, loss, family—all these play out in the classic American context of an immigrant striving toward that hard-won place in the sun. Joy Passanante's wise and passionate memoir is a moving testament not just to her family but also to the deep thing in all of us that keeps turning—and, on some level, never stops yearning—for the people and places in our past that are the soul's true home."

　　—Ben Fountain, National Book Critics Circle Award winner

Germany, June 1945. Major Bart Passanante, waiting to go home weeks after the peace treaty was signed in Europe.

THROUGH A LONG ABSENCE

WORDS FROM MY FATHER'S WARS

Joy Passanante

MAD CREEK BOOKS, AN IMPRINT OF
THE OHIO STATE UNIVERSITY PRESS
COLUMBUS

Mad Creek Books, an imprint of The Ohio State University Press.

Library of Congress Cataloging-in-Publication Data is available online at https://
catalog.loc.gov.

Cover design by Nathan Putens
Text design by Juliet Williams
Type set in Adobe Sabon and Futura

♾ The paper used in this publication meets the minimum requirements of the
American National Standard for Information Sciences—Permanence of Paper for
Printed Library Materials. ANSI Z39.48–1992.

9 8 7 6 5 4 3 2 1

*For my beloved sisters, Judy Passanante and
Jean Passanante, who shared my good fortune in
having such extraordinary parents.*

And, of course, in memory of Bertie and Bart.

CONTENTS

NORTH AFRICA—DECEMBER 24, 1942 TO JULY 28, 1943

SICILY, ITALY—JULY 30, 1943 TO NOVEMBER 11, 1943

ENGLAND—NOVEMBER 26, 1943 TO JUNE 9, 1944

FRANCE—JUNE 10, 1944 TO SEPTEMBER 28, 1944

ILLUSTRATIONS FOLLOW PAGE 192.

ACKNOWLEDGMENTS

THIS BOOK IS a collaboration of sorts. To tell my father's story more effectively, I have integrated many of my father's words and phrases into the narrative without quotation marks. Although I have at times altered the chronology and added contextual details, the saga of the 91st Evacuation Hospital and of World War II is presented as communicated by Bart in letters, diaries, interviews, and personal conversations. I have been true to his thoughts and sentiments, either as he expressed them or as I envisioned them from context and experience.

My gratitude extends to many other people on three continents:

To our current three-generation Passanante clan, Bart and Bertie's offspring—my children, sisters, niece, their spouses and progeny—for their unflagging, loving support and uncountable forms of assistance: Emily Caterina Williams, Liza Bryn Williams, Jean Passanante, Judy Passanante, Regina Corrado, Richard Rodgers, Jack Shannon, Ruth Passanante Shannon, and Yan Shikhvarger. And to Bart and Bertie's great-grandson, Lorenzo James Corrado, who brings such joy to us all.

To Debbie de Schweinitz Abbott, Jan Tureen Abrams, Bonnie Creinin, Susan Davis, Lynn Eder, Cathy Goldstein, Kenny Marotta, Anita Smolens McAuliffe, Tom McAuliffe, Yvonne Sertich, Nancy Williger, and Harriet Silverblatt Worobey—most of whom were my first readers and have been my friends since childhood, and who loved my parents as family.

To inspiring writers Mary Clearman Blew and Alexandra Teague for their judicious critiques of full drafts. To Brittney Carman, Jeff P. Jones, Michele Leavitt, Andrea Mason, Sally Pfeifer, Sean Prentiss, and Rochelle Smith for their astute reading as this work evolved.

To Deborah Ann "Duffy" Taylor, whose aunt, Lt. Margaret House, also served with the 91st Evacuation Hospital, for sharing her extensive knowledge about the unit and for her long-distance camaraderie on my journey.

I am deeply moved by the extended Zangara family for offering my husband and me their generosity, warmth, expertise, hospitality, and time; for giving me permission to use details from their father's diary in my writing; and for making us feel like family: Sabina Taranto; Fausta Zangara, Franco Zappardo, and Valeria Zappardo; Piergiorgio Zangara and Laura Mazzeo; Manuela Zangara and Clint deSouza; and Maria Stella Zangara.

Additional gratitude to Jan Tureen Abrams and Bob Abrams, Cathy Goldstein and Carl Schwarz, and Nancy Williger for enabling my research in St. Louis. Thanks, too, to Douglas Q. Adams for his careful reading and encouragement over many years; to Richard Bradley for his warm perspective on my mother's administrative assistant work for his father at Barnes Hospital during the war years; and to Douglas Hyde and Catherine Hyde Luchessi for generously lending me their father's diary.

I also owe a great deal to my translators—Rosanna Lauriola, Kurt Queller, James Reece, and Sabina Taranto—as well as to my transcribers and other assistants on the many pages of Bart's legacy: my steadfast friend Alice Pope Barbut as well as Amanda Cox, Rachael Guenthner, Jennifer Baillargeon-Hauck, Melanie James, Julia Brumer Levy, Kelly Roberts, Micah Ross, and Cara Stoddard.

I was fortunate to be able to augment my understanding of the journey of the 91st through my heartfelt relationships with 91st Chaplain George Riday and Ambrose "Bucky" Shields. I will always be inspired by their memories as well as those of Edgar Hyde, Harry Meyer, and Bennedetto Zangara. Thanks also to the late Wilda Rush, nurse with the 91st Evacuation Hospital, for her kind words about my father.

Gratitude for memories, information, and support is due also to the late Benjamin "Bud" Milder, Annika Olsson Hofstetter and Christoph Hofstetter, Ron McFarland, Beatrice Wallins, Jo Ann Simanella, Eliot Jonathan Rosenbloom, Ellen Rosenbloom Jones, Jan Boll, Richard Naskali, Prudence Arndt, Jenna Putnam, Chad Burt, Joe Pallen, Helen Cooksey, and Susan Love.

In addition, my work benefited from the following: William "Zelli" Fischetti, associate director, and Kenn Thomas, senior archivist, at the State Historical Society of Missouri St. Louis Research Center; Philip Skroska, archivist at the Bernard Becker Medical Library of the Washington University School of Medicine; Jesse Thomas, library specialist interlibrary loans, and Kristin Henrich, reference and instruction librarian, at the University of Idaho; Gail Wiese, archivist for digital collections and access services, and Jennifer Payne, archives assistant, at Norwich University Archives and Special Collections; Cynthia Hayes, director of Tulane Medical Alumni Relations and Constituency Programs; Mary Holt, history librarian at Tulane University's Rudolph Matas Library; and Helen Weisler, program manager of Tulane University's Graduate Medical Education. Also thanks to Dr. Gijs van der Ham, The Rijksmuseum's senior curator.

Thanks, too, to the friendly, helpful people in Europe who engaged in my search, especially Inge Fild in Wolfenbüttel; Lei Tummers and his son Phillippe in Valkenburg; Herr and Frau Schombar and Herr Bühmer in Geilshausen; Kaye and Jim Thomas of the Huntsman Inn in Falfield; the kind man who worked in the back room at the Utah Beach Musée du débarquement in Ste.-Marie-du-Mont, and the lovely little lady in La Cambe who so moved me that I forgot to ask her name.

Travel and research for this book were made possible in part by a Research Fellowship from the Idaho Humanities Council, the state-based affiliate of the National Endowment for the Humanities. (Conclusions or opinions expressed do not necessarily reflect the views of the IHC or the NEH.) I am also grateful to the University of Idaho and its Department of English for two sabbatical research semesters.

An earlier version of passages from my epilogue appeared in my essay "Visitations" in *Shenandoah* in 2007.

I owe more than I can say to my excellent editor, Kristen Elias Rowley, for her incisive reading and canny suggestions, but mostly for her admiration for my father and for her faith in me over more than half a decade.

I have saved the most noteworthy for last. The only reason this book is no more than flights of fancy and a muddle of papers is my partnership with my extraordinary husband, Gary Williams— researcher, literary critic, writer, editor, and tireless traveling cohort— who read every word in every draft and is in every important way Bertie and Bart's true and beloved son.

A TRIPTYCH

AMHERST AVENUE, ST. LOUIS, MISSOURI, 1950

Her mother opens the door. She has buttoned up her daughter in a gingham jumper and a puffed-sleeved blouse with a Peter Pan collar. The sleeves of her cardigan sweater are rolled at the wrists. The girl jumps down the tall concrete steps from the porch of the dark-red brick duplex where she lives and with the toes of her soft saddle shoes swishes the leaves along the path to the sidewalk. When she kicks the leaves to see how far toward the sky they will fly up, an orange one cleaves to the lace trim of her sock.

Before she skips across the sidewalk toward the lamppost near the curb, she peers down at the other two-story brick houses like hers to where the street ends in a T. She wants to swing on the lamppost while she looks down the street. The lamppost shoots up toward the clouds.

She stretches open her arms to hug the chilly, forest-green fluted column, hops up a little to wrap her legs around it and hug with her whole body. Her arms and legs don't quite reach around, but she hangs on with the tips of her fingers and presses her thighs together until they are tight and keep the rest of her upright so from her slightly raised position she can get a wider view of the street.

The sky is already turning a bruised blue. What does she think of as the column's vertical ridges dig into her fingers and palms? Her gaze is focused on the street, but all that's happening there is the waltz of the leaves, their edges scratching against the sidewalk as they tumble out into the street. Her mother hasn't buttoned her sweater, but she likes it open so she can feel the wind closer to her skin. She knows with certainty that rounding the corner of the street will soon appear a figure, topped with a dark hat and carrying a black bag the size of a big shoebox but with a handle, and he'll have a newspaper rolled under his arm, and that when he sees her on the lamppost, his strides will lengthen and then she will unwrap herself from her perch and leap down and come running toward him on the sidewalk since she isn't allowed to step into the street, and he will increase his speed when he sees her with her toes on the tip-top of the curb and a smile will take over his entire face, and he'll shift his newspaper to the hand holding the bag, and he'll begin to lean forward with his arms spread out, and then he'll break into a run, and she'll jump up and down in place on the sidewalk, her toes curled up and her hands little fists, and then he'll swoop her up and kiss her with his scratchy mustache and she'll fling her arms around him, and her legs, too.

One day, in almost a lifetime of days, she will think of this as her earliest memory. She will remember having seen a photograph of herself as the little girl in the gingham jumper hugging the lamppost—or perhaps the photo was of herself as a little girl in a plaid shirt and the corduroy overalls with suspenders, her thin pigtails plaited with satin ribbons, her elbows dimpling as she clenches her arms and legs around the lamppost. She believes her father took this picture with the camera he bought after the war and developed it in the darkroom he built in the basement of the duplex. The photo was a large print, a black-and-white with crisp white borders. It was curled up slightly so that if, decades later, when she was cleaning out the apartment her mother lived in for four years after her father died, she had found the actual print her father had developed, she might have pressed it in a book— say, in his *Gray's Anatomy,* or perhaps in her collection of Wordsworth's poetry, which also contained a daisy blossom pressed and dried between two waxed paper squares, which, she vaguely recalls, she saved from an era much later in her life, commemorating some romantic encounter with a young man whose name has drifted away. But in the way of it, in the chaotic constellation of losses death presents, that photograph of her wrapped around the lamppost on Amherst Avenue never did appear. And Memory, that trickster, that melancholy son-of-a-bitch, has shaken her up, and she isn't certain what she was wearing or even if it was a gusty October day. Or even if the picture is only secreted, or trapped, in the fly-by-night furrows of her temporal lobe.

But she did find another print, one that, she has begun to realize, reminds her of the lamppost picture that may never have existed. Her mother had saved it in a Pee-Chee folder just after her father died. This other picture, its white border scalloped, its sheen grainy, is a glimpse of a later decade, after the war. It was taken—*by whom?* she wonders. *Where?* In this picture, her mother and father are sitting together in a large upholstered chair. But she doesn't recognize it as a chair in the recreation room or the living room of the house her parents designed and had built in the new suburbs west of the city, in what was then deemed "the country." She doesn't recognize the curtains either. Her mother's hair is clipped short and, even though she can't be more than forty, is already shiny with silver. His mustache is a slim, dark stripe. He is seated in the center of the chair. His wife is behind him. Her hands are folded on each other on top of his clavicle. His hands are folded just below hers, lower on his ribcage. He is leaning back into her. Her black Capri pants are spangled with silver, her sparkly knees splayed out in a perfect diamond that starts in back of him and ends on top of him; the bottoms of her feet meet on the chair just below the crotch of his pants. She is peeking out impishly from his side. His legs are open, feet flat to the floor. She is dreamy-eyed, he is delighted. They are intertwined, as if they had been born to stay that way forever.

CHEVY CHASE, ST. LOUIS, MISSOURI, THE 1990S

Every morning of my yearly summer visit, before the sun could warm the water, I'd wake up in the room of my youth in the bed with the blue ball-fringed canopy and dust ruffle and immediately don my bathing suit. I'd sail downstairs, out the recreation room door, toward the pool. By then, my father, Bart Passanante, had already hosed down the patio and tile that rimmed the water and moved the redwood lounge

I'd been occupying for a score or so of summer visits. He'd place the lounge close to but not under the shade of the Japanese maple in the pool garden. That way, he could maximize my sunlight before the heat and humidity could sink their teeth into my skin, scorch and drain me in turns. As the heat deepened, he'd pull my perch into the shade so that my view would be the daylilies that trumpeted out every day with the precision of a metronome.

Whenever he entered the pool garden on his rounds with his bucket and hose and rubber fishing boots and hoes and weeders, I stared at him, relishing his idiosyncrasies. He poked his grass here and there with what looked like a pronged stick. When he glanced up from his work and saw me looking at him, he dimpled up. He paused from time to time to straighten his back and admire his zinnias and cacti garden, and, if I was there in June, the daisies, which were my wedding flower and which he always timed to bloom when I was back in St. Louis. Occasionally he gestured to show me a plump worm of the sort he used to dig up when he took me fishing, or a sprig of poison ivy. We smiled at each other, and I was happy to be in his presence.

From this seamless-seeming bank of pleasure-days, my memory proffers me two hours in particular, both scenes tinted with the preternatural brilliance of Technicolor. Scene 1: I am perched on the lounge next to a small redwood table, a splintered leg of which my father has bound up with a generous hunk of the adhesive tape he once used in dressing the wounds of his patients. He is nearly deaf by then, and I usually need a pad and pencil to communicate clearly. Though I always keep these supplies at hand when I know I will be with him, and they are now on the table, I seldom use them. We never seemed to need to say much to each other.

Writing away on an idea for a novel, I'm only vaguely aware that he has ducked into the house. When he returns to the patio, he's toting a stack of worn-looking books. He sets aside my notepad and pencil and lays down the books. At first I don't recognize them.

"Did I ever show you my war diaries?" he asks, his voice a little uncertain since he can't hear how loud he's talking. I shake my head, feeling the sting of shame at remembering a Christmas night when our annual holiday party was waning, when he wanted my sisters and me and all our friends to listen to him read from his diaries, and we, deafened by our youthful narcissism, chose not to. Shame, too, at the fact that I am relieved that he doesn't seem to remember. Knowing what I know now, I can hardly believe that I felt relief at the desertion of his memory.

"Would you like to see these?" he asks sheepishly.

"I'd love to," I say, raising my volume. I pluck a book from the pile. It's not a diary but a photo album with black-and-whites meticulously organized and labeled, stuck with black photo corners. As I begin to thumb through it, he beams, then resumes his tour of duty around his lawn.

I spend the better part of the month immersed in these books, and, sometimes when I glance at him puttering in his garden, rubbing the moisture from my eyes.

Scene 2: On the last day of that summer's visit, Diary Volume 4 propped up on my knees, he comes up behind me, startling me.

"I don't suppose you would want to have these someday, would you?" he asks, pointing to the pile on the table. I look askance. How could he even think I wouldn't want them?

"Of course," I shout so he can hear. "We all would. Anyone would."

He nods, though I'm not sure he has understood my exact words. But he has certainly read my expression.

"Well, if you want them, I'd like you to have them," he says. Since he can no longer hear his own voice clearly, his words emerge a little unsteady, and some of the syllables crack and lilt up a timbre. Before I can rise from the lounge to throw my arms around his neck and yell directly into his ear, he disappears around the fence.

He still had his memory then, and I like to think he remembered giving me that gift of gifts that afternoon under the Japanese maple even after he could no longer remember my name.

DELMAR BOULEVARD, ST. LOUIS, MISSOURI, 2005

In the fall of 2005, six months after I cleaned out my mother's apartment on Delmar Boulevard and bid a goodbye to St. Louis so wrenching that my guts buckled under my skin, I opened the acid-proof boxes containing the four diaries my mother had preserved, the four volumes my father had promised would be mine. Every feature of his pages shimmered out at me: his loopy script, his slightly pompous use of grammar, his exclamation points and double-underlines, his hunger for the woman my sisters and I had so recently helped die with dignity and grace.

Beyond their overt subject matter, the diaries brought my childhood whooshing back in unexpected ways. In my father's descriptions of the gifts he bought my mother from the war, for instance, I saw all the knickknacks scattered about the house I grew up in, including some I brought to my first show-and-tell. I also saw the three framed water-colors—a church, a farmhouse, a windmill—that hung in his study and that he eventually gave my two sisters, Judy and Jeannie, and me. Rereading his words so often that they had metamorphosed into litany, suddenly I wanted to know *that* man, the man Alberta Rosenbloom, my mother Bertie, fell in love with and, against substantial odds, mar-ried. Thus, I stepped over the threshold that would lead me not only to Europe to follow his footsteps, but to the frayed edges of memory—a quest that would push me in directions that would sometimes seem to cross the border into obsession as I nursed an urge to see what he saw, to understand what he did, to feel as he felt during the war.

And by then, in 2005, to map my way, I have not only the diaries but four notebooks of letters that Bart wrote Bertie almost daily in an attempt to span the jagged cleft the war had sliced into their marriage. There are 1,365 pages of them. They embellish the diaries, laying bare some of the emotional undercurrents of their life together as well as their life apart. His words reveal an idiosyncratic stylist who revels in the intricacies of syntax and diction, a military officer proud to serve his country, a conscientious physician, a would-be artist, an accom-plished pianist, an American whose ancestral roots are embedded in the sun-drenched terrain of southern Italy, who, except on the sultriest of days, always feels chilled, and the ardent lover—always, always—of Alberta Rosenbloom Passanante, Bertie, his wife.

SIXTY-THREE YEARS EARLIER, from the ship that will take him overseas toward the war, my father writes her the first of these letters. His handwriting evokes the labels on masking tape I remember that he adhered to every medicine bottle and film canister, his meticulous lists of his daily responsibilities as well as the notes he scribbled to all of us whom he longed to communicate with but was no longer able to hear. The same script on the scraps of paper on which he jotted down patches of memory he fought to keep alive as his cerebral cortex played pitiless tricks with increasing frequency on his thinking, his articulating, and even his dreaming. I also recognize, in the loops of his alphabet and the back-slant of his sentences, the loops and back-slant of my own. All these years later, I read into those coils and curves the bodiless intercourse he and his beloved conducted over several oceans and an unfathomable number of anonymous fields.

Here is his letter.

Dearest adorable wife:

Strict censorship forbids me mentioning dates, destination or climactic conditions so judge this accordingly. I love you terribly much and miss you as only you yourself must know. But let me set your mind at rest about me.

First of all the ocean voyage up until now (and we're just a stone's throw from our destination) has been unexpectedly pleasant. Except for occasional consciousness of monotony the trip has been most enjoyable and interesting. I DID NOT GET SEASICK. The first day or so I felt a little rocky and dizzy but I developed my sea-legs quickly. However a good portion of my friends were afflicted with mal-de-mer.

My voracious appetite is being most pleasantly appeased to say the least. The cuisine has been an epicurean's dream. That's the truth. I'm going to hate to leave this ship on that account. I'm sending a menu.

My roommates consist of Harry Meyer, Pearson, O'Brien, Kemp and Riday. They have been very pleasant and humorous. Entertainment is limited, of course, and I have played a great deal of bridge.

I am content in our destination which is not what you and I expected. But I hoped to go there—remember. I won't see Leo Gottlieb.

My strolls on deck have been frequent and for long periods. It is much better there than inside—just the way I like it.

Needless to say I'm in perfect health. I know you are well and that you are keeping warm, eating your vegetables and not being sad.

I hope your financial matters are all cleared up and buy yourself a couple of dresses for me—and I haven't played poker.

There is very little else to write about, sweetheart, but on my return you shall have a chirographic account of everything.

I have been growing a Van Dyke beard so don't worry about my romantic life, please.

Give my love to my family and yours. Tell Buddy when you call him, that I wish him and his fiancée well and that he should give Dora and Alf my love.

If you look at the censored news sheet you'll note I've acquired a little Arabic and just as little French.

Love, Bart

P. S. Have no A.P.O. number yet so until you get it write to address indicated—

More love,
B

Memory is a perilous business at best, slippery and mercurial. I've always been a foot soldier, better at negotiating the steady and the sure. I've heard that many accounts of World War II are tainted, or at least reconfigured, by the years and the cycles of retelling. Knowing that I'm about to do this—to imagine my own version of this story—terrifies me. Two choices are clearly visible: I can lament the thorny predicament of every adult child who didn't ask enough of the important questions while her parents could have offered her answers, or I can forge ahead and tell their story by cutting away and scrapping together what remains—diaries, letters, anecdotes, scant recordings, images from photographs and paintings, memories, and my raw instinct about what he might have felt at certain points of his life—and then retelling it. Perhaps this is the way I, who remained dry-eyed at their deaths, too stunned to be able to imagine a world without either of them, can mourn my father and my mother, too.

As emotions roll through me in waves, I yearn toward his words and pictures as if they could anchor me. The more I delve into my father's work, the more I see his scrawls and visions as a window not just into the war, not just into his fervor for words and music and art, not just into his evolution as a physician, not just into the love he fiercely kept alive for his wife, and not just into what it means to be a first-generation American. I see his blazing need to preserve the story of his life during this absence. I understand what it means to be the carrier of that fire.

Now, nearly three-fourths of a century later, as I am culling through the fragments of a lifetime within a lifetime, I can already see the twilit edge between his story as he recorded it in diaries and letters and my own as I unearth and expose them. His narrative is buffeted, as is mine, by the vicissitudes of memory and desire. And this twilit edge? I hope it never fades, that it hovers in my line of sight always. That it allows me to envision, detail after detail, scattered like breadcrumbs from the fairy tale he read to me again and again, guiding me, in some almost preternatural way, home.

CHAPTER 1
LEAVING AMERICA

And thus a new chapter in my life opens.

Bart and Bertie find themselves standing—no, leaning into each other—on a pier in New Brunswick, New Jersey, before he is to march onto the ferry for Staten Island to board the ship that will take him away from her for who knows how long. It is December 11, 1942. Fog is floating in, and minute ice-flecks chill their cheeks. He pulls her tight to his chest so she cannot see the tears he's fighting back. They've been married just over two years. He's a month shy of twenty-nine, but he's already beginning to feel exponentially older.

As powerful as the pull to stay with her is, he has been waiting a long time, and as he keeps repeating to her, he wants to get this show on the road to do his part for the American war effort. It has been two years and nearly four months—while Bart was training with the other ROTC Army officers at forts in the United States—since France and Britain declared war on Germany. Bertie and he, poring over the *St. Louis-Post Dispatch* every day and shaking their heads over break-fast, have watched with horror as the war exploded in country after country.

Within a month of the onset of war, Germany toppled four European nations. Nine months later, in June 1940, Mussolini joined in the dominoes of war declarations, and the Wehrmacht's goose-stepping troops and tanks clattered into Paris. Within days Hitler struck his shrewd armistice with newly appointed premier Philippe Petain. By complying with Germany's demands, Petain would serve as at least the nominal chief of state and rule over unoccupied southern France (and French protectorates Morocco, Algeria, and Tunisia) from a makeshift capital in Vichy. In exchange, Petain agreed to use military force to fend off all invaders. A year and a half later, Japanese bombers razed the American military base at Pearl Harbor.

Bart and Bertie can almost mark the trajectory of their marriage by the landmark events of the world's inevitable plummet into war. While they were busy planning their wedding, Hitler marched troops into Czechoslovakia, where her stepfather, Alex Rich, the gentle man who raised her, had been born. The month they were married, Stalin began negotiations with Germany for the Axis to include Russia, Bertie's birth father's homeland. Six days before, while Bertie's family was praying at synagogue on Yom Kippur, the Nazis herded the Jews who comprised nearly one-third of Warsaw into a ghetto the size of the tip of Manhattan. One week after their wedding, Italy, the motherland of Bart's parents, moved troops into Greece. A month later, Hungary, the birthplace of Bertie's mother, joined the Axis. They had been married only eleven months when all the Jews in Germany were commanded to wear the Star of David.

Bart had been a 1st Lt. in the Medical Corps for only one year when he married the obsidian-haired love of his life, and the shadow of war was already draped over them. She followed him to Forts Leonard Wood, Knox, and Kilmer, rented bungalows so they could be alone for as many hours or minutes as possible. A photo of them shows her in a white piqué short-sleeved dress, with three strands of rickrack running down from shoulders to hem, white full-moons of earrings, a floppy white bow bisecting the middle part in her hair, which is coaxed back to her neck. Her arm is looped through his; her right hand holds her left. He's in uniform, tie and mustache neat. Her complexion is pale next to her officer-husband's, whose bronzed skin peeks out above his buttoned collar. He casts a ghost of a smile toward the camera. She looks somber, her gaze shifted to the side.

She has been following him not only because she cannot bear the idea of being apart from him but also because she longs to have a baby. She wants to raise a child that is part of both of them, no matter what this uncertain succession of tomorrows will bring. She has consulted a doctor about why she is not getting pregnant. "We'll start with a sperm sample," the doctor had said. So she'd carefully collected Bart's semen in a condom, placed it between her breasts to keep it warm and viable, and sped it back in their rickety Dodge to St. Louis.

As Bart and Bertie stand on the dock, he knows that if it happens he'll worry about her raising a child alone. If it does not happen, so be it. Besides, the United States has finally entered the war, and although the unspeakable is pecking at their thoughts like a malicious crow, the vast velvet curtain has been hoisted up on the entire world, and, damn it, Bart doesn't intend to miss the show.

Without her, on the ferry to Staten Island, the chop of the waves and the viscous fog make his ache feel like a wound. The fog delays their departure on the former luxury liner until the next morning, when they finally head full bore into the increasingly turbulent waters of the unknown.

IN HIS ROOM on board, Bart opens the blank book I imagine Bertie has given him for a going-away gift and scratches with a ballpoint pen into its textured cover:

Dec 12–'42 Depart US
June '43 Africa
B. M. PASSANANTE
#1 LEAVING AMERICA

He folds back the binding. With both hands, he pulls the edges of the pages away from the stitching. He knows that anything could happen. The ship could be blasted by a torpedo; he could be seized as a prisoner or left for dead in some frozen German forest. But the prospect of writing in this book nudges him toward happiness. It will enable him to transform his racing thoughts into the reassurance of words in syntactical order. It will allow him to record details, for some future somewhere, of his own minute story in this momentous episode from what would soon become the past. But most important, every word will ensure that Bertie does not miss any of his life. This chronicle will keep her as close to him as a pen to paper and will be delivered into the safe-keeping of her memory, even if he should not return to deliver it to her himself.

Touching his pen to the first page, he begins his diary:

Dec. 12, 1942. The throbbing of the ship's motors is shaking the table upon which I'm writing which accounts for the wavering in these chirographic lines.

The name of the ship is the Argentina and we boarded her yesterday at about 3:00 pm riding in on train from Kilmer to a New Jersey ferry and on the ferry to Staten Island, the port of embarkation. Some of the more superstitious possibly were not happy about the number of the pier on which our ship was docked. Number 13 was clearly visible for half a mile before we reached the pier.

Everything went off in split second precision. Everyone seemed to know what to do at the right time. And, since the number of troops embarking was tremendous, the job of embarkation was superbly done. I was proud of that.

On the train to the port we were given bologna and cheese sandwiches, apples and candy with a statement that the possibility of a similar unappetizing supper was in store for us. But when we boarded our ship we officers were invited to an officers mess, given a card of admission, and told supper would be served in the dining room at 5:30. There are three shifts of an hour each for every meal. But only two meals—breakfast and supper. At supper we officers trudged to the dining room expecting more of the Kilmer cuisine. But lo and behold! Civilian waiters, politely and with unlooked for alacrity served us a <u>choice</u> [Bart underlines this twice] of two suppers—meat loaf or breaded veal chops—and were apologetic because of the limited choice. We dined in the usual porcine manner washing down our meat, french fries and noodles with very good Maxwell House coffee and good cream. Cake and peaches followed.

Our rooms accommodate six of us with two stacks of berths (mattress included) of three berths each. I have a lower berth!!—My roommates and I get along very well and their humor makes very pleasant conversation.

In contrast to this the enlisted men are herded in berths stacked 5–6 deep in very crowded, ill-lighted, ill-ventilated holes. I was disgusted. Our rooms could be a lot better but theirs could be no worse. Incidentally the best rooms are tenanted by civilian help!

It was early to bed last night while our ship remained docked.

This morning we breakfasted on cooked figs (and they were good) corn flakes and milk, bacon and eggs with potatoes and coffee.

After breakfast the tugs pulled our ship out of dock, and now she is out to sea but will stop for a while to meet convoy. Incidentally I now am familiar with such terms as bow, aft, starboard, portside, etc.

I was just given my life preserver and instructions about abandoning ship, etc.

And thus a new Chapter in my life opens.

I'm tempted to stop right here with that line, to let Bart open his own chapter and then to flee myself. How does one become absorbed in, then resurrect someone else's memory, especially a memory that was already compromised and unreliable years before the person died?

Instead, I say the first twenty-three words aloud. Smiling, I shake my head. They reflect one of the salient truths about my father, and about my mother, too: the fact that they were raised by immigrant parents to become fully acculturated Americans. I can read this in his heightened diction and the slight syntactic stutter he makes with "which accounts for." To be American meant not only to speak the language without self-consciousness but to seize control of it, take it seriously, play games with it, imbibe it, breathe it until it defined and redefined the self. The dictionary at the ready next to the dinner table, the puns bandied about, the word games, the reading by flashlight when Midwest tornadoes and thunderstorms blinked off the electricity, the hardback tomes that lined the built-in shelves, the piles of paperbacks and medical journals on nearly every surface of our house—these images are evidence of the most fundamental fact I know about him: that he was proud to have succeeded in mastering the language; that his parents, who still tripped over their English syllables after half a century in this country, were proud, too. To become Americans, to produce American children—that had been his parents' fervent dream, perhaps even before they stepped onto the gangplanks of the ships that steamed them separately to New York Harbor at the end of the nineteenth century. In the heart of the twentieth century, as Bart, now an American Army captain, steams across the same ocean, his ship is aimed in the opposite direction.

BART BLINKS, BREATHES deep, wheels around, and begins the process of his work, his job—no, his calling. It seems a long time coming. The 6th Surgical Hospital he'd served in for years, assembled with doctors from around the country, was redesignated the 91st Evacuation Hospital for the overseas war effort nearly four months ago, and the Allies, under the code name Operation Torch, have been fighting for five weeks in North Africa.

But for now he has to settle for being the medical officer for one of the few lifeboats. Although he is assured that many rafts are available and knows they are required to wear their life jackets everywhere they go, he looks over the lifeboats carefully, counts them, just to alleviate his anxiety. When the sea swells and the boat pitches and plunges, Bart takes a Seconal and sleeps. In spite of the mal de mer plaguing many of the ship's 5,000 or so military passengers, he makes it a point not to miss even one meal and in fact snacks throughout the day on tidbits he brings up from the dining room.

For the first two days on board, they still don't know where they're going, and now that they've severed ties with land, the trip already seems interminable. But by the second full day at sea, it is clear. He records in his diary: "Conjecture on our possible destination has come to an end. Our southerly course, the warm winds and the pamphlet issued to us entitled 'North Africa,' have settled the question." Soon information, including common Arabic phrases and guidelines for how Americans in North Africa should behave, is pouring daily into their rooms. Skimming a leaflet, he adds, "These Moslems must be peculiar people."

Soon classes in French spring up on board. Bart enjoys learning, and he'll try to learn French though he's all but certain he won't be able to master it no matter how many days it takes to get to Africa. Since he started school, his parents had been so determined to speak nothing but English in his presence that he has little affinity for foreign languages. He'd rather be learning more about medicine, or art.

But now that he's running out of mysteries to read, there's hardly anything else to do besides these ho-hum lessons. After a few days he writes, "The monotony is now as bad as the apprehensiveness of becoming sea sick. I think a week of this pleasure cruise is sufficient." He spends idle time just gazing out the porthole at the convoy. *A beautiful sight,* he deems it, but he feels lazier by the day and soon finds himself spending hours at a time in bed.

One day he wanders into one of the gun turrets that line the ship, and one of the gunners predicts they probably will see little or no action. Bart's spirits sag even more.

But under the bravado the trepidation is always hovering, however erratically. One night he drums his fingers to gunfire from the other ships. It's a safe bet the ships are limbering up a little. He's heard rumors that they're now in dangerous waters. They have become more particular about where they place their clothing and life preservers in case they have to make a beeline for the rafts and boats in the middle of the night. Some are even sleeping with their clothes on. A few days later when the moon ripens—*clear for bombing, calm for submarines*, he thinks—the convoy's course suddenly zigzags, green and red signal lights flash, and an undercurrent of restlessness ripples around the ship.

In spite of the suspended sense of apprehension and the waxing and waning monotony, little by little Bart makes a life for himself. He discovers the ship's library and digs in. He basks in the warm ocean breezes—*How Bertie would love them! Think of it! Sun-bathing in the middle of December!* He keeps his words light, playful: "I continue to astonish my roommates about the amount of food I consume and amount of sleep I do. Aside from some strolling on the decks, playing a little bridge and arising for abandon ship drill I do very little." Bart is a man of small stature. He has always been self-conscious about his height—which, if he admits it, isn't always what he testifies to on forms—though his short legs didn't get in the way of his being a track star in college. He's pleased that he can still do more, and more difficult, callisthenic feats than his companions. As his muscles bulge, his smile broadens.

The Van Dyke beard he's told Bertie about gives him a peculiarly gruesome Mephisthophelean appearance instead of a dignified one, but he talks George Riday, the affable chaplain, into growing one, too. And soon he recruits others. "Moustaches are growing in abandon," Bart reports, "and a few beards are beginning to crop out in the organization. Regulations may stop these hirsute pursuits." He sounds out the last two words to himself, pleased with his rhyme.

He, his roommates, and other cohorts become increasingly creative in manufacturing diversions for this seamless stretch of days. Ambrose "Bucky" Shields, who'd begun a surgery residency in Oregon and joined the unit at Fort Knox, and some nurses pair up with Bart for a few hands of pinochle. One night John Tuhy, a former chest surgery resident, saunters into Room 60 and treats them to a song, "Baby, You're Malignant." Tuhy belts out the lyrics already written by an intern, for which Bart and a few others have entreated the clever but modest Bob Pearson to compose the melody. Bart promises Bertie in the diary: "The song, together with other odd scraps, will come home with me on my return for your perusal. I must feel that you should live all this with me."

In one of his stagy moods, Bart performs raucous impersonations of French generals, Arabs, and Italian and German soldiers—and tops them off with a corny interpretation of Caruso. The boys laugh, and he's just thinking he has his audience where he wants them when Stuart Welch, one of the more experienced surgeons, yells at him through the walls that separate their rooms. He calls Bart a nut and adds some biting remark about dignity. Bart receives Welch's volley of slurs with bemusement.

Soon his room has become a social hub. There, songfests abound, with Pearson, his hands in fists at his sides, his wire-rimmed glasses reflecting the light, supplying the bass. Harry Meyer, who'd begun practicing medicine in New Orleans even before Bart started medical school, and George Riday regale them with their card and magic tricks. The chaplain also performs pantomimes to much applause. Bart is particularly happy in George's company, enjoys his fine-tuned sense of humor. Before now (and after the failure of his parents and sister to indoctrinate him with all that Catholic fol-de-rol, as he calls it), he would have thought a person of the cloth would be the last friend he'd make. But George is different, genuine, not pushy about it. Bart writes: "Our profanity has subsided voluntarily out of respect but he has done or said nothing about our moments of laxity in this respect. At present we are dogging him to read *Elmer Gantry*. He promised he would."

One evening the residents of Room 60, in a more sober mood, play a series of games. When someone suggests the word game Three Thirds of a Ghost, for a minute Bart's heart takes him away, to Cates Avenue, that first summer with Bertie, though not *with* her really, more like watching her, holding her in some place secret even from himself until his bones seem to ache. Every night that summer, after a day of brutal sun, as the Mississippi and the Missouri Rivers that V-ed around St. Louis kept the throbbing humidity from the floodplains in a headlock and the walls of the brick apartment buildings radiated with heat, he watched her. He watched her from his blanket on the other end of the lawn in front of their building. He watched her through the other neighborhood young people who couldn't sleep and who gathered on the lawn every night that July to pass the time until 2 or 3 a.m., when the temperature slid down a few degrees and they crept back inside to sleep nude on top of their sweat-stained sheets.

Every night whoever was sprawled on the grass joined in round after round of Three Thirds of a Ghost. Trying not to stare at the sixteen-year-old whom he watched lift her black thicket of hair from her neck with such slender fingers, Bart ginned out tricky words that might impress her with his gamesmanship, but she almost always caught his ruses and turned them into wins for herself.

Tonight, with the boys, he's glad he's still good at this game. He may have to impress Bertie all over again—when he returns.

The next evening at dinner, he finds himself staring at his baked potato, a thickness closing in on his throat, his eyes welling. When he explains to his askance buddies that his wife always butters, salts, and peppers his potato for him, they tease him unmercifully.

The first night of winter, he writes Letter Number One. He's heard letters will be placed in a mailbox on board ship and left there when debarking—then God knows when she'll ever get them. They have not yet been given an APO number, and they're still using the old Fort Knox address. He hopes things straighten out when they get to Casablanca, but he's worried. He *has* to hear from her.

One night, the moon luminous, he spots a few ghostly peaks of land in the distant horizon—the Madeiras. The peaks fade from sight within the hour, but they've told him that they're now about 450 miles from Africa. Tomorrow night. They should be there tomorrow.

On the deck he and his roommates crane their necks skyward as the usually taciturn Pearson surprises them with what he knows about astronomy. With all Bart's science training, how did he miss learning about the constellations? Their elegant shapes, the stories they outline, the black gaps between the points of light—*that's where the imagination goes,* he thinks. He wishes he could paint the stars.

Before they land, they're served an early Christmas dinner. Bart, a finicky but hearty eater, whose mother and wife have both indulged his pickiness about food, is so thrilled with the feast that he describes it in detail. After they eat, his closest friends sign the back of his menu. "May our return trip be not too far distant and just as pleasant. Inshallah!" writes Harry. "May the courage that possessed you to brave the

taunts of inferior fellows continue to lead you on to even greater vic-
tories than a Van Dyke. *Toujours notre ami* (which by interpretation
means *Bacalao con papas*)," quips George nonsensically. After George
signs his name under his message, he adds, in parentheses, "Elmer
Gantry." Pearson produces his message completely in French, which is
no doubt lost on Bart.

Finally, early on Christmas Eve, he notes from the porthole that a
portion of the convoy has broken off and is probably passing through
the Strait of Gibraltar. The water is greener. Seagulls swoop over the
sea. He guesses they can't be more than twenty-five to fifty miles from
land, and, indeed, they sight it mid-morning. He packs his gear, locks
his footlocker, cinches the belt on his duffel, and is ready to set foot to
foreign soil.

Before leaving the ship, he writes in his diary, "Merry Xmas, Sweetheart. I hope that we'll spend the next one together." But he has yet to
understand the personal consequences of the fact that by the time the
Argentina drops anchor at Casablanca just inland from the west coast
of the continent, the war in Africa has shifted to the East and already
eluded them.

NORTH AFRICA
December 24, 1942 to July 28, 1943

CHAPTER 2

THE FIRST FIELD

I never want to go camping again if and when I get back.

As the SS *ARGENTINA* eases into port, Bart leans over the rails of the deck, the salty wind gnawing at his ears, and gawks at the havoc the Americans have wreaked in Casablanca harbor. He's heard the legends of the *Jean Bart,* and now he spots her, the newest of the Vichy French fleet, much-touted, now sunken in the harbor mud. Bombed shore batteries. Submerged ships—strafed French destroyers, torpedoed battleships, scuttled freighters, minesweepers. He can almost hear the booms of the guns ricocheting over the bay.

Once off the ship, they are told to wait, and Bart paces on the dock for hours, it seems, back and forth, back and forth, squinting into the distance at the daisy-colored sun, the taupe slopes rimming the horizon. He's impatient to step off those planks and onto the sand-flecked African earth, keen to cross for the first time in his life into another country and into an epic historical moment, one that will begin his life as an American serviceman in the thick of war, a practicing American doctor.

From the carved-out chasm between generations, I look at my father at this moment, having just landed for the first time in an exotic port on a foreign continent, and imagine his pulse throbs with adrenaline at the sheer sense of adventure. In fact, I imagine he can hardly believe it—the son of uneducated immigrants, the boy who, before the Army, except for a couple road trips with buddies, had mostly traveled back and forth across the Mississippi River, now thousands of miles from home.

All his diaries and letters indicate, however, is that he is already apprehensive that he will not be able to record in writing all he needs to remember, all the details that compose a life, that create a story, details he has pledged to Bertie. His desire is unwavering: to summon all the words that might—just might—help bridge their absence. And perhaps when Bart writes them, he has at least a nebulous prescience that reading them in the years when his brain launches its chilling war on his memory will help him recall the man he was becoming.

Finally, trucks arrive to trundle the nurses away to their quarters, in a *lycée des jeunes filles,* a school for girls. The men step off the dock unceremoniously, then walk and keep walking. En masse, they march through the French Quarter of Casablanca, then trudge back out of the city—toward what, they are not certain. To stave off a sinking sense of confusion and chaos, Bart focuses on the slice of paling sun edging behind the clouds. The blush recalls the peaches he picked some summers as a child in the orchards in Illinois. They tramp onward until they find a place to bivouac, three miles from the port but ten from the city's center. The stench, the sludge creeping up their heels, the dung piles pocking the field, the grasses chewed into stubble, the puddles kicked up—it's a cow pasture.

Slowing down, the enlisted men, whose baggage and supplies have been taken off the ship, stop to set up their camp. But Bart and the other officers, all of whom have somehow arrived without blankets, without water and food except for emergency rations, slog in desperation back toward town, or, when they can, beg rides, to hunt down a place to spend the night. Colonel Snell is supposed to be in charge, but he seems more intent on finding a place to sleep himself than on giving orders.

They tread through filthy streets past the graying art deco buildings of the French quarter, Arabs, in dingy-white turbans or red chechias and layered mysteriously in soiled cloth, darting away down the potholed streets, and houses with Moorish arches reeking with ordure tinged with odd spices. The sun has vanished, the icy wind has seeped into his skin, and Bart begins to thank the powers that be that he still has an overcoat with him. The final jeep drops them off just in time for total blackout; all the bars are closed. It is Christmas Eve.

They zigzag from one dark place to another, rap on doors. Then one of the men marches up to the imposing door of the Hotel Excelsior and after much persuasion and negotiation elbows his way past the clerk. The men follow him to the bar, where he scoots a stool up to the counter and demands a bottle of champagne. The officers mass around him or take up other stools, ordering more bottles, letting the champagne warm them. But there's a whiff of anti-climax in the smoke-filled air. After draining their glasses, they prowl the labyrinthine streets, hunting down at last a run-down hotel. In a drab and drafty room, Bart lays his overcoat under him and lies down on the cold floor.

It's only minutes after he has fallen asleep that the screech of sirens slams him awake. An air raid. The first. The real thing. His pulse surges. When the noise stops, his heart calms, but he never does return to sleep. In a day or two they'll be headed for the front, he figures.

He spends Christmas day chasing down his bedding rolls and suitcases. His footlocker was shipped a couple days before he left the United States, but who knows where it is now. He unearths his suitcases from a pile but discovers that the bedding rolls are still on the docked ship. In the pasture where they bivouac, over the mud, he spreads the sleeping bag Bertie insisted he bring. He'll have to wait another two days until the pup tents catch up with them. *This will be temporary,* he keeps telling himself.

Since there's been no APO set up, and the cable he tried to send in town was refused, and since the only letter Bart has written Bertie has been stuck on the ship for several days, he and Harry hire a carriage into Casablanca to locate the PO and send her a V-mail. Smudged-faced urchins hang on their legs, begging for bon-bons or gum or anything American. Arabs squat and defecate on the stone streets. He feels bombarded by the strange and the disconcerting.

Trying to keep warm and dry, he spends an entire day bundled up in his pup tent, listening to the patter of rain. At least his and Harry's tents aren't submerged, as some have been, in the build-up of water that has muddied their camp. There's no clean water to wash his grimy hands. He has to cross the field to use a slit trench. "Camp is one big mud puddle," he writes. "The rains have come and the cold pierces to the bones. Just shaved standing up and on the run, begging for two ounces of hot water and one square foot of space near one of the few tents for which we have begged. Our tentage is still not with us. Tonite we will be available for duty in the town hospital if things break like we think they will." He adds, "If I don't cut my throat before then." A couple days later, he declares, "I never want to go camping again if and when I get back."

But soon, in spite of the drenched field and his dampened spirits, he begins to settle into a routine he thinks he can live with. They've been subsisting on emergency rations, but Bart manages to buy fresh eggs and oranges (he can now use two Arabic expressions: *Shahal,* meaning *how much,* and *Bizeff,* meaning *too much).* Finally, they have their baggage and about half their supplies, and the kitchen is set up. He and Harry have built a fireplace; they've hung a wash line. The unit has acquired not only a stove and a few tents to shelter them, but a radio—music, news!—and Harry has brought back a couple of candles from his last trip to town. So now Bart can write letters in candlelight in the pup tents they will have to sleep in for a while longer. *Let it rain, let it be cold,* he thinks.

On New Year's Eve, in search of distraction, he goes to his first party abroad. This one is in a huge sardine factory warehouse, and there are eight nurses to fifty men. He dances a few steps, then grabs his bottle of champagne, sulks on a box in a corner, and drinks himself to tears before stumbling to his pup tent. "Exit—1942," he scrawls.

At 3:30 a.m., he's stunned awake by a racket that ricochets over the skies, the city, the fields, the bay and sea; it's the most earsplitting gunfire he's ever heard. "Wow," he yells, not knowing how else to respond. He sucks in his breath at the fireworks. Anti-aircraft fire, machine guns, cannon, tracer bullets, and what must be a thousand beams of searchlight—all illuminate Casablanca in blackout. Occasionally a plane is caught in crossbeams, and the tracers silhouette it against the cloudy sky. His heart pounds.

In the morning he learns that a bomb plunged down about a half mile from their camp. A slight fear rises. "We feel like rats in a trap," he writes in his diary. "We're camped a block away from an ammunition dump, a quarter mile from Quartermaster supply, one mile from the harbor and in the middle of an area squared off by machine gun nests, anti-aircraft cannon and plane detectors. Phooey." And all this is the work of only a handful of Axis planes. Even so, he and Harry have their eyes on a nearby sewer they can flee to if the time comes.

On the first day of 1943, the sun domes over the frozen water, and Bart longs to tell Bertie what the Germans meted out on the town on New Year's Eve: large craters in the streets, dissection of a small building, about sixty people dead—all Moroccans. But he can tell her nothing of any of this. All their letters are censored. He himself is a unit censor, scissoring out oblongs of text, and he owes a duty to the rest of the men. He cannot afford to be a hypocrite. All he can say is "We have tasted of real warfare á la England and now consider ourselves veterans. The real thing, sweetheart, with all the trimmings— 'God Bless America.' It's not as bad as it would look from America, but one develops a certain callousness and camaraderie, and fears are easily dispelled. It does become tiresome to have to unwrap oneself from one's sleeping bag at odd times during the night." He adds: "Due to adverse conditions we were unable to observe the Rose Bowl game New Year's night. I trust you picked the winner and you always do (???)."

But the need to talk with her is already mounting to an ache. He commandeers a typewriter and bangs out a letter wishing her a very happy new year without sorrow and with good health, asking her to send a pair of gloves, a pint of bourbon, a letter, a letter, *a letter.* Then he asks, "Do we have a family?" He wonders forlornly whether it might be Easter before she even gets his letter.

Two weeks into the new year they finally move out of pup tents and into ward tents with cots. The tent even has electric lights. If only they had heat for the cold nights. If only he had Bertie to spoon with!

He has settled into the habit of writing her almost daily. "Dearest Bertie mine," he begins after more than a month of silence from her, "No letters! This business can't go on much longer." Every day he rushes out to meet the courier who delivers the officers' mail, but every day it's the same story: no word from Bertie. He can blame only himself, advising her not to write until the unit had an APO number, which wasn't assigned until they'd been separated an entire month. If only he'd told her to use the Fort Knox address.

At parties, he keeps his promise to hug and kiss her mentally. Sometimes he dances and drinks to dull his senses. One night, he finds himself retching in the courtyard of the nurses' quarters. Another night, he stumbles outside, glares at the moon, and weeps for love.

For an entire month all he and the rest of the boys seem to do is piddle around camp and entertain rumors: moving to Rabat? establishing a hospital in Casablanca? There's still no medical work, and bickering and squabbling among the men have ratcheted up. He keeps to himself, refreshing his medical memory, studying anatomy and surgery, poring over *Abdominal Injuries* and medical journals. He plays a game he's dubbed "Guess What He's Got" with Tuhy, who's two years ahead of Bart in his training, so he gives Bart a run for his money. Bart works out at the gymnasium beneath the Excelsior Hotel. He lunches at the Roi de la Bière on beans and macaroni with cheese. He sits in a sidewalk café, sucks on a pipe, sips cognac. Back at camp, he spends several days in his swim trunks, sunning on his cot, sometimes learning a little French from a borrowed primer. He boxes with Harry. They barter with a man in a blanched burnoose for a basket of almonds, shell and boil the nuts, butter and salt them, and roast them in their mess kits. He swats at the increasingly irritating flies. "One has to eat rapidly in order to partake more of the food than the flies," he writes.

A shortwave radio tunes in the world, and only the war news breaks up the boredom. British General Montgomery, who had been hounding German Field Marshall Rommel and his Afrika Corps across the scorching Sahara, is finally chasing them out of Tripoli. And the two leaders of the Allied war effort, FDR and Churchill, have been meeting in a villa not ten miles from where Bart's ear has been cocked toward the radio. They've been hammering out the future of the world, and indirectly Bart and Bertie's future, too. *I'll be damned,* he thinks. In a complex array of outcomes of the Casablanca Conference, two major decisions will affect Bart and Bertie more than they can know: a full-scale invasion of Europe would be postponed in order for the Allies to be fully prepared and poised to win; and the Allies would accept no less than unconditional surrender.

These decisions make his letter to Bertie on his first birthday overseas all the more poignant. At breakfast, the boys sing "Happy Birthday" to him, and he gets an extra egg with his bacon. Then he paces around all day waiting for mail. He envisions Bertie, recalls how he used to call her Rebecca—his favorite literary heroine, the stunning, keen-witted Jewess from *Ivanhoe*. His Rebecca. Finally, at suppertime, trucks with about twenty-four sacks of mail pull into camp, and all of the boys take away something—all except Bart. He ends the day in what he admits to Bertie is "complete hopeless sorrow." "I hope you are keeping warm and wearing your woolen undies," his letter continues. "The last word does things to me. Chills up and down my spine. Undies—panties—wow! And I thought I had steeled myself against any such thoughts ever entering my mind. Oh well—it won't be a long war."

CHAPTER 3

BEDSIDE MANOR

I have been doing surgery to my heart's content. I am now strictly a surgeon (at least for the duration) and having been treated as one I am beginning to believe it myself.

BY THE CLOSE of the first month of 1943, rumors are flitting around Casablanca that the 91st may move not to Rabat, as they have been led to expect, but nearer to Tangiers, about ninety miles farther north, to function as a clearing station. Bart longs to tell Bertie about this projected move, and he hates deceptions, but he has to settle for writing her that a change is about to occur. Besides, who knows, he wonders, if she's even getting his letters.

On the final day of January, Bart is sitting in the command car as they travel inland to Port Lyautey on the Sebou River. With every mile, the lighter he feels. The sun has broken through the gloom, and the Mediterranean scenery unfolds before him: cacti, lemon trees, a camel, an ass, and a eucalyptus-lined road. They pass Rabat with its ancient Roman walls protecting the medina, its low, flat-roofed cubicle houses on the slopes, its exotic minarets.

In Port Lyautey, the ground is a jumble of sand and dust, but the air is cleaner, fresher than in Casablanca. He paces around the cork and lemon trees, asks questions. He discovers the men are staying in what were once Vichy French facilities. Theirs will be the first Allied hospital in the area.

By nightfall the ward tents have been hoisted up, and in a little more than a week, their living situation improves: hot water, a shower room, even flooring in the ward tent. There's now a stove in the dining room, so he won't have to rub his hands together before he picks up his chilled fork and knife. He shares a small wall tent with Harry, both grateful for the privacy and electric lights. The boys make a game out of naming their tents—one's called Westward-Ho House; Tuhy and Hyde, who had been accepted to a residency in upstate New York when he joined the 91st, call theirs Tuhy Hyde Out; and Bart and Harry dub theirs Bedside Manor. Before clicking out the light, Harry and he celebrate their move into their new home by toasting old cheese and bread and breaking open a bottle of hoarded champagne.

During their nearly three months in Port Lyautey, the war will grind its wheel of fortune around and back again several times. Bart and his comrades will cluster around the radio, hungry for details. At the onset of February, the Red Army will finally defeat the Germans at Stalingrad. Soon Rommel will churn through the rugged Atlas Mountains around Tunisia's Kasserine Pass. In the havoc of fireballs and smoke, German and Italian troops will topple American units tank after tank, man after man, including the better part of a medical battalion with its wounded. Toward the end of April, the Jews in the Warsaw ghetto will stage an uprising. And somewhere in Eastern Europe Bart's wife's cousins (a young doctor like himself and his brother, a lawyer) are captured by the Nazis. "I sure would like to know how our unit fits in," Bart tells Bertie. "Frankly, I'd like to have some box seats for the shows."

On his first full day in Port Lyautey, Bart examines each of the four tents and wooden buildings of their new hospital, staving off disappointment that he won't be working on a surgery team, at least not yet. He's to be in charge of the surgery ward, though. After all, he's been only an intern, he keeps telling himself, and for only one year at that, when the only practice he had was removing casts and recording medical histories. And some of the doctors in the 91st, the big guns like George Knapp, Stuart Welch, and Charlie Odom, have finished their residencies and have been successful practicing physicians. Odom in particular, with his eight years of post-graduate surgical training and a vibrant practice in New Orleans, is a star. Bart has hoped to tell Bertie he was going to be a surgeon, but he masks his moping and determines to make himself available if not indispensable. That evening a stretcher passes him, bearing a body sheathed in bloody bandages, and he jumps at the case. *Shrapnel wounds—what a mess,* he thinks. He scrapes away dead tissue and sutures closure after closure. He takes care to excise the small bits of metal, irrigating to stave off infection, applying dressings loosely, the way he was taught as an intern at County Hospital in St. Louis. He can't wait to tell Bertie that he's in charge of the first actual casualty of the 91st. He may not be on the operating team, but he's doing the next best thing.

After that, he determines to do all he can to distinguish himself as a doctor. He studies the expertise of Welch and Knapp, examining their techniques over their shoulders, asking questions, learning how to make new kinds of incisions. By candlelight in his pup tent, he scrutinizes articles in the *Annals of Surgery* and his SGO, which Bertie has subscribed to for him. He also reads Welch's paper on peptic ulcers. *Smart man,* he thinks. *Too bad he's so irritable when he's not working.*

When Bart is busy, he's in his element. Some nights he gets only forty-five minutes of sleep and doesn't have time to remove his underwear to wash it. But he's having a lot of fun, he tells Bertie, being "chief mogul" of the surgery ward. In the ward he makes rounds, applies dressings, puzzles through cases: bones and spines, burns, minor injuries, post-ops, a malaria here, an eye case there. When Knapp goes to Casablanca in February, Bart can hardly wait to write her that he's been appointed Knapp's alternate on the operating team and is on call.

Finally, one late night, working alone in the ward, he spots what he believes is a ruptured appendix. He talks to Knapp, who remains noncommittal. *Damn.* Bart can wait, but he's certain he can't wait long or it will be too late. Later that afternoon, when he scans the surgery schedule, he's surprised to see that an appendectomy has tentatively been scheduled under his name. Still . . . anxiety snakes up. What if the surgery is unnecessary? His training has told him not to do it, but his gut says *yes.* And now, suddenly, Knapp has said yes, has assigned it to him, and Knapp himself will assist him.

As soon as Bart cuts his way inside, he sees it immediately, the swelling of that floating finger of the appendix, its startling inflammation. And he can tell from the eyebrows arching out over the surgical masks that it's clear to all the doctors present that he's made the right call. His confidence soars. For a few seconds his scalpel hovers over the lower right quadrant of scrubbed flesh, and then, all the mechanics, all the meticulous protocols rush back to him. When he closes the cecum, then stitches the last layer of muscle, he almost says aloud, almost sings: *Happy Valentine's Day to me.* It is his first appendectomy in the Army, his first in a year and seven months. And he's done it well indeed.

Yet a parade of dull and insignificant procedures—ganglion removals, ingrown toenails, abscesses that need draining, varicose veins—can set him pouting. Occasionally something more challenging comes his way: a thumb is shot with a 45 revolver; a finger needs to be reconstructed, the skin grafted. He sees the artistic in this, the scrupulous attention to detail, the patience he needs to summon and sustain. And at least he's working.

The day before St. Patrick's Day, as Bart is performing a hemorrhoidectomy, he collects an audience, a bunch of the medical crew who surround and heckle him. He calls this audience a gallery. "Look, Gallery," he says. "Look and learn." He's cocky at having gravitated to the center of attention, as he did so often at home and at Soldan High School, where he was popular, a bit of a rebel who could make people laugh.

He's beginning to *feel* like a doctor.

He thinks often about the man who might have done more than anyone else to get him where he is right now. Under the spotlight of memory, he sees him, aquiline-sloped nose and caterpillar eyebrows, stick-thin.

One day in high school chemistry class, as Bart concentrates on pouring from one test tube into another, his teacher, Mr. Teeters, lays a hand on his shoulder.

"I see you like science," Mr. Teeters says. Bart swivels around, nods. "So what do you plan to do after high school?"

"Drive around, play in my band," Bart says, then raises an eyebrow, dimples up.

Mr. Teeters smiles. "I mean," he says, "what do you want to do with your life?"

"I haven't the faintest idea," Bart answers, surprising even himself. "All I can think of right now is be a cowboy." They both laugh.

"You have a knack for chemical things. Have you ever considered becoming a doctor?"

Bart feels his heart speed up. Then a blend of embarrassment and something else, he isn't sure what, descends upon him. Is it inadequacy? Inadequacy mixed with . . . what? The blank, open expanse of possibility? Whatever it is, it is terrifying.

From that hour on, he knows he will be a doctor. There's nothing else he wants to do, and he sets about figuring out how to prepare himself. By the time he graduates, a few days before his seventeenth birthday, he is ranked tenth in his class of over 300. He just needs to move on, he keeps telling himself, and not look back to anything that might get in his way.

Now, little by little, he gains the trust of the 91st surgeons in charge. He's elated to tell Bertie, "I have been doing surgery to my heart's content. I am now strictly a surgeon (at least for the duration) and having been treated as one I am beginning to believe it myself." That notion might even trigger something close to joy if only he had heard even a single word from her since he left her on the shore over two months ago. If only.

When the surgery slows, it seems that all he does is wait for the mail. All his friends and acquaintances have received letters from their loved ones. He's hurt, and a little embarrassed, that he's the only one left. He tries to joke when he writes her: "Mail is now coming in but someone must be removing mine from the post offices and throwing them in the paper basket." Every day, he expects to hear from her. On one trip to the PO to mail her daily letter, he's told that letters will soon be photographed to send on V-mail forms. Another hoop to jump through, but he knows this change is important: by using small letter sheets, censored and then photographed in microfilm negative form to transport more expediently, then blown up for slightly easier reading, the military can save literally tons of space for shipping war materials. He amasses V-mail forms.

His early spring letters are packed with information that makes the war seem as remote as if it were scattered skirmishes on that rust-red dot of Mars, the planet he sometimes scans the night sky for when he thinks he needs an excuse to be alone. He tells her everything he can to will her to be part of his life. He tells her how he washed his field jacket with steam that spurts out of their delousing unit. How he sat through Riday's sermon one Sunday morning. How one gloomy afternoon he walked into the officers' recreation tent and about ten feet in front of him stood a piano (*or something that once was a piano*, he thinks); how he's determined to have it tuned and to practice it (*if it isn't used for kindling first, that is*). He tells her he's traveled to town (it's Rabat, but he can't mention the name), where he's bought some paints and had *Bertie* engraved on his silver wedding ring. "Fine war," Bart comments dryly.

He continues the ritual he inaugurated in Casablanca of buying her gifts: a pair of hand-tooled slippers, an embroidered bracelet, a silver pin. He mails her a money order and tells her to buy something for herself with it—whatever she wants.

He knows nothing about her life since the moment they parted except that she cried after he left her, and he has already endured two months of her silence. "I walked thru the door leaving all that I love and want in life behind. Darling I miss you. . . . I'm writing this one with a morale lower than a snake's belly."

One moonless night on the way back to camp from the makeshift officers' club, Bart is startled by a gamut of sentries—French, Moroccan, and American. They command him to halt, click back their bolts. Sometimes something like this, the smallest click, will remind him that they are in danger here, that they are at war.

CHAPTER 4
ABSENCE

I'm saving all my 'playing house' until I get back darling.

FINALLY, *FINALLY,* ON February 19, two months and eight days after he and Bertie kissed goodbye, he receives his first letters from her. He grabs them, hurries to the privacy of Bedside Manor, flops onto his bedding roll, and reads them over and over greedily, as if he could pull them into his body. He absorbs every word, the loops of each letter, interrupting himself only to toast bread over the tent's homemade alcohol stove for his supper.

When he takes up a pen and paper, it's nearly dawn.

February 19, 1943   Dearest sweetheart Bert:

Life is again wonderful. I am exquisitely happy. My B. M. R. must be about 100 plus this afternoon. I got my first letter from you. I feel funny all over and weak. I was given your 2nd and 3rd letters to me. I wish I get the first one soon.

No, our nurses are not fat and ugly. They are, by and large, just ugly. Those with which I have been working have been very nice to me listening to my sorry tales of receiving no letters from my wife day in and day out. One went so far as to write a letter to me in your name.

I will save it for you. They think I am very much in love with you, which, somehow makes them feel proud of me.

He's so changed, so happy to hear from her that he wonders if everyone thinks he's lost his mind.

Nine days later a spurt of mail reaches him. He pops open two bottles of champagne, and as he arranges her letters in chronological order, her life begins to come into focus. She has a job! And she is learning to play the piano. She has practiced the dashes and dots of her shorthand for Dr. Bradley, her new boss, the superintendent of Barnes Hospital, and already earned her first raise. She's memorized the notes of the musical staff and learned to connect them to plunking particular piano keys.

But although he's been hungry for more news of home, the additional details present him with a new sense of distance and isolation. He wonders how his sister Rosalie celebrated her birthday, if Bertie's brother Harry is married yet, how her sister Rosie is progressing with her singing, if her parents are healthy, if her brilliant twelve-year-old brother Marvin is doing well in school. "Gosh, I just don't know nothin' at all, do I?" he says. "Today I dreamed and dreamed (or is it dreamt). I was thinking about us and finally realized that as long as we've been married the war has been shrouded about us. We never could plan into a clear and happy future, could we?" He beseeches her not to wear any close-fitting blouses she buys to her work at the hospital but to save them for him.

As the storks return to their high nests in Rabat and the trees become dotted with lemons, Bart and Bertie's discussions delve, in a succession of several months, into unsettling territory. He feels an urge to reassure her that he is still—and always will be during their absence—celibate. Just before they moved to Port Lyautey, he wrote: "My bachelorhood is maintained both by circumstances and desire and I love you like fury and think of you q.i.d. and at bedtime for prolonged periods." And then during his early Port Lyautey days: "I'm saving all my 'playing house' until I get back darling," this time using their code, their own code, one that excites him every time one of them says or writes those words. A few weeks later he narrates an anecdote about his debates about fidelity with his Army cohorts: "When Stuart stated that if he had to choose between his wife and his work he'd choose his work, I walked away from him holding my nose. Incidentally he has, recently, more than a dozen times asked me if I had anything 'lined up.' He wants to play house. When I told him that I was waiting until I got home he was very puzzled. 'Funny Thing' he said 'you struck me back home as being the type who couldn't do without it long.' And I said 'Funny but I thought so too.' Be it a year, two, or even three years sweetheart, I'll wait—honest. Just keep writing to me and tell me you love me. That's all I want."

But a later letter from her contains a surprise. Bertie has rescinded: there are to be, she says, no more restrictions on him sexually during the war.

He responds immediately: "Thank you for lifting your 'verboten' on 'promiscuity' or 'sexual necessity' on my part. But please don't feel hurt if I <u>don't</u> <u>accept</u> the privilege you offer. We find here that we can do without and the memory of our lovely faithful wives quickly deadens the male animal urge. Please believe me. When I come back I will still have been yours a hundred percent," then adds "(since our marriage)." When she brings up her offer again a couple weeks later, he retorts, "I disregard your allowing me to break my promise of celibacy. My only thoughts in that regard have amazingly been only in your direction."

While this time-stalled dialogue lurches along, another one begins to braid its way through the letters. It's the first inkling that they are afraid—afraid that their absence will change them and in ways they cannot anticipate. And every month Bart is in Africa there is at least some nod, no matter how hesitant, in that shadowy terror's direction. She promises him that she hasn't changed, but by July, the unease has intensified. He assures her that he's unchanged except for being "more rugged and healthier—but my, what a depilatory this dry climate is—but I'll love you anyway even if you are bald, she says. This afternoon I believe I will go lie on the beach and lose some more of my hair."

In every few letters he creates fantasies of what will happen when he returns—how he'll do nothing but try to make her happy every minute of the day. He'll do dishes, he'll take her to the Muny Opera every week, buy her Eskimo Pies, stare and stare at her. But then, again, the undercurrent of anxiety: "You're so good for me," he writes. "Didn't I appreciate you enough when we were together dolly? How did I ever take naps at home when you were there? I think of those times and feel like a fool." "Remember our Sundays, darling? Remember what preceded ham and eggs?" he asks. His pen hesitates as he lets himself glide back into memory, his synapses busy retrieving images from their double bed with the lace pillowslips his mother stitched for their trousseau.

I CAN ALMOST see the clockworks of his memory on the day he receives the many letters from his young wife, the day he reminds her of "what preceded ham and eggs." A day when his memory is still fine-tuned. I imagine the inside of his brain still fresh and proficient, the mechanical process of encoding and retrieval beneath his skull, the flawless machinations of neurons and synapses. And I'd like to think that the memory of what preceded ham and eggs always lay embedded somewhere in the folds of his brain and stayed with him even when the other particulars of his life plummeted out of reach.

CHAPTER 5

ART BLOOMS IN AFRICA

Keep them, dear, and when I return we'll go over them together.

WHEN SPRING ARRIVES full force to the African earth and catapults into an early summer, and the poppies blanket the sand-colored hills in crimson, Bart, at least for the moment, allows his loneliness for his wife to be swallowed by bathing in the sun and the rollicking sea. Now, the sea froth silvers, the sky lights up with china blue, the grape shoots flower out, and Bart spends idle afternoons trying to wash this color and light onto his sketchpad. Africa has inspired him—its siennas and khakis, duns and oatmeals, the tawny dust, the moonlight burnishing the breakers on the coast.

Long before Port Lyautey, Bart began what would become a sort of journey within a journey—one with art as his companion. Even before he started sketching at Fort Knox, he'd fantasized about being a trained artist. In college, trying to remove his mind from the knotty particulars of anatomy and molecules, he'd paced up and down the library stacks, plucking out books with colored plates of famous paintings.

Near Casablanca, in the earliest days of his absence from Bertie, he traveled to art stores in town to buy pencils, brushes, and watercolors. By his third effort, he'd already noted improvement. "I think I'll keep water coloring as my permanent hobby. What do you think?" he asked

Bertie eagerly. By the time the 91st moved to Port Lyautey, his urge toward art became contagious. "It seems that I've stimulated dormant desires to do water colors around here and one or two of the boys have gone in to get paints," he told her.

On the first day of spring in Port Lyautey, he packs all his water-colors and a few sketches into an envelope to send home. He encloses a letter: "They were done for you. Keep them, dear, and when I return we'll go over them together." Because he doesn't want her to think he's immodest, though, he makes light of his work: "I think yore purty and nacherly love you. But in case you run low in money sell the car, OR MY PAINTINGS (ouch! Who threw that tomato?)." When he hears later that Bertie has displayed his paintings in the living room, he requests that she not show them off to anyone who knows anything about art.

One afternoon in April Bart inveigles the chaplain (though George is such a sociable fellow it doesn't take much inveigling) to accompany him on a painting excursion. They traipse around and perch on a rock near the crumbling wall of an old French fort, then paint together in friendly silence. Bart's beginning to have time on his hands, and he needs to distract himself from his obsessions with Bertie. He sketches and paints—the sides of stucco buildings, tents by the shore, the face of an Arab. Art helps.

YEARS LATER, when my eyes follow the lines and washes of his art-work, I am, from time to time, borne back to a morning one spring when the sun was still pale with first light. I am six years old. Every morning my father wakes up shortly after dawn and walks downstairs to the kitchen. I listen to the clomps of his footsteps on the wooden stairs next to the bedroom I share with my little sister Judy and to the ritualistic snorts he makes through his generous Sicilian nose. That spring morning, I awake with a start. He is standing in the doorway of my bedroom, the room with polished cotton curtains printed with nosegays of lilacs and with the blonde furniture popular in new-minted houses like ours. He seems to be waiting to see if I am awake. I tumble out of bed, and he smiles. We are silent since we both know that my mother likes to sleep late when she can, and he knows she's been up with my baby sister, Jeannie.

He scoops me up and carries me down the stairs. I am not yet fully recovered from complications of the enlarged heart that rheumatic fever has left me with, and after eight months of not being allowed even to sit up in bed, I am under orders not to walk up or down stairs or hills, not to run or skip. In the kitchen he boils me an egg with his two, exactly four minutes. He carries me down another flight of stairs, and I watch as he rummages around in the basement and collects supplies: a bottle of turpentine, brushes of various sizes, hue-splotched rags that he keeps in a metal tackle box. He opens and shuts a wooden box he's sawed and nailed himself, and I catch a glimpse of little tubes of paint. His palette tucked under his arm and protected from his shirt with a chamois, he tosses those and a collapsible easel into the back seat of his black Ford with the ripping upholstery and lifts me into the front.

He heaves up the garage door, and we're off. He backs out of the driveway, pulls away from the young white oak trees that form a perfect triangle on our front lawn, away from Chevy Chase. It still has not occurred to me to ask where we're going. "How would you like to paint with me today?" he offers conspiratorially. My eyes light up. I flash on my memory of him, paintbrush in hand, leaning over the table he'd built over the junior bed set up in the recreation room the year before when I was made to stay in bed all day and all night for all those months. We'd collaborated on a paint-by-numbers picture of a cardinal on a metal wastebasket.

As we drive, I recognize the Pevely Fountain, where on certain summer evenings he took Judy and me. We'd sit in the car, our ice cream cones melting in the gummy air, and watch the soundless show with its mesmerizing spews of water in turquoise and saffron and rose. Now, in the climbing sun, it looks stark and empty.

From the parking lot we walk slowly, hand in hand. In his free arm he totes the tackle box, two easels, and two blank canvases. As he sets up, I wander in circles, examining the ground, the tufts of dewy grass, the twigs and small stones. And when I look up, I see that my easel is facing a waterfall. In memory the waterfall is enormous; in memory light bounces off the tumbling water, rainbows glimmer in the spray.

"Oh!" I say. "Oh!" My swollen heart seems to swell some more. Maybe I clap my hands. Maybe I'm a little afraid of the power of the cascades.

He smooths my flyaway hair out of my eyes and escorts me to the easel, a canvas already balanced on its rim. The easel is so close to the waterfall I can feel the spray on my cheeks. We squeeze tubes onto his palette. He gives me a little brush. While I am painting, he sets up his own canvas on a pile of rocks. Occasionally we exchange brushes.

Perhaps my smile sags because the colors on my canvas are now muddy, and because my waterfall looks nothing like the one whooshing in front of me, nor like the one on his canvas. But whatever the reason, he stoops down so that his face and mine are on the same plane (I can see the smooth olive skin of his cheeks and look into his eyes, as brown as the trunks on the pines in the park) and says, "Would you like me to tell you a secret?" Yes, oh yes, I would.

"This is the place I first kissed your mother." He dimples a bit. I hold the secret tight inside me, where it swells and soothes me for years.

Decades later, it occurs to me that of all the memories that were buried in his brain and taken from him, the loss of this one made me the saddest.

CHAPTER 6

BART AND HIS DAUGHTER RECALL HIS BOYHOOD IN ST. LOUIS

BEFORE THE NERVES in his cerebrum begin to twist into snarled nets, before plaques and tangles erupt and clump, before his cortex shrivels and his ventricles swell, Bart will remember the year he turned eleven and was driven across the river and handed over to a man named Michael Accardi.

Bart's parents still called him Sonny then, one of the few words of English they spoke, though it was hardly recognizable as an English word in the rapid rhythm of their Sicilian dialect. Everyone else called him Bartolo, a name that made him cringe. Everyone else he knows is Italian. His parents are two of the thousands who fled the dismal life of sleeping on dirt floors and digging and fishing out sustenance from the ground and sea. The older ones don't even try to form the flat, Germanic phonemes of English. The syllables they linger on arc out of their mouths, though the edges of the words cling tight to their tongues.

"*Dark corners,* those places were," Bart will tell his eldest daughter on one of those otherwise sunny days when his past and his present are making their initial stirs toward collision, though he does not think of dark corners when he takes that first trip across the murky current of the state line between Illinois and Missouri. He will describe for his daughter what he still hears in his mind's ear, sees with his surgeon's eye—details she, too, recalls, and misses—his mother's happy, crackly laugh, the branching veins of her busy hands as she rolled sheet after sheet of ravioli dough. And when his mind has not been able to, his daughter will contribute details to fill in the sketch and paint the picture he's presented. She will imagine his boy-world, these foreign people who were her grandparents, and, from his memory, will make a memory of her own.

He and she, though at different times, will wonder together what Caterina—who has finally shaken off any awkwardness about *Catherine* and *Jimmy*, the strange-sounding names she and Vincenzo were given with a dismissive scoff at Ellis Island—would have felt, or done, had she known about the dark corners Mike Accardi, the cousin across the river to whom she had entrusted her only son, would introduce him to in the next few years. It did not seem to matter to Vincenzo that Uncle Mike, as Bart was instructed to call him, was in the business he was in. In fact, Pop might have admired his cousin's entrepreneurship; it kept him out of the midnight-dark of the mines Pop himself had to endure. Bart would even bet that, according to Pop, Mike Accardi had a leg up.

All Bart will ever know for certain is that somehow Pop acquired an Essex and navigated the roads in it well enough to visit his second—or was it third?—cousin Mike, who lived in the city across the Mighty Mississippi.

ELEVEN-YEAR-OLD SONNY was excited, craning his neck up at the windshield as he sat crammed between his parents in the front seat of that Essex trundling by the fields of corn in rows, the smokestacks enshrouded in sooty thunderheads—and a stockyard that smelled like the scalded skins of the butchered pigs on his father's cousin's farm in Illinois. Caterina clung tight-fisted to the armrest and exclaimed in Sicilian now and then that she couldn't believe the long road after the Eads Bridge was completely paved.

That first visit to Uncle Mike and Aunt Fanny's house in St. Louis seemed to the young boy like a two-day party—cut-lace tablecloth, glass dishes with snug rows of Aunt Fanny's manicotti, platters of golden-roasted chicken, the lustrous skin loose on the tender flesh, cannoli covering small painted plates, embroidered napkins, and spoon handles looking like silver roses on long stems. This house in the city was so different from his parents' cramped, dark dwelling in rural Illinois, where the few boys he knew were good only for an occasional game of marbles or a fistfight.

There were to be more weekend drives, more visits—Sonny in his place in the center between his parents, his neck stretched so that he would be first to spot the enormous bridge, first to spot the house on High Street and yell, "Here it is! Here it is!" while his mother smoothed the wrinkles from the linen knickers she had sewn him. *Trousers just like the Americans,* she'd proclaimed, trying hard to use only English now that Sonny was at school.

How many visits was it before Mike Accardi, flim-flam man that he was, convinced Caterina and Vincenzo to give him their only son to raise? What words could have been summoned to move the boy's mother to give up her only son? Perhaps it wasn't any of the words Mike must have chosen so carefully, but some inaudible utterance from the same spirit that had whispered to Caterina in Campobello when she was twelve, entreating her to leave her family and journey thousands of miles across the dark, heaving Atlantic.

Or perhaps Mike asked Sonny in English to sit at the piano and play. "Oh," he said to Vincenzo and Caterina in the same dialect Bart's parents used. "Oh! What a talented little Bartolo, our Sonny. Who is his teacher?"

"A nun, comes two-three times a month," they offered, their cheeks already warming, knowing that for a talent such as they had here, that was not nearly enough. Bart pictured the nun in the church basement he walked to dutifully every two weeks from the rented three-room house set back in the field. He knew she dozed as he fumbled around on the piano.

"And see how smart he is," Mike was quick to add. "Already speaks better English than anyone in the family. Do they have good teachers in Du Quoin? Good enough for our Bartolo?"

Instead of answering the question, Caterina and Vincenzo dropped their gazes to the floral carpet. Caterina noticed specks of lint on some of the darker blossoms. But she was already thinking, *No matter. He'll play the piano, he'll learn English. He'll be an American. He can see my clean floor when he comes home to visit.*

DECADES LATER Bart will struggle to revisit himself and his parents at this watershed. When he realizes his brain is beginning to shrink and he scribbles random reminiscences on scraps ripped from prescription pads, he will almost hear Catherine and Jimmy thinking: What *was* there for a boy in Du Quoin who was destined to be an American? Did his simple but determined parents understand more about their son than he suspected? Did Vincenzo know that his own turgid accent on top of his constant rasping from the mine-dust made Sonny reluctant to invite his schoolmates to their dreary home? Did he notice how his son's neck reddened when the hint of a sneer crinkled his friends' eyes as they caught a glimpse of his father in his soiled overalls, even though Caterina scrubbed them between her knuckles every other night?

For a while on High Street in St. Louis, everything evolved as promised. Mike found an Italian professor of music, a wild-eyed man with tussocks of black and pewter hair who played every instrument in the orchestra, and Sonny took his lessons seriously. He started with simple Mozart minuets, but before long the pleasure of the music blossomed and he took on Beethoven's "Für Elise" and "Moonlight Sonata." Soon, he tackled grace notes, then glissandos. His fingers slid, his wrists rose and dipped. But even as the music filled his head, he couldn't help glancing up from time to time at what the man he called Uncle Mike had placed on the piano just before the first time he told Sonny to practice. On top of Aunt Fanny's hand-tatted lace runner covering the top of the upright were two objects: on one side, a metronome; on the other, a pistol. The sheen of the handle told even the eleven-year-old that it had been recently polished.

Every few months Jimmy drove the Essex the eighty-eight miles to ruffle his son's hair and to tuck the money for the lessons into Mike's pocket. The boy Bart must have felt happy—didn't he?—to have left behind his other, lackluster life. No more leaning over the stove to read *Grimm's Fairy Tales* when it got dark, no more trying to ignore his pesky little sister Rosalia. Here, on the piano bench and in his own room in the big city across the river, he could be king of the hill.

Just before the first day of sixth grade, a boy of about Bart's age with a freckled nose strode up to the house while Bart was sitting on the stoop. The boy was scrawny, and his shiny-skinned cheeks looked concave. His hair was the dirty red of the bricks on the houses. As he approached, Bart noticed a stick balanced on his shoulder.

"Knock it off," the kid said. Bart shrugged. No one had ever said anything that stupid to him before, but he wanted to be obliging, so he flicked it off with the back of his hand and waited. The boy socked him in the face, and the next thing Bart knew, he was sprawled on the sidewalk. The boy strutted away, his head thrown back in laughter as he switched the stick in the air like a whip. To walk the three-quarters of a mile to Patrick Henry Grammar School Bart had to cross O'Fallon Park, where he ran into a gamut of boys. There were only a few other Italians at Patrick Henry mixed in with Irish kids. Every day one of them gave another of them a bloody nose or a gash in the forehead. Bart soon learned to keep his distance, or use his feet and legs to give back what he got, and then they left him alone.

He'd seen some Negroes in the bordering neighborhood, too, some houses torn down, some with swaths of cloth covering their broken windows, but he didn't know where they went to school. There were a few Jews, though. The Jews—the rougher boys called them "sheenies"—were a different story. They were fair game. They were laughed at, punched, pushed around. Most of the time they would not fight back. It didn't take Bart long to realize that they must have been instructed not to.

Whenever he didn't win a skirmish, he marched inside to the upright. Forcing his eyes to focus on the keyboard and not on the top of the piano, he practiced, playing over Fanny's banging of pots in the kitchen, over the yowling cats on the fire escape, over the tinniness of the piano itself, until the music was in his head as well as his hands, until it was woven into the convolutions of his brain.

CHAPTER 7

THE BOXCAR TO ALGERIA

Where Harry and I are now we don't know; where we'll be tomorrow we don't know.

RETURNING FROM an afternoon of sketching in Port Lyautey, Bart learns that they are soon to move. *The Mediterranean,* he thinks, *a new phase.* Harry and Bart have heard through the grapevine that two officers are to accompany the baggage by train. They speak with their commanding officer, Fred Lahourcade, an open-faced, amiable fellow who used to double-date with Bertie and Bart at Fort Knox, and are given the job. This means not having to ride in a truck for five days. And they'll have an adventure. Bart's elated.

Before they leave the west coast of the continent, he, Sedam, and Harry take a few enlisted men on a sightseeing vacation. They truck between Rabat and Fes, 125 miles, to visit the ghostly ruins of the Roman mountaintop town of Volubilis, to glimpse the holy city of Moulay Idriss, and to explore Meknes, especially its ancient Medina. They wind through the most beautiful countryside he's ever seen. He soaks in the sights: "thousands of olive trees cushioning the roadside, its monotony broken by patches of fig trees, palms and fields blanketed with poppy, strange cliffs suddenly leaping into view, low rolling clouds severed by mountainous peaks and spread about the hilly sides." "Pardon me for being somewhat dramatic," he adds, "but that's exactly the way I felt." He promises to remember everything for Bertie. Everything.

The next day, the imminent transition is almost palpable in the air: the winds are whisking dust and sand into swirls. But the unit's confusion seems minimal. Those months ago at Fort Knox, Bart never dreamed that the 91st would ever function smoothly, but that's exactly what they're doing. Pride surges under his skin. During its time at Port Lyautey, the 91st Evacuation Hospital treated over 1,300 patients. He feels certain that now they can handle anything cast their way.

Plus, it's official. He and Harry are to take eighteen enlisted men and five days' rations on the train with baggage and lumber. Their destination: Mostaganem, Algeria, about 600 miles from Port Lyautey and 25 or so past Oran, near where the Allies, five-and-a-half months before, launched Operation Torch and soon defeated the Vichy French. The rest of the unit is to follow in trucks. An advance party has already left. He hears from Odom, now a lieutenant colonel and busy arranging their Mostaganem setup, that it's cold there and the train ride is two days longer than by truck. Let it be cold, let it be long. Bart's ready.

When all the patients are evacuated and he completes his duties in Port Lyautey, he laments, "Again I am no doctor." He advises Bertie to expect to miss several letters.

Before he strikes out for the train early Easter morning, he sneaks into the officers' tent and, although he feels rather silly doing so, places both hands on the piano. He rubs his fingers along the keys without pressing them down enough to make a sound. He'll practice on whatever pianos he can find with the sheet music Bertie has sent, and—soon, he hopes—he'll play duets with her. When he returns.

Bart and Harry will be on the train's guard detail, in charge of sixteen carloads of equipment. The train is not slated to leave until evening, but before breakfast, Bart limbers up with push-ups and jumping jacks. He wants to increase his appetite for the last meal he'll eat from a plate until who knows when. After the tents are down, an officer hands Bart a gun. In a photo of him and Harry at the boxcar's yawning mouth, they are balancing M-1 carbines on their laps. It's the perfect artist's composition: both men in their garrison caps spread-kneed, both guns resting on their thighs and pointing outward and skyward, a helmeted enlisted man between and in back of them forming a perfect triangle. Bart's left hand is cupping the muzzle as he might a violin.

Their boxcar is small and drafty, the floor scattered with mattresses for Harry and Bart, who offer some to the enlisted men. They also have a gasoline stove and copious cans of food—mostly chicken, which the mess sergeants who have also been assigned to this duty have been hoarding for them.

The first morning of the trip a euphoria ripples through him. He breakfasts on coffee, crackers, and pineapple and feels the thrill of adventure well up. As the train clangs along the tracks, he writes Bertie: "Where Harry and I are now we don't know; where we'll be tomorrow we don't know—but we've had a wonderful experience and I'm getting fat from it. There are a lot of miles in Africa. Just lots and lots of more and more. Vineyards, fig trees, cacti, date-trees, olive trees abound in vast fertile valleys bordered by high quaint hills, niched by stranger abodes." Then the two officers sit in silence, hypnotized by the landscape blurring by.

At Fes, their first stop, they switch from an electric engine to a steam locomotive. A trainload of German and Italian prisoners whizzes by, no doubt on its way to Casablanca. They rest again at Sidi Maharzin, where Bart bargains with natives for several dozen eggs and orders the conductor to stop the train for an hour at Ain Beida so they can enjoy lunch without the lurching. The conductor shrugs, but brakes the train to a halt. Bart likes his job of controlling the train. He's King of the Cars, Sovereign of the Stations, Ruler of the Rails.

They chug through towns with exotic names that he rolls around on his tongue—Qued Ambil, Bab Merzoka, Taza Guercif—and hamlets with nameless rail stations and huts of straw and stone.

They trundle through tunnel after tunnel in the Atlas Mountains, and soot settles on their clothes and into their skin. Washing doesn't help. Harry and he relieve the monotony by playing a little gin rummy. Bart rereads his stack of mail and takes notes. His hand jerks and his pen skids as the car clanks along, but he manages to record as many details as he can. "Up at 6:30 a.m. after more or less fitful slumber notwithstanding rumbling, squealing and whipping of these box cars with more air-ways than a TB sanitarium," he begins his second day's entry. They expect to be in Oran late that night and will have another thirty-two miles after that. In the meantime, he dashes out to buy lemons for their tuna before the train revs up again.

But before Bart's train can reach Oran, it is diverted to Perregaux with its tiled roofs, roses, and date trees. Perregaux, where the narrow gauge tracks begin and Bart and Harry have to scrounge up trucks to deliver the equipment to its destination. They've been clattering through the countryside for sixty-nine hours.

WHEN I THINK about that train cutting through that wild land on the other side of the mountains that rimmed the desert, I picture Bart most clearly in the daytime, a pen poised between his fingers, his diary open and balanced on his knees. He is squatting on his heels on a dusting of straw over the planked floor, his gaze torn between the terrain rocketing by and the words in his jagged manuscript zigzagging under and over the lines on the page. Perhaps in some ways this trip is an alternative version of the many train rides Bart took from Du Quoin across the river when he was a teenager. But to me—and I am almost certain, to him—this was not simply a train ride.

I examine the minutiae closely. For this man, now in the final year of his twenties, who is almost as hungry to taste the unplumbed world as he is to return to his wife, this is one of the first experiences he writes about at length in both his diary and his letters that bring him not only pleasure but a sense of being integral to the cause, of hovering inside the heart of the action without—not yet, at least—having to witness the horrors of the war that are playing themselves out and proliferating fewer and fewer miles away. Now, as the train churns toward the coast and Bart marvels at the contorted branches and spiny-lobed leaves of cork trees in the red-clay earth—or maybe it was simply the moment he boarded that boxcar—he knows he has been chosen, and he is as much of an insider as he can be.

When Bart arrives in Oran, it is almost the end of April. In a little over a week, the Americans will enter Bizerte, the British will occupy Tunis, and the Allies will trample the Axis' last defense in Africa. Although for now and for the days of this journey, no sound or scent or notion in any region of Bart's brain hints at danger, he wants to believe he's rushing toward it.

CHAPTER 8

THE HOSPITAL IN THE RACETRACK

We've apparently won the war in Africa.

ODOM DRIVES DOWN to meet them in Perregaux, and Bart rides with him over rough roads to Mostaganem, a port city on the Mediterranean Gulf of Arzew. Although in the years to come this city will be considered a major cultural center, now it looks to Bart like just another podunk town, Arabs shuffling from one place to another conducting their business.

But when his truck pulls up in a field of oats, his eyes widen. In front of him is a roofed grandstand with risers. It takes him a few minutes before he realizes that they are to set up their hospital in a racetrack, or at least, a former racetrack. Odom shows it to him proudly. He's already had electricity installed, horse dung removed, the grandstand partitioned. They'll use the grandstand and stables for wards, but they'll have to pitch tents to house most of the hospital. And they'll have to cut a field of oats to pitch the ward tents. Bart stares at Odom. Odom shrugs and says, "General Patton is anxious for us to get functioning soon. I'm giving us two days."

Somehow by nightfall the enlisted men have set up tents and built latrines. As a gesture, the officers let the enlisted men sleep in the pyramidal tents and pitch pup tents for themselves or sleep in trucks. That night two air raid alerts pierce their ears, and the men are uneasy. Rumors have it that there will be a lot of bombing there. But Odom, who seems to have thought of everything, has had a large red cross painted on the grandstand roof, and Bart feels a little safer than he might. In addition, the men are instructed to display the big white cross in an open space between tents to alert enemy planes. The colonel explains that the Germans have respected the red cross so far, but rumors are filtering up from Tunisia that medical men carrying arms are being shot.

Bart gazes out over the Mediterranean Sea—*beautiful but formidable,* he thinks—and sees a flurry of ships. *Something must be pending. Something big.*

The next day he and Harry again set up Bedside Manor, this time on a newly cut field of barley. Within a few days they've spiffied things up with cardboard, cans, paper, candles, and a little ingenuity. Bart's footlocker, topped with a blotter, serves as his writing table "upon which rests the photograph of the most beautiful and most loved girl in the world," he assures his wife. A shower unit is up—the water pumped from trucks—and they hope to have electricity installed in their tents soon. Bucky Shields, who'd worked his way through college by threshing wheat on a Kansas farm, shows the Arabs how to pitch the newly cut hay onto carts. Since General Patton has the town "off limits," they are confined to camp. As Bart's striker, Shorty, digs his foxhole, making quips and adjusting his glasses, Bart does laundry out of a bucket. He steals some gasoline to clean his only woolen shirt.

Bart fixes up his ward, too. They already have two patients to treat who are suffering with atebrine sickness from anti-malaria medication. A few days later, they receive a flock of convalescents, but they're transfers from a clearing station. Bart is assigned four, all with cellulitis. Not very challenging, but better than nothing.

When the rains drench their field, Bart worries about the Allies struggling to capture Tunisia in all this mud and gloom. But by May 8 they all cheer at the fall of Tunis and Bizerte, clearing the way for an invasion on European soil. The details he's gleaned that spring roil around Bart's head: Allied anti-tank weapons penetrating German tanks, gargantuan German motorized gliders on their way to deliver gasoline to Tunisian airfields shot down, grenades and bayonets by the hundreds upon hundreds, even that Nazi general von Armin taken captive. As eager as Bart has been to hear about the conclusion to this campaign, all he can say is, "We've apparently won the war in Africa." He's happy to know that that chapter is over, but behind his words lurks disappointment that he hasn't yet played his part.

The fact that the 91st is not—at least not yet—doing what they traveled over an ocean and a continent to do affects all of them. That fact settles into their skin and, increasingly, prickles and stings. They try to distract themselves. They play ball in the rain; Bart's sore muscles and backaches just make him feel old. He climbs up into the grandstand to hear George's sermon and surprises himself by singing along with the hymns. The chaplain presides over a square dance, but Bart's not much of a square dancer. Bart and Harry truck fifty miles along the Mediterranean Sea and into Oran. But the sky is threatening rain, and the clouds dull the coastline. The city seems dirty; the streets, narrow and crowded. He goes to the beach, but severe wind and sand play havoc with his eyes and ears. Bart and Harry open a snack bar in Bedside Manor (offering, among other goodies, eggs that Bart has managed to score for a dime each), and they soon draw a sociable crowd about their tent, but the food just attracts flies. Bart spends too much time trying to fly-proof his tent. He complains to Bertie that they "know nothing of birth control and shamelessly cohabit on your ears or on the top of your nose." Some days work is so light that he just straightens and cleans his side of the tent. *Bertie's framed photo always needs dusting*, he thinks. Other days, he does very little but sleep.

Perhaps it's this boredom, or curiosity, or the opportunity to practice some gynecology, which he hasn't done since he joined the Army, that leads him to town with Harry and Berg on that first week in May. They've been carefully chosen—Harry the gynecologist, Berg the genital-urinary specialist—to examine, as he later tells Bertie, "a bunch of women for purposes of which I think you know." As they explore the native quarters in Mostaganem, they pass a barbershop, where they're startled to see an old-fashioned blood-letting. They establish their own "pro" station and examine the prostitutes every week. Bart feels good about doing what he can to help keep the women healthy.

Before long, business picks up in the racetrack with varied new cases. But although he scrubs in on as many procedures in the OR as he can, the closest to treating wounds he gets is removing fragments and debris from an officer who has had a detonator explode in his hand. Sometimes an entire week goes by without his getting another case for surgery.

And then, while working on a broken neck case, he loses his patient. This loss represents the first mortality of the unit, and the notion that he has been responsible for that first death haunts him.

A whiff of excitement in the air sidetracks him from his brooding. General Patton screeches over twice, once for a rapid friendly visit and another to address a class in machine records that an adjoining outfit is holding in the grandstand. Everyone's on their toes, and the place literally bristles. While Chief of Surgery Odom gives the general a tour of their wards and introduces him to soldiers who were wounded in battle, Bart surreptitiously glances their way, trying in vain to take a gander at Patton's legendary ivory-handled pistols.

Soon the roses are in full bloom, and each morning the locals bring some to the nurses. But Bart's spirits are wilting. He discovers Bertie has spent her twenty-fifth birthday depressed. "Please bear up just a little while longer. You know me darling—if you give up, I give up and I don't want to. I just grind my teeth and try to smile, always looking toward a blazing bright spot in the horizon where you are standing, searching and waiting for me. Please buy yourself Eads Bridge if it makes you happy." He assures her that he will always keep his wedding ring on, that it comes off only when he operates. "And then," he adds, "whoever holds it for me has to sign a receipt, and when she returns it, I let her mother out of the dungeon." He entreats her to keep him posted "but don't make stuff up just to keep me happy. If you are sad, I want to be sad."

On the Fourth of July, the 91st has no fireworks other than the usual cannon practice seaward. At the beach the strong wind whips the sand into Bart's ears and eyes, but he returns to ten letters from home. "Today I have a heavy heart and a lump in my throat," he responds, "because I keep thinking of those days, years ago when I'd look across the lawn at you with heavy pounding in my chest and longing, love and worship in my eyes. My darling dolly baby, I can't help a silly tear."

CHAPTER 9
BERTIE, BARELY SEVENTEEN

THE SOFT SPRING SUN has drawn Bertie out of the apartment building on Cates and Eastgate, where she has lived for the past few months with her parents and four siblings, and if she uses her imagination and closes her eyes, she can almost see the forsythia buds she loves unfurling in the park. *The air is rich with promise,* she thinks, then wonders if that is a line from one of the books she's reading, piled up next to her daybed in the hall. She is sitting on the front steps near the sidewalk and is looking out at the street when a young man walks toward her. She notes his very tan complexion—one of the novels she devours might have called it "swarthy." And his clothes! He's sporting immaculate white linen Plus Fours, pressed without a trace of a wrinkle, and a yellow knit sport shirt with matching socks.

What a dandy he is! she thinks, sucking in her breath. Certainly as elegant a figure as she'd ever seen in *Harper's Bazaar.* He's holding a bag of popcorn, and when he rounds the sidewalk to turn toward the stairway and her, he offers her some.

They are chatting, but she can't stop staring at his shoes, polished so startlingly white. He is saying something about living in an apartment on the first floor, the one on the west side, the one next to hers on the east.

Why has she never noticed him? Where has she been? Always with her head in a book, she supposes.

And then he says something about expecting to graduate from Washington University in June. She feels awkward about telling him that she is about to graduate, too, but only from high school, especially since she will graduate a year early. She is not accustomed to hiding anything, though, and is just about to disclose this information when the young man says, gesturing with the popcorn bag to a spot in back of her, "Now there is a brilliant guy."

She pivots her head and sees Sammy, his rangy body, his kind face. "Yes, I know," she says.

The young man raises his eyebrows. "Do you know him?"

"Yes," she says, and he's already noticing the full, graceful curves of her lips and her . . . "He's my big brother."

The young, olive-skinned man widens his eyes. She sees in them a swelling of interest and respect, as if—high school student or no—she has just established her credentials. Then he almost spoils it all by making that remark about her lips. *What was it he said? Lips like cherries? No, that couldn't be it. Lips are pretty. Something like that.* She detests flattery and couldn't stand it if she thought he was giving her a line. She is ready to turn her back to him and march inside when he says it, but then something new flickers in his expression, and he flashes just a smidgeon of a dimple in his cheek, and she has an odd suspicion that he might have been sincere.

On the cusp of the summer after Bart shares his bag of popcorn with her, Bertie's mother asks her to go to the corner drugstore on an errand. On her way out the door, she spots him walking down the sidewalk, his arms pumping as if he's in a hurry. He sees her, too. "Oh," they both exclaim, embarrassed. He's just come from the barber, who has clipped his hair nearly to the scalp. Bertie has never seen a young man with so little hair. Bart explains that he is about to leave for his cousin's farm across the river in Du Quoin. What will he do there? Well, hunt squirrels, pick peaches—and, of course, hope his hair grows back quickly. He dimples. He always has his hair cut this short the day before he leaves, he explains before dashing away. *Refreshing,* she says to herself. All the way home she thinks of words and sentences she wishes she had said.

By the time June tumbles into July, it is already the hottest Bertie recalls, with humidity so heavy it hunkers down on her eyelids,

then floods her eyes with warm liquid salt. The tenants are blowing
fuses from running their fans so many hours a day. Closer to down-
town and the Mississippi it is particularly hot. Hundreds are dying of
heat stroke. Her apartment complex houses in its four or five buildings
about eighteen families, nearly all first-generation immigrants, including a multitude of young single people. Bertie is one of the younger
ones. The damp heat is so intense that no one can sleep. The older
tenants sit outside on metal folding chairs and soak their feet in aluminum buckets, ankle-deep with water and, if they can get them from the
milk man, blocks of ice.

Some evenings the younger people grab quilts and trek to Art Hill
to sleep in the park across from the museum and the statue of the city's
figurehead, Louis IX, his cross perpetually raised for the next Crusade.
Other times they just spread blankets on the ample front lawn and lie
on the grass. While evening turns to night and the clouds still hold the
light and heat, they smoke cigarettes. They gulp gallons of water from
quart jars, wrap wet cloths around their heads and necks to try to keep
cool, and play games to pass the time. Bertie has always prided herself
on being adept at games, but almost every time she is about to win
at Three Thirds of a Ghost, Bart steals her thunder. *How clever he is.
How witty.* When he's there with them, she forgets to be self-conscious
about the collection of beads of sweat on her nose, the moisture that
streams down her neck and pools between her breasts. She begins to
wait for him to pull up in his Dodge coupe, which gleams from his
weekend waxing, and join the gang on the grass.

Bertie has a job at an insurance company and has to wake up early,
which she hates to do, especially when she's been up until 2 or 3 in
the morning waiting for the air to cool, and especially since her job is
boring. She's thinking of going to secretarial school to learn shorthand
and do something more interesting, something that involves reading,
thinking. She tries not to think about turning down those scholarship
offers to colleges so that she could help her family, particularly the
younger ones, Rosie and Marvie, whom she adores.

One evening she spies Bart down the street. A little embarrassed
because she's had an eye out to look for him, she starts to veer off in
another direction when she realizes he's making a beeline for her.

"Would you like an ice cream?" he asks when they are facing each
other. She smiles. She could never turn down an ice cream. They stroll
to Velvet Freeze, take a table by the window, and talk. And long after

her chocolate milkshake has disappeared from its tall aluminum container and her napkin is blotted with her ruby-colored lipstick, they are still talking.

Suddenly Bart glances at his watch and stands up. He says, "I am twenty-one years old, and I have never, ever spent two hours talking to a girl before." She nods. Over half a century later, Bertie, dreaming back, will dub that moment "The Beginning of the Beginning."

The next time Bart runs into her, he asks her to walk with him across the street to the playground. On the rusty swing set they swing side by side, and it's all she can do not to recite "Oh how I like to go up on a swing, up in the air so blue . . ." because she doesn't want to sound like a child. He stops, and she stops, too. He digs into his pocket and, as if performing a magic trick, conjures up a ball and gently tosses it to her. By some miracle she catches it the first time and manages to throw it back, and then they spread out on the clover-speckled grass and play catch, and she somehow doesn't drop it *every* time it comes her way. But when she does fumble, he just swoops down to the ground, scoops it up, and in one fluid motion lobs the ball back to her again and again, never once making fun of her.

On their silent walk home, her shoulder grazes his, and she keeps her eyes on the passing lampposts. "Does your mother mind you going out with Gentiles?" he asks suddenly.

She doesn't want to answer that question, and she hesitates. But when she slowly nods *yes,* she looks directly into his eyes and somehow feels better than she has in a long time.

After that when Bertie tours the neighborhood, she admits, at least to herself, that she is on the lookout for Bart. One evening as she rounds the corner to her building, as if she's summoned him up, he drives up Cates Avenue and pulls over in front of her, rolls down the window, and they chat. He needs to go to the medical school and finish an assignment he started in the lab and would she like to come for a ride.

She hurries into her building as if to tell her mother, already knowing there will be no acceptable explanation. So instead of stopping at their apartment, she climbs the stairs to her friend Rosemae's apartment and calls her mother on the telephone. "I'm at Rosemae's," she says. "I'll be home in about an hour and a half." She's relieved that she hasn't had to lie.

She knows there has never been even the most fleeting of notions in her mother's mind that her daughter would be dating out of the faith. It is tacitly understood by everyone she knows that Jewish girls do not date Gentile boys. Daddy Rich has a nephew who married a Gentile girl, and Bertie has heard quite a bit of tongue-clucking and chatter about the subject, but the family has never addressed it directly.

And, besides, her friends (all of whom are Jewish) have been all too eager to convey the rumors they've heard that the Italian boy has been promised to another girl, someone just around the corner. When Bertie asked him, he told the truth. The girl was Italian, from the same town where both his parents were born and raised. The girl is not allowed to see Bart alone, and since she is a good Italian-Catholic girl, she does what she's told. *She's like Bart but not at all like Bart,* Bertie thinks. He wants to be an American, he tells her; he doesn't want to be chaperoned. And besides, he couldn't take this girl to his medical school fraternity parties with her dour, black-dressed mother sitting in a corner and crocheting, could he?

That fall he surprises Bertie by visiting her in the hospital after she has surgery. At first her doctor thought it was hepatitis, but it's really some sort of appendicitis. With a fingertip Bart writes on the dirty window "wash me" in his squared-off block letters. In the hospital she spends the lonely hours thinking about him. She likes his contradictions. He's from a small town but moved to the big city by himself. He has just joined, she discovers, a fraternity—a *Jewish* fraternity. His parents are Catholic, but he refused as a young boy to attend parochial school and declines to enter a church. He didn't read for pleasure until he was in high school and learned from Bernard Ofner—a Jewish friend!—to love books. Bart was a track star in college but doesn't show off his letter jacket. He plays three instruments and has his own band but is studying to be a doctor. He is so . . . different. So *intriguing.*

When she recuperates, they begin to meet regularly, usually at the rental bookshop next to the Tivoli Movie Theatre on Delmar. But she knows they can't be seen leaving the apartment together. So her brother Harry helps them—or their friends, Adolph Schwartz or Stanley Handleman, but particularly Bart's best buddy, Milton Hessel, who lives in the same building as the Passanantes. On any given evening, one of these young Jewish men picks her up and ostensibly takes her out for a date, but instead drops her at the rental shop, where Bart is waiting for her. Bertie hates deceiving her trusting parents, and it aggravates her anxiety even more to see the curtains rustle—and more than once—in the window in the Hessels' top-floor apartment. She's almost sure she's seen Milton's mother glaring down at them with a suspicious eye.

CHAPTER 10
SINGLED OUT

I wonder why people continue to be good to me.

PERHAPS IT'S NOT until I sort through Bart's recollections of Mostaganem and begin to arrange them that I see more clearly the developing patterns that define him on his circuitous journey of learning to
navigate this fascinating but lonely war-rent world. His actions and
reactions seem not only to distinguish him but at times to separate him
from the other young doctors who embarked with him on this particular adventure. I believe that he himself is noticing those patterns and
the ways in which he is different from others. I believe that, in spite of
his customary humility, he's proud that others, recognizing his worth,
are singling him out for special treatment. But it is also evident that
he perceived, perhaps even more keenly, the way in which his being
singled out was trailed by a shadow.

These vicissitudes in perception had been with him since Port
Lyautey, where the most prominent surgeons began to notice his work.
In Port Lyautey, Welch mentored him by expanding his repertoire of
surgical techniques and letting him practice even on particularly dif-
ficult operations, and praising his work. Sedam asked him to take
Welch's place on the emergency operating team in Welch's absence.
Knapp gave him one of his own recurrent appendicitis cases. But per-

haps the crown of compliments came from Odom. Bart wrote Bertie with pride: "Odom told the operating teams that the other ward surgeons were to assist or scrub but not operate—except Passanante." *What a morale builder,* Bart thought.

And now there are the nurses. He's been kind to them, helping them set up their tents and, when he has time, listening to their problems. But why do they always try to baby him, to spoil him? He's one of the doctors they invite to their tents to share the gifts of bourbon and cognac that visiting officers from other units treat them to. He's invited more than most of the boys, it seems. One particularly congenial nurse on the ward, Ann Goforth, has been known to switch names in the schedule so that interesting cases are assigned to him. Another one, Adelaide Mitchell, composes and sends him a loving letter allegedly from Bertie, which, at least for a few moments, whisks away the blues during the endless periods when her words don't reach him.

In Mostaganem the heady feeling of being in some way *chosen* swells when Welch gives Bart private lectures on operative procedures and even offers him some of his own cases and assists *him.* When General Patton honors the unit by requesting that Knapp and Odom travel with him on his general staff as his medical aides, Odom announces that Bart and Welch will form a surgical team. "I wonder why people continue to be good to me," Bart muses.

He's singled out in non-medical ways, too. The onset of June brings him a surprise. At an officers' meeting he's asked to offer a course in Italian. He's begged out of this request before. His vocabulary is limited; his grammar, problematic. His parents speak a regional dialect and never attended school, so he suspects his grammar may be off even if the pronunciation were similar. He's also sure, however, that the boys don't perceive the difference or even know one exists. But the meeting makes the request seem more formal, and he says yes.

As he walks away from the ward and a few of the men pat him on the back, his mind is already whirring away—if he had a primer, even a very small primer, he could learn a lot. That night he asks Bertie to send him one. "Just call me *Professor* Passanante," he tells her. Describing his first teaching experience, for which he spent hours nearly memorizing a manual, fussing over an outline, and trying to muster his knowledge, he writes: "I'm as nervous as a bridegroom and as delighted. (Was I nervous as a bridegroom, darling?)" The popularity of his classes belies his wavering self-assurance.

When it's becoming clear that the Allies are on the cusp of an invasion of continental Europe, Bart attends a meeting about who will be responsible for what in the oncoming assault. Though this is, after all, what they came for, their bravado cannot mask their apprehension. Their unit is to be part of the first or second invasion wave to treat battle casualties on a beachhead, and some of them will constitute an advance medical unit. As the names of the chosen are read, Bart's pulse kicks up, and he thinks about his promise to Bertie to return to her. When all the names are called and it sinks in that his name is not among them, he feels his heart slow. He tries not to glance at Fred, but Bart knows he has him to thank for this release.

The other side of the glossy coin of distinction is a cloudier and rougher one: Bart's deep-seated feeling that he is somehow marginalized.

Even after he finally began receiving mail from Bertie in late February, her letters are still just trickling in. He's had to watch the other men scramble around for letters, carry handfuls of them back to their tents, pass around photos. But now he's, yet again, a month behind in her life. And the most plausible explanation—the only one he can think of really—has been gnawing at him: maybe it's their foreign-sounding last name that's causing the lag.

I recall a phone conversation from a few years after my father's death with one of the cronies Bart mentions in his diaries. The man, by then in his 90s, sounded glad to hear from me, glad to be reminded of my father. But when I introduced myself over the phone, he said, "Oh, Passanante. He was that little Eyetalian fellow, wasn't he?"

Bart's self-doubts creep into his words to Bertie. In town he poses for a charcoal sketch. He has wanted to do it for a long time—in fact, he confesses that he has succumbed to an obsessive desire—but when he glimpses the finished portrait, he sees that the artist has made him look mean and angry. He wonders if that is the way he really is.

When I think of that portrait, which I never saw, a memory swims up. The sounds first: the clunk of the electric garage door onto the concrete floor; the slow thud of my father's footsteps up the basement steps to the kitchen. And then the sight of Bertie in one of her tie-at-the-waist aprons, her face already showing concern barreling toward alarm. Her husband's face has collapsed, his jowls have sagged. He sits down at the kitchen table, drums his fingers on its glass top. He has been passed over for Head of Surgery at the hospital in St. Louis where his patients have been filling the OR and beds for decades. He stares out the kitchen window at the grassy lot next door that he always regretted not having bought himself, now usurped by a house and an untidy garden, too near his property for his taste. She rests her hand on his shoulder. "Bart, Bart," Bertie says (though maybe not as gently as my memory suggests), "remember, you wouldn't have wanted that job. You don't *like* administration. You've been vocal about this. Everyone at the hospital must know that." But even at dinner, when she brings up tidbits of news or serves him spaghetti with her homemade sauce, just the way he likes it, he is still morose.

Years later, when, one by one, his colleagues, some from as far back as medical school, move to establish more lucrative practices in the western suburbs and to live in sprawling new houses with tennis courts and even riding stables, she reminds him again: "But, Bart, you have all you want. You love this house. You can afford to buy yourself a new car every year. You can send your children to any college they want. You have a practice in the city to help people there, not just country club people." But again, the collapsed face, the drumming fingers.

CHAPTER 11

THE GOOD MOTHER

ONE FRIDAY AFTERNOON, Bertie runs into the kitchen, where she always is Friday afternoons, to help with the weekly Shabbos dinner that is so important to her loving stepfather, Alex, a devout observant Jew. Her mother, Lena, is rubbing her cut chicken with a lemon wedge. She sets the lemon rind onto the neat pile of chicken fat, then positions the pieces in her iron skillet, lights the gas burner, and says, "Alberta, I heard that you and Mrs. Passanante's son have been—" Lena hesitates, not always sure of her choice of words in English—"having dates together." In fact, there has been a letter, telling her that not only is that Italian boy going out on the sly with Bertie, but that he is a philanderer, a woman-chaser. Up to no good. If she were a good mother . . .

She lifts a spoon brimming with paprika over the skillet and sifts the spice onto the chicken thighs and breasts.

Bertie is, for these few seconds, stunned, paralyzed. She watches her mother coat each piece evenly. Then she rallies. "Yes, we've talked with each other a few times," she admits, sounding casual, but she can almost hear her heart pump. "He's funny," she offers as if in explanation. She wonders what the Hungarian translation might be. "I mean, he makes me laugh."

Lena nods, with a fork turns the chicken, wipes her hands on a hand-embroidered dishtowel. Bertie waits. From the icebox Lena takes out the compote she made yesterday and removes the saucer she's used to cover it. "And Adolph and Stanley?" she asks, but Bertie knows that is no question.

"Milton is picking me up tonight," Bertie says. She, too, chooses her words carefully.

Lena looks up. "He's funny, too, Milton," she says. She doesn't need to say the rest of the sentence Bertie knows she is thinking—"and Jewish."

During the next two years, she and Bart do, sometimes, make dates with someone else. They are careful not to talk to each other under the Hessels' window or near the buildings. Bart gives his red-headed Italian girl an ultimatum. He simply cannot get to know her with her mother or aunt always chaperoning them every moment they are allowed to see each other. But there's nothing simple about his motive. He is thinking about Bertie all the time.

YOWEE. THEY AIN'T KIDDIN'.

There isn't much else to say at present, darling, but I know you want me to win this war for you so I'll just have to go out and do it.

IN MOSTAGANEM, a dominoes-like series of instances occurs that curdles Bart's mood and threatens to drain his confidence. One of them begins with an unexpected conversation. One morning on his way to the ward tent as he passes Colonel Snell, the colonel motions him aside, his lanky form leaning over the shorter man like a willow arched toward the ground, and confidentially informs him that he is recommending him for promotion. *Amazing,* Bart thinks. Making a beeline back to his pile of V-mails to report this exciting news to Bertie, he's ebullient. Eleven days later, the hottest and sultriest they've had in Africa, he finds out that his promotion has been, as he tells her, signed, sealed, and delivered, on its way up the military channels.

But two weeks later, he hears through the grapevine that all promotion recommendations have been returned. *Until after the invasion,* he surmises. Their bids will be pigeonholed—and his daydreams crushed—until the next go-around. He immediately writes Bertie: "Ain't that hell? Oh well! Another thing to look forward to is shot to pieces—there are so few around here. It really will be boring now. Do you love me anyhow—even if I'm not a major?"

The next evening, when Bart walks into a drinking party of a group of his lieutenant friends, he's met with a sudden lull. "What?" he asks.

"What's going on?" Finally one of them tells him without any attempt at tact that he's been a heel for "working" the colonel for a recommendation when there are so many captains ahead of him, so many who deserved it more. Bart turns away, speechless. He downs drink after drink, trying to numb the pain, and even so, his gut feels like it's filled with nettles. He'd give his right arm to talk with Bertie.

On May 19, while Bart and a few others are dancing at the Signal Corps beach house club, Bart has other worries. Mostaganem is bombed. The erratic flashes of light make his heart thump, and he's glad the boys can't hear it in the booming noise. Two nights later, as he will describe in his diary near dawn, he is "playing poker when suddenly the lights blink out and sirens begin screeching the red alert. Meanwhile we heard planes overhead in the moonless sky and then hell burst loose. The tracers and anti-aircraft fire were severe and their target was directly over us. I picked up my poker chips and ran to my tent, picked up my helmet and dove into my slit trench where I found Harry comfortably seated. The firing lasted 15 minutes while shell fragments and shrapnel fell all over us, some piercing the tents and some beating out a rain patter on the tin roof of the grandstand. Yowee. They ain't kiddin'." Afterward, the boys exchange witticisms, as if to cover the chill spreading from their spines. The next morning the men pick up shrapnel from the ground and gawk at the holes in the tents. When Bart is assigned as ward OD, he walks around with his helmet on just in case.

By mid-June the temperature spikes to 112. The ward tents feel like furnaces, and the blistering heat is wearing him out. He muses that the intense St. Louis summer might even seem cool by comparison. All he does after his routine work early in the morning is hunt for a piece of shade for the rest of the day. And they're still wearing woolens. Even though the air cools at night, he's had to sleep with the tent flaps open. The moon shines onto his face as strong as sunlight.

Wild rumors fly around that the 91st will move somewhere—perhaps Bizerte?—between June 10 and 12. But on June 11 they are still in the racetrack when they learn that the six days during which the Allies have been pummeling Pantelleria (the island nearly equidistant from Tunisia and Sicily) by air have concluded in victory. He hears that the bombing was so intense that when the British troops finally landed, the Italian garrisons on the island immediately surrendered. Now the

Allies have an air base, and it's only a hop, skip, and a jump to Sicily and the rest of Italy. Bart grins.

The third week of June, they are instructed to pack for a rugged voyage, and Bart sends home as much as he can so that he can travel light. They can take with them only their bedding rolls and whatever else they can carry. Their footlockers are to remain in Africa, and their overcoats will be stored in supply. Since he can't send back Bertie's letters without having them censored, he decides to strap them to his back. Change hangs heavy in the air.

A week later, Bart sadly says farewell to the advance detail—six lieutenants and three captains, including his buddies Shields and Hyde—who will probably participate in one of the early invasion waves. He knows he may never see them again. Within a few days all patients are evacuated and the hospital is disassembled, but for ten more days they just sit and wait for orders. Everybody has moved out but them, and once again they are eating out of cans and mess kits and reading by candlelight.

One day before the 91st finally moves, accompanying Capt. Whitworth, an eye doctor, to examine an Italian prisoner with an iritis, Bart sees about twenty Italian prisoners working on a French farm. Astounded that they are unguarded, he mingles and converses with them for half an hour. They are pleased to speak with an American who knows Italian. Every one of the prisoners seems content; for them, the war is over. For Bart it has hardly begun.

CHAPTER 13

BERTIE AND SAMMY

BERTIE DOES NOT want to come to terms with the fact that she's been shying away from her brother Sam. She feels guilty about him, about sneaking around him, and lying, though not about Bart's religion, or, rather, his parents' religion; she doesn't give a fig about that. She doesn't really think about her own religion except, of course, to please her father. She has heard from her mother since she was a little girl the story of how the eleven-year-old Sammy sat at the bedside of their first father, Jacob Rosenbloom, a week before he died; how the boy had solemnly promised his father he would not get married until his little sister Bertie had a husband to take care of her. Her mother's Hungarian accent thickens and her voice breaks each time she recounts that story, which she does often. Bertie has noticed lately that Sammy never seems to pay attention to girls, and Bertie suspects the reason involves more than the fact that he has his head in his studies all the time and is earning money to help support the younger ones.

One day when Bertie runs into her house breathless, having spent three-quarters of an hour too long necking with Bart in the Tivoli Theatre balcony and worried that her mother would ask where she's been, Sammy is waiting on the sofa in the living room, his hands in his lap.

"Shall we take a drive?" he asks.

He drives her to the corner of Westgate and Delmar, pulls over, kills the motor, and says, "Bertie, I want to ask you a question, and I assume you'll answer me honestly."

Her pulse quickens, and she is already phrasing his question in her head, hearing it in his soft, sincere voice, and knowing that to lie would be unbearable, when he surprises her. He does not ask if she is seeing Bart, if she is being devious.

"Are you in love with Bart Passanante? Is he really—" his hands drop from the steering wheel to his lap. He chews his lip—then blurts out, "a soul mate?" Bertie feels a rush of weightlessness. What a burden this secret has been for nearly two-and-a-half years. How awful to have to betray someone you love for someone else you love. She turns toward him and nods.

"And the differences in religion?" he asks, the question hovering in the air.

She thinks about what words she will use to answer; she does not want to be flippant or seem disrespectful. She shakes her head. "I don't think we have any differences."

Sam nods slowly, taking in the information in his usual thorough way, sorting it, weighing it. Finally, reaching for the ignition, he says, "Then that's settled. I'll talk with Mother. Then if you promise to date others, too, you can bring Bart to the house."

CHAPTER 14

A CLIFF AND AN OLIVE GROVE

*What I see around me ain't Hollywood props and I got a good idea that
real live ammunition is being used.*

BEFORE DAWN ON JULY 10, hundreds of Allied ships land in force
on the southeastern coast of Sicily. Bart hears they've tricked the Axis,
who expected a landing nearer Tunisia. General Montgomery's British
army has walked into Syracuse, and now General Patton and his newly
designated Seventh U.S. Army have lunged into the south and taken
Licata. *A momentous day!* Bart thinks. And soon he learns that wad-
ing from the landing craft to the shore of Sicily with the general was
Odom himself.

Now, again, Bart fills with hope. "I'm going to enjoy this party (I
think)," he writes. "Chin up for this next phase, dolly."

Three mornings later, the convoy begins to rumble for up to fourteen hours a day over nearly 800 miles. In the cab of the command car,
Bart jounces over the pitted roads. He takes in the arid land studded
with rocky hills, where herds of camel dip their heads and nibble at the
ground. Along the way they camp in open fields surrounded by anti-
aircraft guns jutting from the hilltops. Bart squints past prison camp
after prison camp, but he sees nothing that resembles a battleground.
They roll over the border of Tunisia, gas up, and pull into a dried-up
wheat field. Although far above olive trees and cacti scores of bomb-

ers zoom back and forth, grazing their heads, Bart has no idea where they're going, or even where this war is taking place.

It's not until the last day of the journey that he finally sees some of what he has wanted to see. From the hilltop town of Beja—which has been struck many times since the first weeks of the war in Africa—to Mateur, the gateway to the capital, a wide, war-scarred swath unfolds before them: "Shell craters, tons of twisted steel which once were German and Italian tanks were strewn about the road-side and on the hills—a picture of vengeful devastation." Hillside signs warn them of mines. And from Mateur to Bizerte, he notes signs of success in the hundreds of busy airfields, the thousands of vehicles and U.S. and British soldiers. Mateur has been shelled fiercely. "Bizerte," he writes, "is a mass of ruins—not a house or building is without holes or it is strewn all over the streets. The enemy air installations and docks on the harbor are a mess of mangled Nazi planes and ships. We did it up good this time."

In fact, so much damage has been done in Bizerte that the 91st sets up above it, in an olive grove on the lip of a cliff. That evening, skin coated with dust, stomach growling, he stands on a cliff overlooking one of Bizerte's harbors. Their rugged stretch of ground is blemished with anti-aircraft and pocked with a few bomb craters, but it's shaded by the silvery olive trees. He hangs all his belongings from nails on one of them. He jerry-rigs a half-shelter and mosquito net over his cot.

Bart feels happy. His gaze sweeps across the harbor. Barrage balloons float above it, and the full moon slides over the other side. It is a deep orange and flings a path of gold across the water, silhouetting the ships at anchor. *Their* ships. This is one of the most beautiful sights he's ever seen.

"I'm O. K. and hope I stay that way," he assures Bertie later. "These days are most eventful as you can guess. What I see around me ain't Hollywood props and I got a good idea that real live ammunition is being used. Things around and about us are spectacular to say the least and the more I see of it the more I want to wave the good old America flag. The organization has an unusually high morale and we are all anxious for that front seat which is imminent I hope."

For several long days he watches other convoys pull out of the harbor on their way to Sicily, less than 200 miles from where they're waiting now. Even Harry and the other officers in the advance detail are still waiting—on the docks, where Bart visits them. "Here we are sitting on Bizerte Harbor and the war in Sicily is nearly over while we wait for a ship—I'll be damned," he says. Ed Hyde is the only officer who has made the trip across the water, and the boys say they get little information out of him except "man, oh, man!" There has been no mail for some time, and Bart suspects he knows where it's going: to the place *they should be now.*

Even before they arrived, he'd heard that several other evacuation units were at Bizerte receiving casualties from Sicily. But none have come their way. He wants so badly to get to the action in Sicily already—and not just clean up after the Brits, or even Patton, for that matter. He has his reasons though he'll keep them close to his chest, at least for now. *It's only a matter of days,* he thinks.

But before the 91st leaves Africa, Bart will hop a jeep to Carthage and cast about the ancient ruins. Above him a mass of bombers and fighters will cover the skies. *Beautiful,* he'll think. *Beautiful.* The next day he'll discover that these planes have bombed Rome. Along the trip, he'll shake his head at the wreckage on the docks and the airfields loaded with Nazi airplane debris. Before the 91st leaves Africa, Bart will watch Nazi prisoners disembark and file past. *Ill-kempt, ill-equipped, and sickly Italians,* he'll think. *Arrogant Germans. Supermen. What warriors—phooey. The silly bastards.*

Before the 91st leaves Africa, Bart will learn that Mussolini has been arrested by his own Fascist Grand Council.

Before the 91st leaves Africa, Bart will swear: "I'll be damned. I'm itching, disappointed, expectant. So damned near and yet so far! And my former roommate is beating me to the front seat—the dog."

Finally, after they've been living hour to hour in makeshift shelters and out of musette bags for fifteen days, their orders arrive. Whoops of joy, thumping, clanging—their racket lingers past midnight. Still . . . no real action for the 91st, though. That night he writes Bertie: "Yes there is no change—I have no more fingernails. I won't have any heroic facts to relate to my darling when I get back. It seems that just when we're about to get in it—somebody holds us back for a rainy day. But we still have hopes and it's only a hop, skip and a jump away."

The loading thuds on until noon the next day as they back their twenty-five trucks and trailers and those of two other organizations onto the front end of an LST into a space designed for tanks; the decks are jammed with vehicles. On July 28, after seven months and four days in Africa, they are finally on the move. A large, white hospital ship in the lead, their convoy is speeding out to yet another country, on another continent he has never seen, across another sea.

In the morning they steam by an island. *Pantelleria?* he wonders. "And so we are off to Sicily—" he writes. He is thinking, though, of more than just the cutting open and suturing up of bellies and legs, but of something more personal, and in some ways more problematic. He's thinking about the faces of the enemy, wondering how much they'll look like him.

CHAPTER 15

COMING UP IN THE WORLD

By THE 1930s Mike Accardi, coming up in the world, had bought and moved his little family into a four-family apartment building on Oakherst Place in St. Louis's West End. But for years before that, on High Street, when Bart wasn't practicing the piano or scuffling with the boys in the playground, Mike took him places. They went to the Forest Park Highlands, or to Sportsman's Park, where he and Bart cracked open peanuts and yelled their throats raw as Rogers Hornsby slugged arc after arc over the fence, or gawked open-mouthed at Jesse Haines's knuckleballs, or pumped their fists at the Stecher-Londos wrestling match. When they stayed out until two or three in the morning, nobody bothered to wake him for school.

One evening after dinner, when Aunt Fanny was drying the dishes, Mike told Bart to start his homework, but Bart just kicked his short legs under the table. Bart looked up at Uncle Mike, his oily forehead, his boxcar ears, then out the window. He could almost hear the whack of that bat outside two stories below, almost see the end-of-summer dust cloud up over home plate.

"A-look, Sonny," Mike said. Bart winced at the name. Mike always used his stumbling English now that the boy was living with him. "If-a

I have a five-gallon can and sell eight of them for 45 dollars, how-a much I make?"

"What will you do with the money?" Bart asked, suddenly interested.

Uncle Mike raised his bushy eyebrows, pinched Bart's cheek. "You wanna' new ball glove?" he asked, then guffawed.

"Three hundred and sixty dollars," Bart said. Uncle Mike glanced down at the jottings Bart had made on the butcher block paper Mike had put in front of him, then gazed at him with affection, but also with something new, as if someone had just overturned a hat of gold coins onto his table, right over the book and the paper and the cut-lace tablecloth.

Now each evening as Bart scribbled out his math homework, Mike pulled up a chair to the dining room table and brought his new son other puzzles to solve, all involving cans and parcels, gallons and vats. Years from then Bart will not recall when it was that he first saw the whole picture, when he figured out exactly what Mike actually did, what he manufactured and sold in five-gallon cans, sometimes in bulk, to the slick salesmen without accents who pulled tight up to the curb in their Chryslers and Hudsons, or to the blank-faced customers who chain-locked their apartment doors behind them.

Years later Bart would recall one winter night as a turning point. A December or January—the ice on the curbs glowing a sickly yellow under the lampposts. Before they left the house, Uncle Mike waited for him to finish practicing the piano. That was one thing he was unambiguous about—Bartolo had to finish every word, every equation of his homework, then practice the piano for one hour every day. But that night, Bart noticed in his peripheral vision that Uncle Mike seemed fidgety, hovering over the piano bench, his hand disappearing over and over into his trousers pocket to come out with the tarnished-looking watch he always said was his father's though Bart suspected differently.

Mike led Bart across the street to a garage where he parked his black Buick coupe and unlocked the door, then closed it behind them. He opened the trunk of the car. He picked up a ladder from a corner and moved it just so. As Mike ascended the ladder, he motioned for Bart to stay where he was, and suddenly his upper half disappeared into a hole.

"Need your help," he could hear Mike call from the hole. Then he saw Mike's shoes on the top rung. Mike backed slowly down the ladder, grunting under the weight of a forty-pound can, which he handed to Bart. Bart could hear the liquid slosh inside it.

For more than an hour they dropped off cans of alcohol, Uncle Mike gabbing about the Cardinals in his thick Sicilian lilt. Occasionally Bart hefted the can for Mike, nodded at a client from under his cap, but mostly he just listened to the man who was glad to have a son after all those years of waiting, even one he couldn't claim as his own.

I must have been inured, Bart will tell his eldest daughter seven decades later, shaking his head rapidly as a goose shakes off rain, as if he still can't believe all the places Mike took him—the men seated around on folding chairs, decks of cards and jam jars of murky, amber-tinted liquid on the table, the hillock of coins and bills in the center, their hard-edged Sicilian syllables and laughter filling the room as their short arms reached to sweep whatever they could away. By then Bart knew how one thing could lead to another, how the man he called Uncle, the man with his new little boy who could figure out the arithmetic for his business, wouldn't stop at just taking his new son with him to deliver whiskey. He wanted Sonny to have it all, and he would show him *his* territory, all of it.

Bart quickly learned the ropes. Sometimes he drove with Mike back and forth over the Eads Bridge to haul a trunk-full from the stills in Collinsville. One day a blue-uniformed man Mike introduced to Bart as Sergeant Dempsey reached through the car window to shake Mike's hand, and Bart saw that when the sergeant withdrew his freckled arm, there was a twenty-dollar bill in his palm. Afterward, at home, Uncle Mike opened and shut the garage door, and Bart muscled the heavy cans up the ladder for him to stack. Bart's biceps soon bulged handsomely.

Sometimes they stopped in dives with cigar butts on the floor and chinks out of the wooden bar as if someone had taken a hatchet to it, sometimes in dark alleys or in brothels, where Bart might catch flashes of garish satin slips, hear things a young boy studying to be a pianist should not. But this was indeed Mike's territory, and no one objected to his bringing the boy with him. In fact, the men who met Mike's young sidekick seemed to enjoy having him around. Like his father, they ruffled his hair, even pinched his cheeks. He spoke English without tripping on it, and no one hooted or looked down their ugly noses; the kid could help them read for one thing, newspapers, signs, even contracts. Besides, he was funny and used to being teased. He followed Mike Accardi around like the puppy he always wanted but was never given.

AFTER SPRING BURST upon St. Louis and the pyracantha flared up in banners along the city parks, summer took hold and the heat closed in, and Bart's parents wrote Uncle Mike a brief letter requesting that Bart come visit them. They missed their boy, and it had been several months. It would soon be July, and there was no school then, and Bart didn't have to play the piano every day during vacation, did he? And since they promised to let him return to St. Louis to go to school and to continue his piano studies, Uncle Mike bought Bart a train ticket to Du Quoin.

The day he was to travel to Illinois, Bart waited in the living room for Uncle Mike to show up to drive him to Union Station. But Mike was late. He'd been delivering. By now, Bart knew, Mike had fine-tuned his system. He'd simply park in front, knock, and walk in the door. He'd be carrying a valise, one chosen with great care, the dimensions yielding evenly and snugly to the contours of a five-gallon can. Bart could almost see Mike stepping over the threshold of the faded brick house of his second to last customer of the day, a man who rarely said anything, who looked like he left his couch only when he shuffled to the door to accept another delivery. He must have motioned Mike inside and nodded to his wife to bring him and Mike a cold Coke. Why should Mike say no? Bart could take the next train.

At last Mike honked the horn, and Bart sprinted down the cement steps and slid into the back seat next to the remaining undelivered valise. The coupe lurched forward, then sped. They were within a block of the 18th Street station when they heard the siren.

"Oh, no!" Bart yelled in spite of himself, but Mike turned to glare at him. Bart bit his lip and tried to fix his gaze out the front window, away from the police officer who was taking his time sauntering to the car to give Mike a citation. Since there was no way to hide the suitcase, Bart moved as far away from it as he could, until the armrest dug into his waist. His pulse raced.

"Hello," Mike said politely even before the officer reached the window. Bart didn't recognize this policeman as one of those who tipped his hat or pretended to look away when Mike was transporting or delivering. Mike spoke in a rush, Bart flinching at his accent. "I'm-a sorry I was speeding, but I got to get my nephew to the train. His parents are waiting for him in Illinois. You let me take him rest of the way, I promise I come back and you can take me in, whatever you need."

The officer peered into the back seat and nodded at Bart. Bart sank into the seat, for once wishing he were even smaller. Mike opened the door, and before Bart could move, the officer reached in as if to grab the suitcase in back, but Mike said quickly, "My nephew, he like-a carry his own case."

The officer smiled at Bart. *Give the boy his due,* he must have thought. *Someone needs to make a man of him someday. Those dagos need to get a leg up.* The two men walked Bart to the train, the policeman elbowing others out of the way and Bart lugging the suitcase, the contours of the metal five-gallon can knocking against his thigh. At the train, the policeman gestured for Mike to help Bart board, and as they hurried to step into the passenger car and Mike grabbed the valise, Bart felt he could finally breathe. He slumped into the nearest seat, and as the train whistle shrieked, Mike swung the valise onto the overhanging shelf, wheeled around, and hurried off the train.

Of course, by that first visit home, Bart was more interested in helping Mike than in going to school or even playing the piano. One afternoon they dropped off a can at a smoke shop on Choteau, not far from Jefferson. The proprietor sat behind the counter, his skin a treebark dark, his laugh so different from those of the *paisani* at the taverns, this man's laugh soft, as if his vocal cords were lined in flannel. The "cutting," Bart knew, was what folks did who bought the whiskey from Mike but wanted to make some money for themselves (or "theyselves," as the man said). The man motioned Bart through a curtain into an over-stuffed back room and showed him. Bart already knew enough of the business to figure that the amount of water was greater than the amount of alcohol by around seven gallons. He knew the alcohol was generally 100 proof, and estimated the dilution brought the percent of alcohol to about 75 or 85. Uncle Mike always said that would do—at least for some.

Bart knew he shouldn't ask about this aspect of the trade. The people he'd seen with Mike had an unsettling air about them with their long, bulging coats and hats that nearly obscured their slits of eyes, and it was best to keep in mind just who he and Uncle Mike were.

BART WILL REMEMBER the first time Uncle Mike showed him the still in the attic over the bedroom closet. Bart loved the idea of a secret entry. Mike would carry a ladder into the bedroom, open the closet, push aside the mothball-stinking coats and dresses, and, palm flat on the ceiling, push up, and after a grunt, a square of the ceiling would give way. When it was time to manufacture the product, a friend or relative would "cook" the liquid, just sitting on a small stool, chain-smoking cigarettes while he watched a five-gallon can fill drop by drop. Bart's job was to figure out how many cans of alcohol could be distilled from so many gallons of mash. He'd learned more than he wanted to know. But what he will remember most is the stench of the mash that oozed from the attic through the wooden panel in the ceiling and seemed to fill every room. That smell could make him vomit.

Sometimes he'd be walking home from school and a waft of that odor would smack him just as he turned the corner of High Street. Later on, he wondered why they weren't raided more often. When the police finally did come, in some odd ways he felt relieved. It took them only a couple minutes to find about 100 five-gallon cans stashed above the bedroom.

Uncle Mike was wearing a long coat and kept his hands at his sides, rubbing against the wool, the rubbing betraying the calm on his pale face. Then he said to the lieutenant with the red hair and pug nose, "Maybe we should come to an understanding." But the lieutenant shook his head.

"No, Mike,' he said in a serious tone. Bart thought he could see two gold teeth when he opened his mouth. "I shan't do that." Bart had never heard the word "shan't" before. It wasn't until years later that he realized how lucky they had been. There were kids in his class whose parents had been shot by other gangsters. At least Uncle Mike maintained his independence in the business.

When Bart entered Beaumont High School, he became even more tuned into Uncle Mike's bootlegging, and more uneasy about it. It seemed to him that every week there was news of a shooting. Sicilian gangs, particularly the Green Ones, waged war with other gangs, some primarily Irish, like Egon's Rats and the Cuckoos, and with other Sicilian gangs, like the Russos. Whispered in the same breath with gory accounts of bullet holes in walls, streams of blood, mutilated bodies abandoned in alleys and tossed over bridges, all these names became words in Bart's personal lexicon. Fanny's mouth increasingly tightened, Mike was jumpy.

Mike once took the boy to a double funeral—Shorty Russo and Vincent Spicuzza, kingpins of the Russo gang, which had already been the perpetrator and victim of bloodshed in the war instigated by the ruthless Cuckoo gang. The rumors buzzed citywide that the two Sicilians had been hired by thugs in Chicago to kill Al Capone. But someone had tipped off Capone first. Their bodies, pistol-whipped, kicked, and bullet-torn, were shipped back to St. Louis, a nickel enclosed in their stiff fists. One of the truckloads of floral wreaths that decorated the church was signed by Capone himself.

SICILY, ITALY

July 30, 1943 to November 11, 1943

CHAPTER 16
THE REAL THING

We have the box seats I ordered. It's the real thing now darling and vacation is over, at least temporarily.

It is already July 30, and Bart is impatient as the packed LST tries and tries again to squeeze into the small dock at Licata, near where Patton launched his sweep up through the heart of the island. Despite the lack of a destroyer escort or plane protection (and a bout with sea sickness), the crossing has been smooth—no torpedoes, no planes, no bombs. They sighted land at 5:10 the evening before, but because unloading would have been tricky in the blackout, the ship spent all night bobbing in the harbor. Even the poker game in the dining room fell flat, and he threw down his cards at midnight. The men had packed their cots before they landed, but Bart wove his way to a jeep, lay fitfully on a bunch of paraphernalia, and popped a Nembutal to catch some sleep.

Now, heartened at the spectacle of the hundred or so Allied ships swelling the harbor, he muses, *How silly of anybody making war on America.* American troops have occupied Palermo for a week now, and the fighting has shifted toward Messina, in the northeast corner of the island's triangle. Bart is eager to be ashore. He can hardly believe he's in Sicily. In spite of his efforts to control it, his heart races.

Stoked on melons and grapes several Sicilians have brought them, they convoy eleven hours to Palermo. The coast roads toward Agrigento, into which Patton's armor roared just two weeks before, and those over the mountains inland are rugged. The trucks wind and bump through towns, past compact stone buildings, cobblestone narrow streets—beggars, children with smudged faces, women in tatters, signs of poverty everywhere. But as they pass, the people wave, smile. Bart is amazed. *Aren't we still at war with Italy?*

When the 91st's convoy finally pulls into Palermo, Bart sucks in his breath at the sight of the white building looming up before them. The large letters at the top read *Medicina,* the medical school. An American flag has been hoisted in the front courtyard, which is landscaped with young flat-leafed trees and palms that have graceful arches mirroring those of the first-floor windows. The entryway is flanked by fluted columns. In back, flat-topped, sand-colored mountains rise above the trees and the sparse buildings. Inside, his quarters remind him of his junior intern quarters. He even has a cot and a mosquito net, a bath, running water. And he's been assigned to one of three surgical teams; his is the midnight shift. He writes Bertie, "We have the box seats I ordered. It's the real thing now darling and vacation is over, at least temporarily."

Although there is always an aura of confusion around what is happening to the 91st, Bart will piece together the story of the war around him from the radio, which has blared out warnings of an impending invasion and asked people of occupied countries to prepare. He and Harry and clusters of others, jostling for places around the radio, will hear how, when Eisenhower broadcasts the Italians' intention to surrender, the Germans, who have anticipated this and are at the ready, will disarm the Italians and move into their defensive positions. How the Germans will recapture Mussolini from house arrest on the highest peak in the Appenines. How Allied forces will finally drive through the rubble-choked, once-elegant city of Naples in the wake of the Nazis having gutted factories, burned artwork to ash, sunk every vessel in the harbor, and blown up sewer lines, soaking the city with disease-laden water. Bart and Harry will cheer and toast until their throats are raw and their blood pulses with whiskey.

During the three months and ten days that Bart will live and work in Sicily, events will transpire that will bend the trajectory of the world. But the most intimate way Bart experiences the war comes from the wounded whom he bandages and transfuses, cuts and sutures in his ward and on the operating table. He learns about the plight of American destroyers like the USS *Shubrick* by working intently on the severely burned victims. From a pilot with a flak wound he received from a bombing mission, he learns about the attack on the toe of the boot, the Allied landings at Salerno, less than 200 miles away, and as Bart continues to receive trainloads and planeloads of casualties, he learns how ferociously the Germans are waging their counterattacks. What a tough job the English and Americans had attempting to cross the Volturno River, how arduous to slog up the peninsula under fire. How wounded British commandos had been left with no food and no treatment but first aid for three days. How the weather and the land have also played their roles in enmity and execution: the rains swelling the rivers, the treacherous currents, the slick, steep slopes and rock-strewn mountains. He will eventually understand that this is going to be a longer war than he, or anyone else, has predicted.

But for now, late into the final day of July, Bart tours the Medicina complex, examining it from various angles. For a second he closes his eyes against the plunging sun and envisions, instead of the barren hills in back of the building, the trees along the streets near home—the silver maples and oaks, the hickories and elms, the scallops and star-points of their leaves, soon to be burnished and flaming in fall. He takes a gander at the Italian prisoners, working hard to unload the equipment and baggage. In spite of their sweat and grimaces, they look happy, grateful to be able to work for their food. The only trouble they've had with the prisoners apparently is that when they're returned to the stockade, a *larger* number walks in than came out.

The 91st is barely settled in when at 4:00 a.m. he is jolted from his cot by a barrage of anti-aircraft. He fumbles for his shoes and helmet. Bomb after bomb plunges down. Later, when his pulse is steady again, he writes, "The anti-aircraft was furious and continuous but seemed utterly ineffective. We were helpless—crowding in the corridors or looking out the windows—glass broke, the building would shake with each bomb and even the concussion waves were felt." One shell exploded in the street in front of the hospital. Patients screamed. Bombers concentrated on the ships in the harbor, a stone's throw away. After a bomb hit an ammunition ship, there was a momentary lull. Then the injured began to roll in. Many came in dead—or with chunks of flesh chewed off, head injuries, compound fractures, shock.

Bart doesn't finish in the OR until mid-morning, and the wounded are still pouring in. His shift officially begins again at midnight, and when the patient traffic slows at about 3:30 a.m., he tidies up the hospital in preparation for General Patton's visit. As medical officers, they have already identified the deserving recipients for Purple Hearts and have put all the air raid injuries in one room. After Patton passes out the Purple Hearts, he declares the war in Sicily will be over by the 22nd of August. A big push is supposed to start that day or the next, and Bart wants to believe him. He's proud his unit is Patton's pet. He longs to tell Bertie about the general's visit, and about the air raid. Instead he writes, "I have time to write lengthily to my baby but rummaging about my mind I find that all the spectacular things I want to say are all censorable. It must be enough to say that finally we got what we have been looking for—and plenty. I have a hunch now that the midpoint is passed and I'll then come back to you and live again—"

The next night, again the hills light up with those ghastly yellow flares, strings of bombs plummet and shake the ground. For an hour the walls and floors quiver, and the windows rattle with every terrifying blast. He sleeps only a few hours, just enough to prepare for the 200 patients the night train will deliver from the front to be gurneyed in, bringing the count up to 790. The bed count is 400, but at least there have been 500 evacuations. He can't imagine how overwhelming all these patients would be if the Italian prisoners weren't working as litter bearers and general cleanup men. Bart has never worked this intensely. He tries to focus on only what is in front of him—the swath of skin, the snake of intestine, the pooling blood—tries to work with his usual concentration and precision. Still, his scalpel makes wavy incisions.

Finally the skies are quiet, and he can let his mind wander to the fantasy that's been brewing in his brain for days, perhaps even before the shore of Sicily telescoped into view. And now, he has time to see if he can put his plan into action, to do all that a rootless impulse inside him has been urging him to do.

That night, before his shift begins, he looks around the grounds for Fred. He'd finally confided his plan the night before, but he knows that any commanding officer might see a problem with his request, might very well say no. "So, you'll ask the colonel?" he'd asked Fred. Fred, flashing his characteristic half-smile, reassured him. He didn't even look particularly worried. But Bart has been hesitant to ask, or even to mention the plan whirling in his head. The war makes being here so complicated. *Hell, the Sicilians are still the enemy,* though he has trouble thinking this way. The next morning, he secures the colonel's permission. Yes, he will be allowed to travel to Campobello di Mazara, the town he'd known as The Old Country since he was born.

Early the next day Bart takes C rations, a jeep, and a driver and rides along the north seacoast with its rocky outcroppings, its blue, blue water below, its cacti and bougainvillea. Then he dips inland, where the terrain gives way to fields striped with rows of grapes and olive trees, to a dingy-looking town of low, flat roofs.

What is swimming in his head on that bumpy way west in the country of the enemy? A murky vision of the fluid facts that defined his family? Of that other self he can still feel gnawing away at his memory? The boy called *wop, dago,* the teenager knocked to the street and kicked by other children of immigrants from other countries? Here he is now, he almost has to remind himself: *Dr.* Passanante, a U.S. Army captain, rumbling toward a place he thought he'd never see and was never sure he wanted to see.

He drives straight to the city hall and finds his way to the mayor's office. The mayor stands up, shakes Bart's hand heartily, and gives him the directions he's asked for. When Bart thanks him, the mayor opens his hands as if he were welcoming Bart to every room in his palace. Then, as Bart is about to turn down back toward the door, the mayor says, "Your father's brother is in the building."

He finds his uncle, Calogero, a bony, balding man, stooped and gap toothed, who, when he learns Bart's name, embraces him as if he doesn't want to let him go. He takes his nephew by the elbow, and they weave up the streets, the uncle chatting in Sicilian, elongating his consonants as the syllables gallop up and down the scales of sound, and Bart straining to understand. He learns that his grandfather, Bartolomeo, for whom he is named, and his grandmother, Vincenza Passanante, are now dead. His mother's mother, Francesca Indelicata, he knows has been gone for a dozen or so years, and his mother's father, Stefano Riggio, vanished even before his daughter boarded the boat that would cross the ocean to deliver her to that promised land of America with those streets paved with gold. On top of the hill, he passes the tiny church his mother sometimes talked about, still standing though bullet holes pock its walls.

When he gets to the wooden door of the stone and clay hut with the dirt floor where his mother lived for the first twelve years of her life, his mother's sisters, Maria and Anna Riggio, seem almost to be waiting for him. Perhaps it's because he's wearing an American uniform or they recognize him from a photograph, or perhaps because he looks so very much like his grandfather, but they run to him. They cling around his neck, bury their gray heads in his chest, wail and weep. He takes in their frayed dresses, their sallow skin. They kiss him hard, one cheek and then the other, again and again. Then his father's sister Caterina joins them, and before he knows it what seems like the whole neighborhood has shoehorned into the house, all speaking at once. Someone sends someone else out for ice cream, and from half-empty cupboards, they scrounge up almonds, a melon, wine. While Bart tries to figure out who is who, one of his aunts—Maria or Anna?—fries him one of the eggs she's been hoarding to feed the family. They all huddle around him to watch him eat. When he has scraped his plate, a throng parades him to his father's home, just two rooms though there is a floor. Everyone in this house is dressed in threadbare and mended clothing and looks ill-fed and haggard. He ransacks his memory and pulls up the notion that somewhere in the countryside his father's family once owned a small vineyard, maybe also an olive orchard, and maybe even a wine warehouse in town. Of course, that was before the war.

Seemingly countless numbers of these good people come and go, swell the house. He leaves money and cans of stew, hash, pork and beans, crackers, and cocoa for his aunts and uncle. When his Aunt Maria insists that he take the last of their eggs with him, his eyes heat up.

As the jeep bears down the road back to Palermo in blackout and the waning full moon sneaks above the saw-toothed peaks, a sentence from a warning speech by General Patton floats back to him: "Many of you have in your veins German and Italian blood, but remember that these ancestors of yours so loved freedom that they gave up home and country to cross the ocean in search of liberty."

He will never forget these four hours with this enemy who embraces and kisses him, who dampens his cheeks with their tears. "I will never forget," he writes Bertie after he returns to the hospital. Not their heart-wrenching poverty, not their faces when he said goodbye and left them red-eyed and helpless looking. He recites it aloud, as if it were a vow.

When he returns to the hospital, he hears a rumor that the Germans are intending to flatten Palermo, though he is too exhausted, and too distracted, to stay awake and worry. But he can't help hearing and seeing the most ragged of echoes and images.

CHAPTER 17

DARK CORNERS

It is 1932. Bart is driving the business car up Highway 40 and heading west over Eads Bridge in the dark. He's beginning to wonder how he's arrived at this place. Not at this road, the bumpy highway that leads him from one flat state to another, not this bridge, which spans the Mississippi, from which, if he stretches his neck and glances back, he can see the smokestacks of Peabody Coal belching out orange flames that lick the blackened sky on the other side, but this place in his life. If only his father hadn't broken his leg. If only Uncle Mike hadn't been caught. Bart shakes his head, steals a glance to his right as if someone were in the passenger seat, but all he sees is the smeary window, the harvest moon an eerie smudge behind it.

What was he doing back in Illinois anyway, and at that hour? He'd cut his ties with Mike Accardi, or at least begun to unravel them since his folks had moved to St. Louis. But Uncle Mike and his father had already joined forces—wasn't that really why they'd moved to the city?—and Bart had known enough to stay out of it. At least he thought he had. But something nags him, makes him squirm, an itch on his conscience.

Soon he would pass Washington University on the Hilltop, and the itch makes him twist in his seat. This is the reason, he knows. This was why his father had joined Uncle Mike's business. And already it looks likely that, if they were careful, they would have the money to send Bart to medical school and perhaps even Rosalie's husband Jack to dental school. They've been putting away pennies. And if his father hadn't . . . if Uncle Mike hadn't . . . well, who knows really?

And how long can this last? Business is already on the downswing. They'd all heard about the Volstead Act, seen it looming closer in their sights. But instead of scaling down, Uncle Mike had come up with the scheme to bolster their business by investing in some distillery across the river. It made Bart edgy, especially given what he'd been reading in the papers. And then there was all that business about remaking the car. Truth to tell, he hadn't minded helping the folks get the Dodge coupe to the guy with the grease stains in the shape of a sickle on his cheek. He hadn't minded waiting in the cigarette-stinking back room most of the day while the grease monkey hammered and drilled so that the trunk could accommodate twenty-five gallon cans of alcohol, hadn't minded while someone re-enforced its rear springs so that the 800 pounds were balanced and the driver could enjoy a smooth cruise over the bridge and up the road. That long, dark road where, for the third time since Pop had broken his leg, he found himself driving on now.

Bart is more uneasy now, much more. What will his mother do if his father is sent to jail as Uncle Mike had been? There had already been one sting, and now Mike is cooling his heels in Union, Missouri, for possession of a barrel of whiskey in a basement beneath that pharmacy on Grand. Or, rather, for those stamps he counterfeited for the bottles.

Suddenly a car skids in back of him, swerves to the side, and surges beside the coupe. He glances in their window. Three, maybe four, faces. Meaty noses. Slick-backed hair. Scowls. One hidden by the rim of a hat. Other Italians? He looks at the road ahead. The car is blocking the return lane. At least there's no traffic from the east. One of the men jabs his index finger in the air toward the side of the road—at least Bart thinks it's only a finger—and he hesitates for an instant, but the car edges closer, and he knows that a one-eighth turn of the wheel will thrust it right into the new paint. Bart lifts his foot slowly from the gas, eases on the clutch, presses the brake. Slow motion. As if he's disembodied, somebody else. If he were the praying kind, he'd do it. He'd heard of cars of roving thugs; Prohibition had sure brought out the best in everybody. *This is it,* he thinks. He stops. Hands gripping the wheel, he focuses his gaze straight ahead, hears the other car door slam. Then, a knock on the glass. He fumbles for the handle, cranks down the window.

"What are you doin'?" the man at the window asks. No accent. He doesn't sound at all like Mike or his father.

He thinks of the 800 pounds in the trunk. Of the twenty-five gallon cans. Of what his father would say. Of the pointed finger that may have been . . .

"I'm a driver," Bart says. He hears the crickets, hasn't noticed before that he's had to raise his voice to talk over their racket. "For Mike Accardi." He wants to look this thug in the eye, but can't.

"Like I say, what're you doing?" The man's voice is now impatient. The other men, Bart can see from the corner of his eye, have gathered around their car. One has a cigarette. He can smell the smoke. He wishes he had a cigarette now.

"Hauling liquor. From Collinsville." Bart gestures with his head toward the trunk, then turns toward the man at the window—white T-shirt, skinny arms but muscular—looks up into the face. What surprises him is that the man is about his age.

The man's skin has a bronze sheen to it in the moonlight. Yes, dagos, Bart decides, but of course doesn't say so. The man with the sheen to his skin nods, signals with his thumb to the others, pivots and walks to his car.

As Bart rolls up his window, his hands are trembling. He remains in the coupe at the side of the road long after the cloud-streaks billow up and shroud the moon.

CHAPTER 18

A STRANGE EBULLIENCE

I wish you were here to see these unusual (for us) and beautiful things rise out of destruction and squalor.

IN SPITE OF the wreckage from the spring's and summer's bombing of Palermo, in spite of the absence of his wife, in spite of the trainloads of wounded that already overflow the wards, Bart's descriptions of his early sojourn in Palermo suggest a strange ebullience. When he takes the time to inspect the damage in the city, although he notes the dirty holes in the walls where people in rags cluster, the beggars, the nauseating odors, the buildings splattered with metal or nearly crumbling, his artist's eye also sees a gorgeous city unfolding before him. He and Knapp tour the town in a carriage. He marvels at the domes and monuments, the stone archways, the sculpted draped nudes rimming the fountain, the gardens with palm trees. And the cathedral—what a monstrous and beautiful structure, with its carved statues and marble, its silver and gold. In the chapel of Santa Rosalia, his thoughts turn to his sister Rosalie, who is finally pregnant. He'll be an uncle! "Darling," he writes Bertie, "I wish you were here to see these unusual (for us) and beautiful things rise out of destruction and squalor. I'd like to wrap this city up for you and send it to you."

About ten days later he's asked to escort Ollie Atkins, photographer for the *Washington Daily News* and, now, for *The World Tele-*

graph and the Red Cross, around the unit. They amble along the corridors and peek into a few rooms: the photojournalist in his owl-eyed glasses, the doctor-soldier dimpling at his guest's winsome grin. For Bart, underneath the easy camaraderie a sense of the magnitude of this ephemeral time must be inundating his consciousness. Isn't he still the child bootlegger, the foreigner, trapped on one of the lowest rungs of the social ladder? And yet, here he is now, *Dr.* Passanante, helping an elite photojournalist create history.

Neither of them knew then that the photos Atkins would publish would affect millions of Americans and others around the globe—and for scores of decades in a foggy future that Bart has not even begun to envision.

It is over seventy years later as Ollie Atkins' photos are parading before me from government archives, click by click on my laptop screen, that I alight on two images that zoom me back, deep into 1943. The first image depicts a nurse bent over a patient on his side, next to a small table with a basin. Above him is a bottle, and a tube curves down into his veins, although I cannot see the actual veins, or even the arm. He is receiving plasma. My eyebrows arch. I am almost certain—I so want to be certain—that this is the gift Bart gave the photojournalist, this moment made eternal by the power of art.

The other image is a haunting photo of a narrow Sicilian street, paved in oblong stones, rubble swept to the sidelines, the walls and balconies of the buildings flanking the street slanted at an angle that causes the white light radiating from the background to seem like a character of its own. In the center: a man and a woman, backs curved over a table, a wine bottle placed in the corner, a cat staring up from the street at the photographer (and now at me, down that dank time tunnel). And that light—that light looking as if it is roaring in from the background, just missing illuminating them. The legend reads: "A Sicilian family dines 'al fresco,' eking out a small measure of civility amidst the detritus of war." I think of Bart and of all the measures of civility that he was able to eke out—and all that he was not.

WHEN THE ITALIANS hear Bart speak in their mother tongue, with their accent, sometimes a crowd gathers. Some of them offer him friendship and eclectic gifts, which he accepts with pleasure: a pink silk embroidered bedspread, green bananas, a 100-year-old Malacca walking stick embedded with a sword. One of these new acquaintances, Trovato, a friend of his father, who now lives in Palermo, insists that Bart come to his home for two-hour lunches, where his American guest gorges on seafood and spaghetti and meat and apples and toasted nuts, as well as for Sunday dinners with three kinds of wine. (Trovato must be connected to the notorious black market, Bart suspects.)

Bart experiments with the Kodak film Bertie sent him, buys chemicals to use for developing it, borrows Hyde's daylight loading tank and learns to use it, delights in the results. His surgery is going well, too. After only three weeks in Sicily, he performs his first abdominal operation without supervision. One night, though he's been standing up so long doing surgery that his feet feel like someone has pounded them with sledgehammers, he performs nine operations himself. When he figure-eights a spica bandage around a surgery site, he thinks, *Artwork. This looks like artwork.* He just might be a surgeon yet.

Then, on September 8, exciting news comes at supper. After watching the celebrations in the street, he hurries to his quarters to pass it along to Bertie. "Darling mine: just a little over three hours ago our big chiefs informed the world that Italy had surrendered unconditionally. We took the news with a great deal of joy. From what I saw this evening the people here are also joyful. Shouts of '*Viva l'America*' and 'it is over' filled the air. To them it means their sons will soon be home. There will be a long night of festivities here I believe—even in blackout, altho' the moon is half full. I think most of us are dreaming of the day when we shall cheer at the end of the war—with this difference— we shall cheer in victory instead of surrender."

And his promotion finally goes through. He's *Major* Passanante now. Legs pumping, heart pounding, he rushes to his cot and pulls out a V-mail form to tell Bertie. How proud his family will be. The rest of the day he can think of little else—Bertie, Mom, Pop, major's leaves, Bertie, Mom, Pop, major's leaves . . . Bucky and Harry have also been promoted, but Bart is buying, and several nurses join them for thirteen bottles of Seagrams until some of the boys, including Bart, celebrate themselves sick.

In a little room of the officers' quarters, he and a few of the boys open a bar and dub it The Sundown Bar. They have decorated its walls with a colorful mural for which Bart has contributed a drawing. The bar is popular, and even the celebrities troop through it—Jack Benny, Anna Lee, Larry Adler, Al Jolson, Bob Hope, Frances Langford. And they now have a piano near their quarters, writing tables, chairs, a radio! One letter describes even more conveniences and pleasures. "Looking about me today I found I'm living in a civilization approximating that which I left in the states. We have allowed civilians to open a tailor shop, a beauty shop and a barber shop in our quarters. We have a seamstress quartered with the nurses. We have a place for peddlers of linen goods. We have a town (fairly large city) within walking distance which has gradually become wide-open. We have a long line of neighborhood women who vie with each other for our laundry which is ordinarily done much cheaper by the nuns in the building. We have a colored quarter-master 2 blocks away who does dry-cleaning for us without charge. We get a pack of cigarettes daily in our ration. We have meat three times a week, at least. The pastry in town is wonderful. <u>Should I complain?</u> I want to come home to you dolly—but let's win the war here first—shall we?" He'll be home for Christmas, he assures her. Someday he'll want to retrace all this with her, he says.

But the undercurrent of gloom, more intense than any related to being annoyed at Army regulations or living arrangements, or even to missing Bertie, has been gaining momentum. By early October it has roiled into a desperation of sorts, one that threatens his commitment not only to his work and his unit but to the way he defines himself.

CHAPTER 19

SHOOTOUT

I came home and there was blood all over the snow on the front lawn.

BY THE TIME Bart was 20, as he was in February 1934, he was already intimate with blood. He'd shot squirrels and hunted birds and deer on his cousin's farm many summers running. For the last three years he'd pored over blood slides under the lab's microscope, squinted at the platelets with purple-stained circles. But all that was different from what he was about to see as he drove home from the college that night. As he parked his black Essex that late afternoon, those carmine marks on the front lawn must have looked, at first, like some work of art gone amuck in an inconceivable place. But as he angled toward the house, he saw that something was terribly wrong: two large pits carved into the snow patterned with pools and ribbons of what he now recognized as blood.

Three days earlier, when Mike and Fanny Accardi pulled into their garage behind their building, two men were waiting. The larger one was Herman Tipton, stogie bobbing under his turned-up Irish nose, shaded by a bright white hat, the boss of the infamous Cuckoo gang. He and his sidekick drew their overcoats back to expose the barrels of their revolvers. They ordered Mike and Fanny to get out of car and escorted them by the elbows to their living room. Then Tipton demanded money. When Mike emptied his pockets and pointed to the crumbled bills, Tipton announced that unless he came up with $2,500 cash in three days, they would take him for a ride. Mike was picturing this ride when the telephone rang. Mike spoke with his cousin Vincenzo Passanante in the dialect of the dreary Italian town they were both born in, explained to the glowering Tipton that Vincenzo wanted to take him to a show, and before much else could happen, Vincenzo entered the apartment. Mike begged the other men (by then two more men had joined them) to let them go. To which one of them responded, "If you don't get that money by Monday, we'll bomb your house and bump you off." The Cuckoo gang had already bumped off more men than he could count. The cousin exited, and Mike agreed to scrape up the money. What else could he do?

What he could do was go to the police, who'd been waiting for a way to get rid of the Cuckoos, whose most recent gang war had left the city's buildings pocked with slugs, armored sedans roaming back alleys, and curbs littered with bloody bodies. The District Attorney soon joined Mike in the station. They could use this dago two-bit crook to put these thugs away.

What happened a few days later on February 26 at the house Bart had called home for over seven years became St. Louis's own soap opera. Tipton called three days later and demanded that Mike bring the money to Eleventh and Pine and "bring that looker wife" of his. Mike, exactly as the police had instructed him, said he was afraid to leave the house. Tipton finally agreed to collect the money there.

When the sky had blurred into a battered blue, two men in overcoats mounted the steps as eight detectives waited in silence. Mike cracked open the door, and havoc shattered the windows, splintered the wood. Revolvers and shotguns blasted the air. Overcoated men barreled down the steps, firing away. A detective knotted a tourniquet over his wound and, his blood blossoming out, led the chase outside. One man toppled backward in the yard, his left leg dangling; another dropped facedown onto the sidewalk and fired his final bullet before collapsing for good. The snow was rutted by two dead bodies, stained with the blood of three men, one of them unarmed.

Since neither of the dead men was Tipton, he was tried for extortion.

The front-page copy the *Globe Democrat* and the *St. Louis Post-Dispatch* cranked out with mug shots of all the key players titillated the imaginations of the three-and-a-half million city and county residents for over a year. The audience was hooked as soon as the *Post*'s lead paragraph set the scene: "While housewives in Oakherst Place, a secluded West End side street, prepared dinner in the kitchens of their homes last night, eight detectives sat in the darkening living room of the apartment of Michael Accardi, a bootlegger, at No. 5952."

As the snow shrank and the red buds exploded into flower, Bart fretted. He snipped columns and collected them in a cocoa-colored manila folder. He paper-clipped it closed on all four sides to ensure that the flimsy columns he'd taped together were organized in one place. On the tab he wrote "SHOOTOUT" in big, block letters. In felt marker on the front, he recorded "Feb. 27, 1934," and under that, "I came home and there was blood all over the snow on the front lawn." Bart cringed at the all-caps headlines ticker-taping out into the universe, at the way the reporters called Uncle Mike "the bootlegger Michael Accardi" as if all four words comprised his name.

As night after night the papers reported Mike's story, Bart couldn't help noticing that Mike recalled more details, and that he recalled them differently. He remembered more about his bravery, more about his leadership. In Mike's newly illuminated memory, Tipton ratcheted up the volume and his threats. ("You dago, you see this gun? I'm going to crack it down on your head. I will fill your belly with bullets.")

Within fourteen months the trial, which Bart did not attend, trailed to its sorry climax. Bart shook his head at the judge with the Irish name who was clearly on the side of the Irish. Imagined Tipton's attorney's swagger as he cross-examined those stupid Wop witnesses who could barely speak English. Obsessed about the grainy photographs that resembled mug shots: Mike's thin lips pressed together angrily, meaty Italian nose taking up much of his face, and those black-browed eyes—their crazed look, their cartoonish evil. And then there was Fanny, as lovely as Myrna Loy or Ingrid Bergman, but pictured in a fur coat, a dead ringer for a gangster moll.

Perhaps the most painful moment came after the fate of all the participants in the debacle had already been set in motion, when it was clear that the prosecutor's dreams to use the feckless Sicilian and his ignorant cousins to take down the powerful Irish gang would be dashed. After the jury snickered at Mike's inflated story and after it was inscribed into legal history that Mike once operated a still in the house he'd brought Bart up in.

That moment came when the key witness for the prosecution took the stand: Vincenzo Passanante, Bart's father. Perhaps it was what Bart couldn't see and couldn't hear that gnawed at him more than anything else: the way the star witness, when asked to describe the events he'd months ago detailed for the police, repeated four times, "I don't remember." The way the prosecutor reeled and jabbed the signed statement toward his witness's face, demanded that he read it aloud. The way the witness hung his head, the way he was made to wrench up the volume so the entire court could hear. How Bart's father's cheeks enflamed when he murmured his own surprising confession, one that had nothing to do with murder or even bootlegging, the confession finally loud enough to be fully understood, to produce murmurs that bounced off the courtroom walls as ear-shattering as an assault: "I can't read. I never been to school."

The papers blared the story within hours. "Witness impeached on cross-examination," they said. The headlines screamed, "I Don't Remember" and "Says He Can't Read."

"All I felt was shame," Bart said after the jury declared Tipton and his henchmen not guilty. "All I felt was shame," he said again and again over all his remaining decades.

I'd like to think, though, that, with time, what swam up into Bart's gray matter was the conviction that his parents, who'd kept him out of the fray, who were using their own money (acquired legitimately or not) to ensure him a college education, were determined that he would be a better person than they were, that he, by God (or by whatever powers they could summon), would be a successful American.

I'd also like to think that, after Bart spotted the blood on the snow and marched through the tainted drifts toward the house, as he turned away from Oakherst, away from his blackened past, he noticed the way the lampposts glittered the ice on the sidewalk, and that he heard a gathering murmur, rich and mellifluous. And that he kept his head forward as he strode toward it.

CHAPTER 20

THE SPREADING BLACK CLOUD

It shouldn't be such a long war.

THE DESPERATION THAT infuses him in Palermo begins with the little things—niggling frustrations here and there, paltry disillusionments, a pale specter of paranoia. The photo shop returns the film of his relatives not only unprinted but scratched irreparably. Then there's the post office's new ruling that now prevents Bertie and everyone else from sending candy to soldiers overseas. "Is it possible that the candy is a necessary 'home front item' to line the guts of those poor two-fisted, hard-fighting fat-bottomed 4-F's dearly defending St. Louis? Gosh, baby. I'm sorry to use up our space for stuff like the above but I'm mad at the St. Louis postal departments," he complains.

Moreover, his second trip to Campobello is hotter, longer, dirtier. He takes a circuitous route, out of his way—four hours this time—so that he can drop off one of their Italian enlisted men in Santa Margherita to visit his kinfolks. In Campobello the men are all home from the vineyards now, and they join the other relatives in nearly suffocating him with attention. In fact, the number of relatives keeps multiplying. To entertain himself, he flashes his wife's photograph at every opportunity. The women make him spaghetti (they follow his instructions not to use onions or garlic) and kill a chicken or two and somehow feed about thirty people in the cramped house.

On the drive back, he has to find his way in blackout, and his mood turns the same color as the mounds he sees in silhouette. Even his promotion casts a shadow: it makes him feel, especially now that his hairline is clearly receding, old.

Unsettling surprises seem to multiply. Rumors from people who have heard him speak their language in Palermo must have made the rounds because Bart begins to attract random Italians who do not claim to be related but still vie for his attentions. Some of these self-proclaimed friends won't take no for an answer. (One, for instance, brings him a vase and expects Bart to pay him for it.) Random others from Campobello arrive unexpectedly at the hospital, bearing gifts from the countryside and vineyards: wine, figs, almond brittle. Some even expect him to drop his duties and drive them back to Campobello. As good as he feels about having opportunities to help his parents' family, and as much as he knows his parents will take great joy in his connecting with their kin, their unpredictable appearances and assumptions about what he can and cannot do during his workdays burrow under his skin more than he wants to admit. And as the Germans, furious with their allies for surrendering, swoop down over the Italian skies with bomb after bomb, the casualties just keep flooding in.

One afternoon after they've once again dive-bombed the harbor, Bart, who's been working since 5:30 a.m., is just about to stop for a bite to eat before returning to the operating table when his 75-year-old great-aunt (his father's mother's sister) and her son drop in on him at the hospital. They've brought him a basket of eggs, cookies, and a melon from his aunt. He's grateful for the eggs; he hasn't had one since he went to visit them. They chat for a few minutes, and he's about to send them on their way, when the great-aunt asks him to give her a physical exam. Right then and there. He is anxious to get back to the patients, but he wants to be a good boy, to make his relatives happy, to please his parents so far away. So he finds a nurse willing to help, takes out his stethoscope and Baumanometer, applies them to the appropriate places on his great-aunt's body, and declares her healthy.

But the most prominent trigger of his downward spiral happens when George Knapp, who has been named acting chief of professional services while Odom is traveling with Patton as his surgical consultant, assigns Bart to an overflow medical ward. The trains have delivered forty new cases at once. So now Bart is first a medical ward officer treating patients with malaria and sandfly fever and only second a surgeon, and he's questioning his ability in both fields. "A wrong day," he calls this. "A strictly wrong day!"

Trains chug into town loaded with patients who jam the wards. Bart seeks out Knapp and tries to persuade him that he should be allowed to return to surgery. Knapp agrees and Bart is back on surgery the next day—but two days after that, Odom calls him in to tell him that because they've had another record admission, two wards are again full, and even if Bart is a surgeon, he'll have to take the wards. Bart protests, and the colonel turns stern and cold. He informs him that insofar as Bart isn't running the hospital yet, he has no choice but to return to the wards. Even before he closes the door behind him, Bart's morale plunges.

Then there is the spreading black cloud of boredom. After the war is won in Sicily and the fighting shifts to the mainland of Italy, the work slows, and Bart is faced with idle time. He stares into space, beginning to wonder where he'll be going next, feeling the ache of Bertie's absence. "There is only one star I can see shining," he tells her. "That is you. Beyond that I think no more." When there's a full moon, he can see her in it. If only she didn't seem light-years away.

The first week of October brings another setback. Odom tells him in what Bart is sure is a deprecating tone that he is dissolving Operating Team 3 and assigning the ill-tempered Major Rose, who shares the graveyard surgery shift with Bart, to orthopedics and fractures. And Bart? He's to be what he will come to call "High Potentate of Ward 15." "Ward 15, my dear wife, is the crap ward—reclassifications, chronics, jaundices and some G. U." He's being pulled out of surgery altogether, leaving junior officers in surgery wards. "I have 42 beds, and as far as today's rounds go, they are just that to me—42 beds."

Just when he thinks things can't get worse, the paranoia he's been fighting down about being marginalized swells to a head. On October 13 Italy declares war on Germany, but that, to Bart, is a matter of indifference. He confides in Bertie. "Taking a shot in the dark I asked Knapp what the idea was. Why was I getting pushed around? He was piqued at my attitude and bluntly said 'If you want to know, your work in surgery lately has not been of a conscientious nature.'" Rose apparently told Knapp over a drink that Bart wasn't taking care of patients and helping the ward surgeon. Knapp told Odom. Bart feels betrayed.

Odom reminds him how he's bent over backward to treat him fairly. He also admits that, having gotten wind of Bart's discord with Rose, he was concerned about the lack of team cooperation, which he believed was causing Bart's surgery to slump, so that was why, when the surgery bogged, he broke up the team. Some part of Bart knows that Odom was trying to enable the team to save face. And now what must Charlie Odom, the fair-minded colonel Bart has respected and considered a friend, think of him?

Even Bart's body begins to betray him: chills, fever, headache, backache. The rancor ripples up and spreads. He entreats Bertie to help arrange a transfer for him. There's no place for him there, he's a persona non grata, he tells her. He suggests she ask her boss if Bart might transfer back to St. Louis, to Barnes Hospital.

Then Harry tells him that he's been granted permission to join the advance detail. This, the job Bart did with Harry last time! After that, he keeps more or less to himself. After he says goodbye to Harry over coffee at 4 a.m., he misses him. All the other men are getting on each other's nerves. Bart tries to keep his focus where it belongs, on being a good medical doctor even if he can't be a good surgeon.

That night he lights two candles to gaze at Bertie's flawless face through the cracked glass he's patched with celluloid tape fashioned from X-ray film. "My darling, as I look at you now I remember every little thing about you. Little things that I once took for granted—things you did because you wanted me to be happy. Three years ago this evening we were brought together by law—that we must never forget. But what is written unto eternity is the fact that long before that we were tied by a bond far greater than an early union. How else would you have moved into Cates Ave.? Three years ago today we made a home—a completely happy one jealously guarding it with every fiber of our being. We still have one darling—we'll fit the pieces together again. Here's a toast for us tonite, 'We'll live again.' Happy Anniversary, my darling." He slips into bed, finally—or at least for the remaining hours of this night—at peace with the world.

Soon, his handwriting reverts to his usual generous up-and-down manuscript, his tone returns to humorous, and he reassures Bertie that a few pneumonias have relieved the monotony of his medical practice and he is now even enjoying his work. He asks her to send him a book on physical diagnosis to refresh his mind and to help him design a more effective system for examining patients. "I guess I'm a medical man after all," he admits. "If nothing has been done about the transfer, then forget it. It shouldn't be such a long war."

But Adolphe Menjou, one of the celebrities who's visited Palermo, has predicted the war will drag on until June 1945, and Bart fears he might be right. Even so, Bart tells Bertie, "Darling—when spring comes—then begin to look for me."

CHAPTER 21

ENTER SPRING

One Sunday afternoon when an early spring enters St. Louis just boldly enough for Lena to open windows and invite in wafts of lilac and crabapple, Bart is a guest at the Riches' house on De Giverville. Lena is getting used to the Passanante boy. He's already galloping along in his internship. He works so hard he's even been living at the hospital. She has to admit she loves how he gulps down her paprikash and capon (but so politely), how he always thanks her as he consumes platefuls of her roasted veal breast. In fact, if you ask her, you couldn't tell the difference between Bart and a nice Jewish boy.

After dinner Bertie washes dishes and Bart wipes them dry, a task he isn't allowed to do in his own house since Italians believe that housework is women's bailiwick, that men have more important things to do. But in this house he's seen Alex swipe the window ledges with a dust cloth, bake apple tarts for Sunday breakfast. As Lena spoons leftovers into a few red-striped bowls to save in the icebox, Bart suddenly turns and says, "Mrs. Rich, is it all right with you if I marry your daughter?" Lena stands still, stares straight ahead, but Alex pipes up from the living room, "Maybe you should ask me first." Bart smiles, says, "First things first." He knows which one of them he might have to convince.

Bertie raises her eyebrows, keeps washing. This blurting out has caught her by surprise. She has been, for years already, resolved to be patient, to wait, as all responsible adults do, for Bart to finish medical training, perhaps to establish a practice. But she wants to be with him every day—and, yes, every night. Though they haven't explicitly discussed it, this move has seemed increasingly obvious—inevitable.

Lena finally looks his way and nods. This is no surprise to her either, of course. How many Sundays has he been a guest at her table for dinner now? It's almost as if it has already happened.

Bart glances from one to the other of these strong women. He picks up another plate, and as he circles it with his dishtowel, he looks at Bertie and half-asks, half-announces, "How about October?"

Bertie lifts her hands from the dishwater, turns to him, sees that dimple, and tries not to cry.

When Bart comes home that evening, his father is sitting alone at the kitchen table with a deck of cards in his hand. He is so short that his feet barely reach the floor. He holds up his hand so as not to be distracted from his game and his ghost opponent. Bart takes a chair and waits to get his attention, revising his rhetoric in his head. "Pop, I want you to know something. Bertie and I are getting married in October," Bart says.

Jimmy shuffles the deck, slaps the cards in a messy row onto the wood table, covers them and uncovers them with other cards. "Do you know," he says, in his almost impenetrable accent, "that she's a Jew?"

"Yes, I do know that, Pop." Bart keeps his tone polite, away from ridicule or sarcasm.

Jimmy slowly swipes the cards into a pile, edges them back into a deck, shuffles again. He slaps the deck onto the table. "But Jews are crooks," he announces, as if that were a fact that his college-graduate son should know since everyone else seemed to.

Bart is prepared for something like this, doesn't let his voice waver or hint of emotion, doesn't acknowledge the irony given the source of the declaration. "Do you know any Jews?"

Jimmy thinks a minute, shakes his head. "No, but I heard."

"Is Bertie a crook? Are her parents crooks?" Bart asks.

His father walks slowly to the back of the kitchen and grabs a jug of wine from the shelf-papered sill over the stove. For several seconds, he hesitates, considers the question, then shakes his head and turns to face his son. "No," he says. "No. But she's an *American* girl. Why not a good Italian girl?"

Bart's mind flickers to Bertie's parents, one from Hungary, the other from Czechoslovakia, hears their accents in his mind, and is about to respond in the most tactful way he can, when his father pours wine into two jelly glasses, shoves one to him across the table, and raises his glass.

"*Salute,*" he toasts.

CHAPTER 22
A WORLD LIGHT-YEARS AWAY

I lived the day with two hungry but wonderful painters.

IT IS LATE OCTOBER, and Bart has already begun to shiver as soon as the sun dips down when he meets two artists, Zangara and Buttitta. They've brought their sketchbooks, pencils, and paints with them to the hospital to trade sketches for cash. Bart watches as Welch poses for Zangara, and something about this unassuming, young-looking artist compels his attention—this long-necked, lean man with fine facial features, a swath of wavy hair, and eyebrows pointed up in the middle like upside-down V's. Bart admires the delicate, precise way he angles his brush. As they ease into what will be their first of many conversations in Italian, Zangara drafts him a vision of his life as an artist—how he uses not only pencils but oil paints, water colors, even pastels; how he studied painting nudes and engraving at the Academy of Fine Arts; how he worked in architecture; how he wants to make art in the United States. Bart is mesmerized.

Bart sprints up to his room, grabs the new leather-bound photos of Bertie, and rushes them down. He presses them into Zangara's hand when he is finished with Welch. Zangara promises to return them with sketches he's made from them. Bart writes Bertie all of these details except about the sketches of her that he's commissioned. He predicts that if this man has any luck, his name will be known to the future.

The next day Bart waits around for him to bring the sketch, and when he walks in the door, he is happy to see the artist, and not just because the sketches are worth every cent of the $5 he's agreed to pay, but because he likes his company, is fascinated by his knowledge of art. When the conversation circles around to oils (Bart has always admired oil paintings), Zangara offers to paint him and Bertie for only $30. "*Out of friendship,*" Zangara says! From then on, seeing Zangara is the highlight of his days.

While Buttitta paints Bart's portrait, Zangara gets to work on a painting of one of Bertie's photographs. The artists invite him to their house where, in a room with canvases of still lifes, landscapes, and American officers' portraits stacked and leaning against every wall, Bart watches Zangara work, admires his careful eye, the transition of life to canvas. Later, he tells Bertie, "I lived the day with two hungry but wonderful painters."

He dreams about dabbling in oils when he returns. In a small way, he's already gaining a reputation as an art critic. "I didn't advertise for the honor," he says, "and when some artistic work is bought the owner comes to me for comment. I suppose I should say something milder than 'It stinks.'" Occasionally he strolls to the studio to check the progress of Bertie's portrait. When he sees the finished work, his striking wife's face rendered in those rich oils still shiny-wet on the canvas, he's delighted.

By the end of October, their mail dwindles, their food rations diminish, they're told not to send any more laundry. Everyone now knows the 91st is to move soon, and signs that the unit is preparing are ubiquitous—everyone doing his share of packing and numbering barracks bags and boxes. But no one knows where. Since they are to take none of their hospital equipment, they'll have to be in a place where they can be easily re-equipped, Bart figures. He hopes for England, but all he knows for certain is that this time they'll travel on a larger ship. He amuses himself by drawing two happy conclusions: (1) there will be less nausea this time, and (2) it will take at least two torpedoes to sink the ship.

The morning of the day they are scheduled to embark, Bart is packing his bedding roll when he's called downstairs to see a visitor. It's Zangara. Although Bart's words about this moment are confined to a single sentence, I can see him, this artist, fellow Italian, who less than three months before was considered an enemy, his long legs moving at a fast clip to make sure the American ship doesn't glide out into the bay and disappear forever without his parting gift. His worn jacket is spattered with the first raindrops of the day. He is clutching something to his chest, a package wrapped to protect it from the November storm clouds. When Bart comes down the stairs, Zangara extends the package—an oil painting.

Their Sicilian-dark eyes meet—Zangara's round as oversized marbles, opaque as a moonless night; Bart's the shade of the chocolate bars he's been handing out to the kids on the street.

CHAPTER 23

ARMED AND READY

His name is Zangara and given half a chance I think we'll hear about him later—after the war.

WHEN I FIRST read Bart's description of his days in the boxcar to Algeria, I had no doubts that I, too, wanted to travel there. I wanted to ride that train and see what Bart saw, feel his thrill. When I began to investigate trains in Algeria, though, what I found was not what I wanted to find. Website after website, including one linked to the U.S. State Department, warned me not to travel there—*terrorists, warlords, closed borders, disorder, Do not travel after nightfall, avoid minor roads, Closed border to Morocco.* So that was off the table. But my musings about Algeria planted an idea that began to sprout. My husband Gary and I would follow Bart's footsteps in Europe. And a visit to the homeland of my Italian grandparents with its compelling but still sketchy story of Bart's friend, the artist Zangara, topped our list.

Late one night a week before leaving for Sicily, I Googled his name, along with "Palermo," "artist," and "war." Nothing significant came up. I added "Buttitta." Zilch. I tried other combinations—WWII, World War II, Sicily, etc.—still zilch. I paced around the house and decided to simplify my search, keyed in "Zangara Palermo 1943"—and *presto!*— I was surprised to be clicking on a site for the Museum of Geometric and MADI Art in Dallas, Texas. "3 Italian MADI Artists," the site informed me, the last of which listed is Zangara. Although I'd studied art history, MADI art was new to me. I scrolled down the museum's colorful page depicting cubes and semicircles rendered in brightly tinted plexiglass and read: "Piergiorgio Zangara was born in 1943 in Palermo, Italy, where he received his first artistic instruction from his father." The words flashed at me as if in neon. I was feverish to know if *this* Zangara, whose ultra-contemporary superimpositions seemed to backlight hues of the Mediterranean world, who was born the year the 91st Evacuation Hospital Unit served in Palermo, was the son of the portrait painter who befriended my incipient-artist father.

Somehow I already felt connected to him. The younger artist, practitioner of a movement so contemporary that it seemed as though it might be fabricated in a post-modern novel, who evoked images that are more cerebral than celestial, was of my generation. I would be born four years later, not quite two years after my father returned from the war.

Piergiorgio, Piergiorgio. I repeated his name, stumbling over instead of rolling the *r*'s on my tongue. How exciting it would be to meet him in Palermo. Searching for a web address, though, I felt let down to discover that he was based in Milan. And then, the following day, I told this story to a friend, who said, "Why don't you call the museum in Dallas?"

I reached a kind-sounding lady named Mary Anne. I assured her that I knew she could not give me contact details for Mr. Zangara without his permission, all the time hoping that I could charm her (or at least pique her sympathy) and that she would give me his email address. In the time it took her to key in my contact information I did my best to impress upon her the urgency of the situation. I blithered on about fatherhood, immigrants, artists, fathers and their children, the importance of generational connections and of history itself—working myself up emotionally and feeding her more information than I felt comfortable doing. She chatted about how pleasant and friendly Piergiorgio (which she pronounced with a Texas cadence) and his wife Laura were, how much she enjoyed their occasional visits to Dallas. She promised she would try to contact him before I left.

A day or so after our conversation, she emailed me to tell me she had reached him and briefed him about my request for information about my father. There were so many confusions in our chat that I wondered exactly what she had told him, and in what language.

And in the ways of fairy tales, just as I was about to zip shut the laptop case before leaving the house for our trip, a message popped onto the screen—not from Italy, but from Dallas. I scrolled down to the word I was looking for: *Zangara*. A message from Mr. Zangara. "It is possible that my father knew Ms Passanante's father, because in 1943 he painted many portraits of US Navy and Army officials who were in Palermo at that time." I whooped, then dashed off a note asking Piergiorgio (yes, I was already calling him by his first name myself, at least in my head) if we might meet in Palermo, and as I locked the back door, I hugged the laptop to my chest.

It was nearly midnight before the plane was to take off, and I flicked on my email for one last time until we could find a suitable place in Sicily to read our messages. And there he was. His mellifluous name in my queue. He sounded eloquent, gentlemanly, kind, helpful, eager. Just the sort of son his kind father, who had befriended a fledgling artist, a doctor in the Army that had just conquered his country, would have had. The letter, which was translated by his daughter, told me that, while I was in Sicily, Piergiorgio would be running an international exhibition in Milan. But he included an invitation: "However, my sisters live in Palermo and they have many of my father's paintings which they show admirers and collectionists who want to see them. I have already spoken to them and told them about your trip to Sicily. If you want, you can call them and take an appointment through my niece Sabina who speaks English." He also offered Sabina's contact details and suggestions on where to find his father's work. I recited Bart's prediction aloud: "His name is Zangara and given half a chance I think we'll hear about him later—after the war."

I wrestled my notebook from my already packed suitcase and emended our ballooning agenda to include the places where we could view Zangara's art. We'd already listed the hospital in the medical school where Bart worked and where the windows had been blown out by bombings, the officers' quarters in another building across the street, the nearby harbor, the sculpture and landmarks that brightened his outlook. And, of course, the renowned cathedral and its chapel of Santa Rosalia, the patron saint of his vivacious, loving sister.

I repacked the notebook next to our pile of guidebooks and panoply of maps, as well as several folders of enlarged photocopies of Bart's

1943 snapshots, an annotated typed version of his diaries, copies in Bart's manuscript of most of the hundred or so letters he wrote Bertie while he was in Sicily. Excitement kept me awake most of the night, but I was confident we were armed and ready.

CHAPTER 24

EXPERIENCED TRAVELERS,
THE TWENTY-FIRST CENTURY

OUR HOTEL was in the quiet fishing village of Castellammare del Golfo, on a sweeping half-moon of water which from our balcony we could see lapping the shore. We were between Campobello and Palermo, each about thirty-seven miles from Castellammare in different directions. *Perfect,* we thought.

As we squeezed into our dented rental Smart Car the next day, we felt exhilarated. But as Gary steered us closer to Palermo and grappled with the most harrowing traffic we'd ever encountered, the cacophony of cars with drivers slamming on their horns at our apparently too-slow 100-kilometers-an-hour speed, Vespas whipping around us, Audis and Fiats zooming so close to our car that two of them knocked the side mirror askew, my enthusiasm turned to terror. Hearts walloping our rib cages, we parked inside the city as soon as we could, far from every place on our list.

Although we thought of ourselves as experienced travelers and had spent months preparing for this trip, we found ourselves haplessly embarking on false starts and circumambulations covering uncountable kilometers. We tramped, often in the wrong direction, along the shoulders-wide sidewalks, rutted stone cutting through our soles, in an attempt to find the streets, monuments, and buildings my father saw—to explore the terrain, to experience what remained. We began by mis-identifying a landmark building so that our search for everything else was off kilter. Collapsing geographical dominoes. We made an unnec-essarily wide semi-circle around the city while trying to find the hospi-tal. When we did find it, raindrops were puddling in the courtyard, and the view that Bart's camera had captured from the officers' quarters across the street was obscured by clouds.

What we seemed to do best was imagine. We imagined Bart's explo-ration of what he'd called a ghost town. We saw through his eyes the bomb-toppled walls, the razed tile roofs and wrought-iron balconies and terracotta window boxes of flowers and statues of the Virgin and her Savior Son. Banks of rubble clogged the sidewalks and shards of glass and metal coated the cobblestones. Italian prisoners swept up scattered debris. The resplendence of the surviving cathedrals and pal-aces was muted by soot and ash.

We'd reserved the last day we were to be in Palermo for locating the subjects of Bart's photographs and Zangara's paintings. One of the first items on our itinerary was to track down a pair of sculptures that Bart had photographed but did not identify. Two alabaster-looking nudes: one lying down, her arm resting on a lute; the other standing adjacent to her, one hand covering her crotch, fig-leaf style. We'd shown the photocopy to various guards, policemen, and caffé owners, trying to ascertain where it was. We found ourselves drifting about the Piazza Pretoria for about twenty minutes and randomly shooting pic-tures of the statues flanking a fountain that filled the piazza before we realized that the fountain included the sculptures we'd been hunting down. That experience became an archetype of all our explorations in this maze-like city.

I indulged my obsession with recreating my father's perspective not only by snapping the same shots he did but by tilting the camera to capture the exact angles he chose of memorials and churches and fountains and laundry flapping from balconies, and by waiting, cam-era poised, for ten or more minutes by the Catedrale to take a picture without gawkers and recapture some sense of an Italy at war.

Along a wide avenue lined with palms and marble benches, we trudged to the Excelsior Palace Hotel, where Bart had celebrated Har-ry's birthday, and arrived in time for a splurge lunch and some propi-tious advice. We were banking on finding a concierge or even a desk clerk who could help us find the city library, the Biblioteca Comunale. We'd had no dependable Internet source since we left America, and no one seemed to know where we could find the building. I was beginning to wonder if it existed.

The hotel was, as Bart said, *swank*. "Swank, swank, swank," I chanted above the screeching of the cars and Vespas. Inside we poked around, soaking in the ambience and imagining Bart (though the polished moldings and fresh painted murals indicated that the building had been renovated since the war) as he was then, about the age of our younger daughter. I sneaked into the Ladies to finger-brush my hair; I patted my ruddy face with water over a marble-topped sink.

Then we found the front desk. *Melania,* the name tag of the woman behind it read—and she was as lovely as her name. Long black hair and Oxford-degree English. Trying not to sound too desperate, we asked her where the library was and how to get there.

"Are you guests at the hotel?" she asked.

"We plan to have lunch here," I said before Gary could offer her the opportunity to reject us. I launched into my story, already fine-tuned by practice, about our purpose in Palermo. She smiled and nodded, fiddled with her computer, scribbled an address on a notepad, frowned slightly, picked up the phone. In a few seconds she said, "I can tell you how to get there"—she glanced at the clock on her desk—"but unfortunately it will be closed, and it will not be open until next week."

Next week we would be in New York City about half-way home to Idaho. My watch read 12:25.

"What time does it close?"

"One o'clock," she said.

"Come on," I said to Gary, reaching for his hand but snagging his wrist.

"We'll be back for lunch," I called to her as we hurried out of the marble-floored lobby.

"Wish I weren't lying," I said wistfully, almost panting now.

And there, miraculously, just outside the door as if waiting for us, was a taxi, the first one we'd seen—an advantage of hanging out in pricy hotels. We entreated the driver to rush to the address on the notepad (we had to thumb through our pocket dictionary to find the Italian for "fast"). As we were being tossed back and forth in the cab, Gary ran his index finger over a map and I clutched the armrest.

"Oh no!" he said. I turned to him in alarm. He pointed to a spot on the map. "This place is exactly where we started out this morning, near the Quattro Conti!" The four corners Bart photographed, the woman with her hand over her crotch.

Oh no! indeed.

Spotting traffic congestion ahead, we directed the driver to let us out near the Piazza Bellini, where we'd spent a good part of the morning and were, according to the map, close to the Piazza Quarante Martiri and the address Melania had looked up for us. Without waiting for change, we fled from the cab. My watch said 12:45. My heart thumped. Packs and purse flapping against our hips, we sprinted up the street to the so-called Piazza, which looked like a cramped parking lot enclosed by a ring of closing offices and darkened shops.

We ducked under an archway, and a guard stopped us. In answer to our question, he walked us back across the street to a narrow lane that led the other way. We rushed up that lane, button-holing anyone we met (a shop owner closing his shutters for lunch, an old woman shaking out a tablecloth), and ran the way they pointed, in circles to back alleys and dead ends. Almost everyone we approached fingered an extensive arc in the air for directions. Finally, a man in a dark office told us in an Italian I could understand, "Go through the church." On the other side of the church, we spotted an unassuming sign for the Biblioteca Comunale.

By the time we shoved open the heavy, carved door to the library, we had less than five minutes to spare. Already, well-dressed men and women were crowding out the doors as we walked in. A stocky man sitting in a modest chair by a modest table—I thought of him as the Minotaur—stopped us. "*Chiuso,*" he barked. *Chiuso*—one of the first, and most useful and frustrating, words I learned in Italian. Closed.

We spun out our story as fast as we could—in French, our only common language. I was nervous about the time, and I knew I must look like a desperate virago with my sweat-beaded cheeks and untidy hair. He told us (I think) that the library actually comprised two buildings, but the other one was *chiuso* for renovation. He explained that this building contained no art painted after the 18th century. We explained we had been assured by the artist's son, etc., etc., etc. He had never heard of the artist or his son. He quizzed the workers gingerly walking out of the building about Zangara and about paintings from the time of *la guerra*. Everyone said no.

It was now 1 p.m. He shrugged his shoulders and bobbed his head toward the door. *Grazie,* we said, our own shoulders drooping.

Damp and cranky, we headed toward a guidebook restaurant to bury our disappointment with a hefty Italian lunch, but—again—*chiuso.* Eventually we stumbled onto a restaurant set up in a tent squeezed between two booths in a colorful market. It was beyond our budget and touristy, but it was open, and offered a captivating view, the gold church of San Domenica burnished almost blue in the sun. After we downed a *mezzo litro* of wine and filled our bellies with fresh mullet and bass, we felt recharged.

Gary pushed his plate littered with fish bones away and smoothed the map flat. We were halfway between Sant'Agostino, where Piergiorgio had indicated we could see more of his father's work, and the harbor, where Bart described the bombing. We strode first toward the harbor and its bevy of sailboats, their sails down, masts jutting into the blue, blue above the buildings and scallops of mountains silhouetted in the background. The side of a building looked bombed out, but everything had been repaired.

We turned up the Via Cavour toward yet another place on our list: the Grand Hotel et des Palmes. "Prioritize," I begged Gary. "We need to find Zangara."

Gary, who was already a foot or so ahead of me on the pavement, called back, "That's what we *are* doing." But I eyed him dubiously. "It's on our way, and we'll ask there," he assured me. I panted to catch up.

In the hotel I felt self-conscious in my clammy travel clothes. Its marble staircase and scarlet carpet, its modern stained glass skylight, its potted palms, murals, and mirrors—all gave an aura of splendor. I asked the uniformed, English-speaking desk clerks where to find the Galleria della Congregatione della Pace so that we could see the portraits of Sicilian nobles that Zangara had painted. No one knew where or what it was. I sighed, ran my finger along an antique vase, and marched out the door.

It had been complicated to prioritize, to figure out what order of finding and seeing made geographical and chronological sense. And somewhere along these winding paths we had both realized that we couldn't possibly find everything we wanted to.

On the street corner just outside the hotel, Gary again unfolded the now torn map, and we set out for the next destination. "Well, at least we can visit the church, the one that allegedly has the big altar piece by

Zangara. Of course it might be *chiuso*," I said, already trying to resign myself.

The church was nearly hidden by a warren of market stalls proffering linen and household goods, which we wove through to enter the building from the side door. Although it was a medieval church that had been renovated in Baroque splendor, Sant'Agostino had a more intimate feel. At the door I hesitated, took in the rose window, the gilded stucco, the sculpted cherubs, and scanned the worshippers. No tourists here—only modestly dressed, olive-skinned women, one genuflecting, another two or three slumped or stiff in pews. I tiptoed in so as not to disturb them. I whispered to Gary that he should take photos of the altar pieces.

Gary looked skeptical, whispered back, "But all those paintings are very old. Painted long before the war."

"Just do it! Pleeeeze?" I mouthed at him. He shrugged and clicked the camera while I worried about the impact of the flash.

When we exited the church, my spirits were sinking. "At least it wasn't *chiuso*," I offered. Chuckling, Gary reached for my hand, and we plodded toward the train station.

GARY AND I had visited Sicily once before, years before we read the name Zangara. As our ferry had pulled into port, and the sunlight had just barely scraped the pinnacles of the hills and dawn had feathered the sky with scarlet, I'd stood on the bow of the ship, teary-eyed. We had wanted to see the land of Greek temples and churches whose pillars looked like those in mosques, but the immediate reason for the trip was family. I'd wanted to take Gary to the town that in the 19th century had spawned my grandparents. We'd rented a car and followed the confusing roads to Campobello di Mazara.

Somehow we'd managed to track down Bart's cousin Vito Critti, whom I'd never met but whom Bart had corresponded with for several years. Vito and his wife Antonina were warm, generous hosts in spite of our having had to rely on the (we hoped) universal language of gestures and on our rusty French to relate to each other. Through Vito's photo albums and framed black-and-whites, we took a virtual family tour of various Crittis and Passanantes (including, we were surprised and pleased to see, photos of my sisters and me). Vito also guided us on a literal tour of the family home of Bart's now-dead cousin, whom

Bart had seen in 1943 and whose framed photo we viewed on the television set.

But before we arrived in Palermo this second time, to follow Bart's war story, I had fostered the conviction that the triangular island would give me what I had fantasized about for so long. Certainly, I could not perform the miracle of swindling death—and I'm not sure I would want to—but maybe I could conjure another sort of trick, not at all dependent on magic. I could edge close to my parents before my birth, see what my father saw and sensed those years of his absence from my mother, and even see what he did not see.

BACK AT THE HOTEL at last, we flopped backward onto the bed and stared at the ceiling. Although the specter of my failure at finding Zangara's artwork was billowing around me, I promised Gary he never had to drive to Palermo again.

Nevertheless, I steeled myself, and half out of politeness, half out of a little remaining hope, I dialed the number Piergiorgio had given me. His niece Sabina, who answered the phone, sounded as if she had been waiting all her life to hear from me. She spoke English beautifully—she was a substitute English teacher and worked for Alitalia. Her voice was young, warm, and ebullient. It took a few seconds for it to sink in that she was my father's Italian wartime friend's, the artist Zangara's, granddaughter.

"I am so happy you called," she said. Then she told me that her aunt Fausta (Zangara's daughter, the sister of Piergiorgio) would like to invite us to her house in Palermo on Saturday, two days from now, to see her father's work and talk about her father and mine. For a moment I was stunned. Then my anxiety spiked. Saturdays the trains didn't run regularly. That meant *we would need to drive back into Palermo. Palermo*—where we'd wrestled harrowing traffic, etc., etc., etc., and where I'd had to cover my ears at the noise and hide my eyes at the oncoming vehicles while Gary gritted his teeth.

I thanked her profusely and was about to say no-thank-you, but Gary was already smoothing out his map. "Saint Gary," I said *sotto voce.*

I felt guilty involving Gary in another trip to Palermo, but he assured me, pointing vaguely to the map, that this time we could avoid the tricky heart of Palermo. "No problem," he said. "Easy." My husband is the poster child for optimism.

Later that night, sipping wine on our hotel balcony, watching the pink, blue, and yellow stripes of light from the bars and restaurants along the crescent of the town along the bay, I let down. I didn't talk about my anxieties about driving again into Palermo, and I felt, finally, restored. And that is exactly what I was thinking, exactly the English word I was hearing in my head, when I was struck with the truth— which is that we *had* been looking at Zangara's work.

"Restorations," I announced, breaking the uncharacteristically long silence. "Restorations," I almost shouted.

That was it. Zangara must have done *restorations* of paintings. An artist recently unemployed who must make a living, an artist carefully trained in details of the history of the church—that's what he does. Restorations. I clinked glasses with my fellow detective. That was it.

CHAPTER 25

BART AND BENEDETTO

On Saturday afternoon, only five minutes late and much more frazzled than Gary had anticipated, we found the apartment of Fausta Zangara and her family. Fausta's husband Franco, a burly man with kind dark eyes and an abundant mustache, met us in the parking lot and escorted us upstairs. When Sabina opened the door, I felt like I was greeting a friend of my daughter, one I'd known since elementary school. We spontaneously kissed European-style, a peck on each cheek. We shook hands warmly with the other two generations of Zangaras: Benedetto Zangara's daughter Fausta and Fausta's daughter Valeria. The walls were nearly covered with framed paintings, drawings, and pastels. I inched close enough to one painting to see Zangara's signature. Art books filled more than a wall of bookshelves. Fausta brought us a tray with a bottle of water and two glasses. She was a beautiful middle-aged woman with smooth skin and stunning blue-green eyes. She must have had some Norman blood, I thought. Everyone else had eyes as dark as mine.

Since Sabina was to serve as translator, all eyes were on her as soon as the words in either language left someone's mouth. Fausta agreed that her father may have known my father because after the libera-

tion (after he lost his commission as an officer in the Italian Army),
he began to earn money by painting portraits of the Americans from
models and photographs. I had already heard this from her brother
Piergiorgio, but I was happy to hear it again. And I was already certain
in the way of the faithful that her father was the same artist who'd
befriended mine.

I opened my folder of photocopies and showed them a picture of
Bart smiling on a sail boat in Mondello, the nearby beach resort Gary
and I had found so peaceful just before we drove into Palermo that first
morning. I used my father's Italian name—Bartolomeo—and his Italian nickname, Bartolo. They asked to see the other photos and seemed
excited by them, surprised that we had photos from their city in 1943.
They tried to help us identify those pictures Bart had neglected to
label—mostly rooftops, bombed out buildings and street scenes, some
featuring cherub-faced, dark-haired children who reminded me of the
Sicilian cousins I'd grown up with, and of my sisters and me. But the
photos were nearly seven decades old and grainy; everything had been
rebuilt.

Franco brought out a bottle. Sabina said she didn't think she could
translate the name for the contents of the bottle, but it turned out that
it was the same word in both languages. *Anise,* they told me. I sipped
from the glass. It felt good to relax a little, even if the alcohol content
was augmenting, as I suspect it was, the carmine flush on my perspir-
ing face.

On my copy of the diary transcription, I had highlighted in yellow
all of Bart's sentences that mentioned the two artists, and I read them
aloud. I began with the first passage in which Bart meets Zangara,
dated October 27, 1943. "The only really interesting thing happening
today was my acquaintanceship of two artists—the real McCoys. They
came over to pick up some change doing sketches. One of the artists,
the better, named Zangara, gave me a little oil painting on wood which
he knocked off in spare time." Sabina started to translate but was confused. I was suddenly aware of how colloquial my father was, and I
felt compelled to translate into contemporary standard English expressions like "the real McCoys" and "knocked off in his spare time" so
she could understand what she was translating. Fausta was clear-eyed,
intense; she leaned forward into the conversation. As Sabina translated
the sentence stating that the artist was "anxious to work in the states,"

Fausta looked askance. She turned to Franco, opened her hands, said something to us I didn't understand.

"She says she didn't know that about her father," Sabina explained. I wondered if this desire was true, or if Zangara had said that merely to forge a connection with the Americans. When I was done reading from the diaries, Fausta spoke. Words tumbled out, the Italian rising and falling, reeling out in ornate, lilting lines. I caught a word here and there, nodded. She was talking about her life with her father. I was mesmerized by her speech, her earnestness, her intensity. While Fausta spoke, Sabina stepped in frequently to translate, and her voice was becoming hoarse. I was learning facts from Sabina, and I was feeling emotions from Fausta. Her father had taught her to paint before he'd taught her to read—I flashed on the waterfall I'd painted with my father, its rainbow sprays—and much of the framed artwork in the room was hers. I glanced again at the gallery wall behind her. I also learned that the older artist Zangara kept a diary, too, and my heart leapt with the notion that perhaps Bart was mentioned in that book.

I read more of Bart's words out loud. "Out of friendship they are going to paint me and my wife for only $30.00," he says. I wanted to believe that this transaction was truly, at least in part, a gift of friendship. After all, how many officers spoke Italian? That must have made some impression, perhaps leading to something more than a commercial connection, to a bona fide, if brief relationship. Fausta asked me what happened to the painting her father gave mine, or to the painting of my mother that Bart bought from him. I recalled nothing about it, I admitted sheepishly. In fact, I'd been troubled by this missing piece of this particular puzzle. I didn't recall ever having seen the painting—or the oil painting that Zangara had taken the trouble to bring my father as a farewell gift. Did my mother, who was particular about pictures of herself, dislike it? Did my parents give it to one of my grandmothers? Did it get destroyed when the basement flooded, as it often did after a Midwest squall?

It was getting late, and I was beginning to wonder if we were overstaying when Fausta asked if I would like to see some of her father's work. *Yes, oh yes. Please.* A flurry of activity. She ducked into a back room and seemed to float back into the living room with a large portfolio and lay it before me. She unveiled his art piece by piece, giving us time to admire each one. This cornucopia of Benedetto's paintings and drawings, some of them matted, ranged from miniature to poster-size.

On several of them was a date with the signature, indicating that they were completed several decades after the war. Some of them depicted religious figures. Others, striking-looking women, including Fausta. One of the drawings (a semi-nude in black and white with a splash of red) reminded me of the sensual sort of picture my father sketched of my mother. He once sketched her nude, lying on her side, dressed only in a skirt above her knees, her hair draped to the floor. I told them about that drawing. They seemed a little surprised, but I liked sharing the intimacy.

With Fausta's permission we photographed some of these works. My favorite, rendered in shades of sienna, was one of her as a teenager sitting on a chair. It reminded me of a drawing a high school artist-friend had inked for an illustration in our literary magazine. She depicted me reading; she captured my awkward teenage posture, my long, straight hair, my gaze intent on the book. I was thinking about the connections between the Zangaras and me when a quick look at my watch startled me. We'd been there for two hours; it was time to go.

After I gathered my notebook and folder from the couch, we embarked on a profusion of thank you's—*grazie, grazie, grazie mille*—when Fausta said something else, and I could hear and see that it was a question.

I looked to Sabina. "My aunt wants to know if you would like to take one of the paintings," she said. I stared at her, confused. Fausta said something else, with more fervor. She was nodding yes, I was nodding no, but the sort of no that meant, *I don't believe this is happening to me.* "She wants to give you a gift," Sabina continued. "It would be her pleasure."

My heat-ruddied face wrinkled up, my eyes filled and spilled over, and Fausta ran to me and held me tight.

CHAPTER 26

THE ARTIST BEFORE *LA LIBERAZIONE*

IT WAS SOME months later that another of Zangara's daughters, Maria Stella, emailed me a copy of Benedetto's diary, and even more months had passed by the time I had it translated into English. Only then did the picture—a mere sketch really—that Bart's words had drawn for me of his artist friend blossom into nightmarishly vibrant color.

I can still envision those two at the instant of farewell, both men about to pivot out into their separate futures, and I can also see what Bart did not.

I see that while Bart was camped in a muddy cow pasture outside Casablanca, waiting for his career as a doctor-warrior to be launched, Zangara had already begun to move his new bride from place to place in an intrepid effort to keep her safe. I see how an airstrike caught Zangara as he walked to the school where he taught, how at home pieces of shrapnel shattered the glass of his lamps, how when the schools were inevitably closed he had no way to support his wife. How wild dogs scavenged on the streets. How blanched-faced men with baskets roamed the ruins, scrounging for anything they might exchange for food. How he became ill and, to make money, accepted the dangerous task of restoring the Church of Santa Maria la Nuova, in a public square that was no more than a mass of debris and close to the sea, where bombers hovered and dropped their cargo on the ships nearly every night. How the Fascists mistook him for a spy. How he and his family hid in the basement while hundreds of planes smashed Palermo for three hours. How he and his now-pregnant wife dodged fragments of glass and stone and felled electrical cables as they left Palermo for Monreale and safety. How columns of stunned-faced people clutching dirt-smeared children and pushing carts swarmed out of the city as it became, increasingly, flame and ash. How at night as the cannons thundered he watched the fireworks of the sky's bombardment through a crack in a stable door. How he rented a *carretto* to take him the eight miles back and forth from Palermo to retrieve his wife's dowry and allay her rising anxiety about protecting it from looters, and how on the way back he walked behind it without food as the heat beat into his skin. How when offices began to close in the city and more and more buildings were toppled and gutted, he moved again, to the windy hilltop town of Borgo Schirò where he waited in line in the relentless sun for drinkable water and prayed that malaria and typhus would not find them. How the booming of the cannons from the Allied landings at Pantelleria, then Sciacca, only sixty-two miles away, kept them awake all night. How a plane shot up the square where the people stood in line for water and children were playing. How he and his wife found another stable and huddled on the straw on the ground. How from the next place they watched terrified from a kitchen window as a bomb exploded into fire on a caravan of German cars carrying soldiers. How from the porch they witnessed the bell tower of the church irradiated by a flare and trembled at the crash of a bomb that struck just outside the village. How they bolted again for the countryside outside of Partinico, and when their car broke down, waited facedown for three hours in the grapevines before hiding at midnight under sheets in the bed of a truck.

How in spite of all the terror of the fast-encroaching Americans and their bombs and tanks, Zangara knew that where they had taken over meant the end of danger. How on the road back toward safety, he could see for the first time the faces of his enemies, the nets on their helmets, their dark glasses, the stars within the circle on their vehicles. He could hear their foreign-sounding voices, but he could see that they did not look like enemies at all; they looked like liberators.

SOMETIMES I WONDER how I might have cast this story if the details of Bart's diary had matched those of Zangara. The what-if's mount up. What if the war had exploded and flamed in, say, St. Louis? What if he had been an officer for the losing side? What if he had had a pregnant wife and had had to keep moving and hiding her and the baby in order to keep them alive? What words would I have chosen from *that* diary to represent all of Bart's memories from the war?

By the time Gary and I waved goodbye to the Zangaras and to Sicily, the raw story Zangara somehow managed to write lodged in my brain. I had a vague sense that no matter how much pleasure my being the agent of my father's memory was or would be, no matter how many of the details I would pass on to another generation were those of a man often at leisure who felt he was winning something eminently worthy, some sense of burden would take its due. I was already discovering what I should have known already: that memory was a moving target, that I was changing it inexorably as I selected or jettisoned or interpreted or embellished the details of Bart's legacy and translated them, as if from some distant, elliptical language, so that I could write my own pages for a future he could not know.

I was still to discover that more often than not I had to rein myself in in delivering to the twenty-first century a picture of Bart's life during the war. The words I'd been poring over for years now were precise, evocative, and expansive. What he ate, the way he shivered with cold, the books he devoured, the movies he saw, the gifts he sent and received, the stacks of letters he read and reread before organizing them into packets, how he slept, what moons and tides and flares and explosions and deaths he witnessed, even the narrative particles he may have wanted to forget—all these minutiae were essential to his story, all were stunning. All were synergistic cells of his memory, which I was willing to abscond with in my longing to embody them and, then, lend them to my own kind of art. But I did not know then that, ironically, the more digging, the more obsessive tracking down, the more culling and selecting I would do from these thousands of details about his life during his long absence from my mother, the more poignant would be my sense of loss.

CHAPTER 27

STRANGER AT THE FUNERAL

JUST BEFORE WE LEFT SICILY, I told Gary a story about my life he'd never heard before. I'd like to say I started spinning it out the moment after I lit the candle for my grandmother at the church celebrating her patron saint, Santa Caterina, but I'm not certain I did. It sprang up fresh and raw from my subconscious, and it occurred to me that before this moment I may not have understood that it *was* a story.

The story began thirty years after Bart's father testified at the trial, when my grandmother Catherine's daughter Rosalie suddenly swooned to her mother's feet in an elegant St. Louis shop. An hour later, her brother Bart was at her side in the hospital, but his well-trained doctor hands, which had by then already saved hundreds of lives in the bloodied heart of battle, were powerless to help her, and she died.

Afterward Catherine—given her Sicilian legacy, which included wives and mothers hurling themselves into the graves of their beloveds—was determined to die, too. For more than a year, she concealed the tumor ripening inside her, her belly curdling and corroding with the beast she had succored until it was so fulsome her son could see it bulging from her aprons. Soon she, too, died, Bart's hands again powerless to help.

Though he'd never had much truck with religious rituals, he honored her request for a two-day wake with an open casket. My memory of the funeral parlor is swathed in the surreal. In memory—though, really, how could this be true?—it was decorated carpet to ceiling in shades the color of blood.

At the wake there prevailed an un-Sicilian-like solemnity, a sense of inevitability. After glancing at the shrunken body of the woman I'd loved dearly, I studied the carpet. When I raised my eyes, they looked directly across the casket at a stranger, a gap-toothed man, a pie-round face on a short, square body crammed into an ill-fitting suit. He smiled broadly at me. "You Bart's daughter?" he asked in an almost impenetrably thick accent.

"I'm Joy, Bart's eldest daughter," I explained, wondering who this new Italian who'd decided to pop into my grandmother's wake could be. I was surprised I didn't recognize him. Though I hadn't 100 percent mastered the Who's Who in the family's Italian contingent, who seemed interconnected in some invisible web that I found baffling, I still had a sense of what everyone looked like. I knew they all lived in north St. Louis where they did unusual things for a living like make sausages and serve God as a nun, that all of them considered themselves our family somehow, and that all of them loved children and adored my father the doctor.

At that moment, my father came toward us. I noted that the stranger was even shorter than my father, who was the shortest man I knew. The man turned to Bart. "Bart, why you no introduce?" He left off the last word as I'd heard many of my relatives do. His stubby hand sculpted the air. Barely glancing his way, my father uttered some Italian name or other I didn't recognize.

Trying to be polite and maybe a little charming—after all, it was usually the Italian side of the family who made me feel best about myself, often calling me *bellissima* and *brillante* when I clearly was neither—I smiled as endearingly as I could. Then I said something like, "I guess I must have missed you at family gatherings."

The man no doubt could tell I was trying to figure out why I'd never met him before because he gripped Bart's shoulder, grinned, and said, "Tell her where I been."

My father, who usually enjoyed the camaraderie of others and always respected his elders, flinched. He didn't smile back. I was suddenly conscious of the body in the casket that separated me from the two men and of the room's bizarrely sanguine glare. One of Bart's hands squeezed the other in front of him. He shook his head, swept his gaze to the side.

The man repeated, this time with a gravelly chortle, "C'mon. Tell your daughter where I been."

Bart's bow-shaped lips turned down at the corners. Shaking his head, he said, more to the body in the casket than to me, "In jail." His voice was so thin and brittle that the impact of the information took a while to penetrate into my brain. By that time, he had gone away, without saying *goodbye* or *excuse me,* away from the man with the gap-toothed grin, away from his mother's casket, and even away from me.

Scores of years later, about to leave the homeland of my ancestors, I was prompted to tell Gary this story because I suddenly remembered my father's expression at the moment before he'd floated ghostlike away at his mother's funeral. It was a look I had never seen him cast a family member—one I now recognized as an expression of unmitigated disgust.

But that was not to be the end of the story. A few weeks after Gary and I returned from Sicily to Idaho, I removed the paper clips binding the newspaper columns in a cocoa-colored folder with my father's meticulous label. The top article fluttered out onto my desk, and what struck me first was the legend under the photo, "Michael Accardi, a bootlegger." Then some neural code snapped open, and I found myself staring into a suddenly familiar face.

ENGLAND

November 26, 1943 to June 9, 1944

CHAPTER 28
TORTWORTH COURT

Wotta war!

THE RECORD OF Bart's memory of England begins on the seas, before he knows for certain where the raging waves will deliver him. The imposing USS *Santa Rosa*, a prewar pleasure liner now stripped for troop transport, bobs for two days and nights in the Palermo harbor before weighing anchor on November 11 for its still secret destination. It is tethered together with other ships, and Bart notes that, given the ominously full moon glancing off the water, it's the perfect target for an air attack. They are, apparently, waiting for another ship that was sent to pick up the survivors of vessels that were bombed and torpedoed off the coast of Algeria—exactly where the *Santa Rosa* is slated to pass on its way to godknowswhere. Bart's station, as a medical inspector for the ship, is in a particularly dangerous place, on B deck, starboard forward—but he'll have a good spot to see the show . . . *if there is one,* he thinks.

They are barely out to sea when an air raid alert keeps him awake and watchful until 2 a.m. Escorted by cruisers and destroyers, they sail through what the sailors call "torpedo alley." Hugging the north coast of Africa, the ship pitches and rocks its way through the Mediterranean; the men whine, moan, vomit. The sea calms in time for Bart to rove around the deck and glimpse Oran, which (so long ago, it already seems) he toured with Harry and where he took snapshots of a statue of Joan of Arc triumphant on her horse before returning to the hospital in the racetrack. He wakes up the next morning at 5 o'clock to gawk: brilliantly lighted on the African side, the Spanish city of Ceuta; silhouetted against a dark horizon on the European side, the Rock of Gibraltar.

They steam past Tangier and into the Atlantic, past Spain and to the Azores and then, oddly, north by northwest. By their twelfth day on board it becomes clear that the ship is charting a circuitous route. They still have no idea where they're going, and the scuttlebutt is that the ship is being stalked by subs. On November 14 a destroyer explodes four depth charges, and the *Santa Rosa* lurches at the concussions. The men and women are alerted, run to their stations, and wait in silence for twenty minutes, trying to remember to breathe. The explosions, the rumors, and the ship's long, meandering path fray the unit's nerves, but hours of bridge, poker, rationed Coca-Colas—and, for Bart, a "bird-bath" using a basin of fresh water—ease their edginess, at least a little.

After nearly two weeks, as the dishes at breakfast shift from one end of the table to another, the ship steers up around the coast of Ireland. It heaves down the Irish Sea, and soon Bart spies the cliffs of Wales and knows now that they will be landing at Swansea. He writes Bertie proudly that in spite of two bouts of seasickness, he has missed only one meal.

Although they drop anchor on November 24, the day before Thanksgiving, the Army is still solving the problem of gathering enough trains to distribute the troops throughout England. So the 91st holds its holiday dinner early, aboard ship. That night they're told their "final destination" is to be North Tidworth, a town about seventy miles southwest of London. But the Army is still abruptly changing its mind, keeping its men and women in the dark: the destiny of the 91st is not to include North Tidworth.

On Thanksgiving Day, 1943, at 4 a.m. in the brisk Welsh air, the troops board the trains and in a few hours stop at an English hamlet. Bart happily greets Harry, who's gone ahead as advance officer and arranged for trucks. The trucks ramble over the countryside and into what Bart thinks at first is a park. As they wind down the tree-lined approach, a building comes into view, and then he can hardly believe the vision that is evolving in front of him. When the truck stops, they all tumble out and gape. "Tortworth," someone says.

Tortworth Court is one of the thousands of British country homes requisitioned for war purposes, Bart will find out later. But for now, it's a castle from a dream. He takes his time describing it. He doesn't want to miss a detail: "Before us stood a huge brick and stone castle-like structure, now known as a duke's country estate, similar to the manors read about in novels. I got one large room in which there is a fire-place, a sink, flat wooden beds w. mattress, blankets, and linen. I share it with White, Welch, Waggoner and Harry. There is plenty of closet and cupboard space. The lavatory is in an adjoining brick building within the estate's walls where there are hot showers and even tubs. Of course it is cold and the coal is rationed but we are more than satisfied." What is just as exciting, stacks of mail are waiting for him. And he's thrilled to have letters from Bertie making verbal love to him, which she's been doing since he arrived in Algeria.

Before he crawls into bed, he admits he's worn out. But at least for this and the months he will spend in the heart of England, he is safe.

On the first day, glad to have freedom of movement on land, Bart walks alone three miles in the rain to Huntsman's House Inn, a pub in Falfield. He indulges in five pints of ale, walks home, then returns that night with friends. They down more ale, stout, and a few Scotches. They sing and dance to risqué tunes played by the 300-pound woman proprietor. They stumble home, unsure of the way in the blackout, rain, and mud, and for the first time in weeks he sleeps well. That jaunt sets a pattern for the next six months at Tortworth Court, a pattern that seems to revolve around anesthetizing himself through alcohol to the horrors of the war he's hearing about on the radio and to images that linger under his eyelids and make his heart gallop. His world becomes, for the next months, the radius around Tortworth Court and in the relative cultural mecca of Bristol, the villages and pubs of Falfield and Berkeley and Alveston and Cheltenham where there are Scotch and ale and pianos to play, a PX, and a village seventy miles away called Shrivenham.

What a difference from the bombed-out hospital and the rubble and ash of Palermo streets this manor is! Even the small amenities—the hot water in the room, a proper shave at a sink, the right to wear a brown star on his African campaign ribbons representing his "participation in the Sicilian Affair," as he calls it—make this seem like a different universe. Soon he has time to ramble around the grounds and make small discoveries that give him pleasure: an old church, a pet cemetery (some of the little graves dating to 1850), the fish in the larger lake, and especially the plantings. His mind drifts to daydreams about playing with his niece- or nephew-to-be. Maybe he can take the little fellow (or *little girl,* he reminds himself) to see his cousin's farm sometime and they can pick peaches together. Maybe they can . . . the possibilities he sees grow every day.

During that winter and spring, though his radio brings him news of some of the fiercest fighting yet—months-long bombardments at Anzio, only thirty-three miles from Rome, and Monte Cassino, Italy's most prominent monastery—Bart is, much of the time, virtually, bizarrely, on vacation. From the end of the first week at Tortworth, when he raised his eyebrows at what he called "amazing and strange trees, shrubbery and vines," he spends as much time as possible outside exploring. He treks over empty meadows in the bracing English winds over blankets of fallen leaves and fields of wildflowers. He gathers snowdrops and plucks daffodils. He delights in the grace of the magnolia blooms. He asks George, or maybe Stuart Waggoner, whose long face and fleshy lips Bart himself has photographed several times, to take a photo of him: gloves suspended from his one hand, heavy brown jacket zipped to the collar, he stands in front of a backdrop of yews and a purple beech, in a meadow thick with bright blossoms that just cover his boot-toes.

He frequently hops a bus or a truck, sometimes even an ambulance, and rides twenty miles to Bristol for art books and supplies, sheet music, movies, dances, sandwiches compliments of the Red Cross, a Scotch and soda and elegant lunch at the Grand Hotel, an exhibit of French contemporary art. Knapp takes him in his command car to the London Philharmonic to see pianist Myra Hess. Bart hunches over the piano in the mess hall or the pianos in pubs, determined to master the "Warsaw Concerto," which he first heard at the officers' club, for Bertie. It's in a movie about the struggles of Poland against the Nazis, but it reminds him of home. He canters on horseback through the countryside with the chaplain and nurses. He sees a Technicolor film on field transfusions, plays basketball in a homemade gym, stays up late reading—Cecil's *Textbook of Medicine, As You Like It, Archy and Mehitabel,* anything Bertie sends him. He jogs up and down the stairs for hours as he develops photographic prints and enlargements in his make-shift basement dark room. The personnel throw a costume dance, nurses donning evening gowns and eighteenth-century French court period wigs, an English string orchestra playing minuets and even a Virginia reel. He helps the 91st host a Christmas party for village children.

In spite of, or perhaps because of, the pleasures and distractions, an acute sense of uselessness and boredom sharpens within him like a knife edge. "What a frail, vacuous existence," he writes. "Things just go on slowing—we just wait." A few days before Christmas, about the time of the 91st's first anniversary overseas, he sits in front of his wife's picture, the one she sent him in November with the white, gauzy, ruffled collar, and has, for the first time in his life, a crying jag. Maybe *next* Christmas he'll spend with her. But he remembers he said that last year.

To escape from being dragged down into melancholy, he and Harry take trips—Scotland, Stratford-upon-Avon, London!—to sightsee the buildings and monuments and museums he's read about. One evening after a musical revue at a theatre in Piccadilly, Bart and Harry venture out into the city blackout under a half-moon to dine on widgeon at an elegant French grill in the Dorchester Hotel. A few cocktails and several beers lead them into a conversation about how much they miss their wives. Bart slips Bertie's photo from the billfold she's sent him, and Harry takes out Marilyn's photo, and they flash their wives' pictures "to give them a treat of the place too." They laugh at themselves so heartily they don't even mind the bill.

At any other moment in time, Bartolo Passanante, only one generation away from sleeping on a dirt floor in a hut in Campobello, might be said to be living a dream. But he is torn. He has a job to do, and he is not being asked to do much of it. His work in Sicily already seems far away. Why aren't they busy saving soldiers' limbs from gas gangrene, eyes from shrapnel, and feet from grenades instead of mending injured motorcycle policemen and hapless soldiers who accidentally shoot themselves in the abdomen?

In January Russian troops cross the 1939 Polish border. Bart writes, "We begin to think that perhaps the Russian campaign may alone decide Germany's fate and without our help. Could be? Of course we Americans are doing a big part in being here—a big threat." But in truth it will be weeks until he can write that the medical officers of the 91st finally put in a full day of work. Two months later he bemoans the situation: "Today the Russians have reached the Romanian border, Cassino is a stalemate, Anzio beach is stale, and we threaten to start a second front from here."

It's clear they are preparing for a full-scale invasion of Europe, but there's no telling when or where that might be. Bart's sense of restlessness accelerates. With the help of one of his roommates, he lugs a field stove from one of the tents into their room. But in spite of the welcome heat, he ushers in the month of March still gloomy, just staring at the fire until lunch. He decides to send home all of Bertie's love letters "for lifetime safe keeping." He can't afford to take the chance of losing them in the Channel. *Whenever that might be,* he says to himself with a sigh.

CHAPTER 29

SEARCHING FOR A BRIDGE TO WALES

How Green Were His Valley.

TO HELP DEFUSE the tension of waiting, Bart buys a bicycle from a local man at a pub, and close to the end of March, he and Waggoner collaborate on a plan for an excursion. They have the kitchen staff pack them a lunch, and stopping at two pubs along the way, they pedal toward the Severn River. They bike north along the Gloucester Canal, then cross-country over hills and back down again. Bart scouts the landscape for a northern bridge to Wales. He writes Bertie later that he "strained to see," on the other side of the Severn, "How Green Were His Valley." Richard Llewellyn's much-loved novel *How Green Was My Valley* was prominent in Bart and Bertie's bookshelves. I suspect that this book, chronicling the life of a boy and his family of coal miners in Wales, recalled for Bart his own boyhood, his father's daily return home in the dark from the mines of Illinois with coal-blackened overalls, soot-streaked face. Or perhaps he was longing to see the same vision of the idyllic, grassy valley that the boy in the book remembers before the pristine town was pockmarked by slag heaps. But Bart and Stu cannot find a bridge, and, disappointed, they pedal, more slowly now, back to Tortworth.

Feeling once again bitten by the art bug, Bart decides to fill his waiting hours with more serious attention to watercolor techniques. He borrows a watercolor instruction book from Orwan Hess (who, within a decade after he and Bart part company, will become renowned for developing the first fetal heart monitor). Except for his short-lived interactions with Benedetto Zangara in the fall, it's the first time Bart has had access to formal art instruction, even if only from a book. He begins a painting project that, at least for a time, fills his vacant hours and suppresses his anxious thoughts. After biking and walking back and forth the two miles to the tree-shaded yard of St. Leonard's Church for three days to study it, he pencil-sketches it, then uses watercolors and the new brushes George bought. At least he's learning.

Otherwise, he is just marking time. One lonely night he tells Bertie he would give a year of his life if he could hear her voice. Just one little sentence—a few words. In response, she asks if he would like her to make a phonograph record for him. He pounces on her offer, asks her to "send lots of them at frequent intervals in case some get here broken—even if you run out of things to say and start counting or recite the alphabet. Just imagine 'Dear Bart: A. B. C. D. E. F.,' etc.; or, 'one and one equals two' darling." He feverishly awaits her record, advises her to send it cushioned in cotton. The minute he sees the first one waiting with the other mail on his bed a month or so later, he searches frantically for a phonograph and finally finds one in the 128th Evac's quarters, where he barges into a room of six officers and places the record carefully on the turntable. He hears it once in silence, then thanks them and walks slowly downstairs, but before he can bring himself to leave the building, he reels around and races back up. With a sheepish grin, he asks the officers if he can play it again. Later, he thanks Bertie for what he calls the most thrilling moment of his life. In another month she sends another record. This time the record gets stuck on the last line—and he hears it over and over. "I love you," "I love you," "I love you," she says to him again and again and again.

On one of his trips to Stratford, he and Harry stay at a Guest House for Officers run by the Red Cross. When he uses their phone to call Tortworth for news, Waggoner reads him a cable: he's "AN UNCLE of a boy." When he returns, he writes these words in his diary in capital letters. He'll cable Rosalie as soon as he returns to Bristol. The other news that evening reports that the Germans have bombed one of their hospitals in Italy, but even that horror cannot quell his excitement about his new nephew. His namesake.

Bart doesn't learn until ten days later that the birth has been excruciating for Rosalie, complicated and, Bart suspects, mishandled, and his sister is bereft. The baby, Anthony Bart, is deformed. His foot is angled sharply out of position at the ankle, and if an orthopedist who knows what he's doing doesn't do something quickly, the baby will never be able to walk as other boys do. Bart demands the best physician for his nephew, and the doctor he engages, through Bertie, saves Anthony's foot. It takes Bart weeks to calm down.

ALTHOUGH A PAMPERED CHILD, Anthony will never make trouble for anyone and will eventually marry a good Catholic girl, a timid woman with some pretty features and buttercup blonde hair, and sire two children.

Thirty-four years after Anthony's foot is repaired, Anthony's father, Bart's former friend and former brother-in-law Jack Manzo, and Bart will find themselves on opposite sides of Anthony's bed in a St. Louis Catholic hospital. For the moment, Anthony is no longer screaming from the cancer that is eating its way through his bones and blood and tissues. Bart's eyes do not meet Jack's. And it is not because Bart has been unsuccessful in cajoling or ordering the nurses to administer a little more morphine. It is because of the facts that have burned beneath Bart's skin for nearly thirteen years: the way Jack began seeing that awful woman just months after Rosalie died; how Jack wept and confessed to Bart, begged his forgiveness, promised he would wait for a respectful while; how Jack could not, did not wait; and how Bart's mother draped herself in black for two years of mourning, moaned and sobbed and begged Jack not to be with another woman so soon, and waiting was the very least he could do to honor her only daughter, his beautiful, faithful wife; and how Jack ordered her to leave his house and never return, the house built from money that she and her husband had given him to start his dental practice, the house where she'd rolled out miles of sheets of dough for ravioli and stirred boiling pots of sauce even when the temperatures spiked to 101, the home she'd help raise his son in and had planned to die in; and how he sent her packing with only a trunk and a suitcase; and how she began to grow her own cancer secretly in her belly. Suddenly Bart hears that

Anthony is not only groaning but uttering words, and sees that his nephew is reaching out to him with one arm and to his father with the other and asking something of each of them. And then Bart sees the pleading expression, hears the words, understands that what he's asking them to do—no, begging them to do—is simply to shake hands. *Please. Please.* It's his dying wish, the only thing, now that the nurses have refused to increase the morphine, that Bart can do for him. And possibly Bart hesitates, possibly he extends his hand over the emaciated body shackled to machines and bags of liquid toward his only nephew's father before he snaps it back to his thigh. But even if he *does* inch toward that gesture, his head is shaking from side to side, his mouth is saying *no,* and the Sicilian blood roiling with hate in his veins is also making him cry.

CHAPTER 30

BLASTER PASSANANTE

The air is filled with impending movement. I can feel it again.

AT TORTWORTH preparations for this "second front" are very much a part of Bart's life. The preparation to work wherever they're needed jump-started about a month earlier, just a few days after Fred Lahourcade took over as company officer and asked Bart what work he would like to do in this new setup. He knows he's the only doctor consulted about his work preferences and that this is an enviable position to be in, but *what a way to make enemies,* he thinks. All the doctors are assuming that on the continent the unit will be functioning as a surgical hospital, and Bart expects to be on a surgical team. But he's still not completely sure what he wants. He tells Bertie that on a surgical team he would be just an assistant doing minor debridements the head man didn't want. He sees himself putting on casts and holding retractors, not the work of a surgeon. He only wants a medical ward, Bart finally answers Fred. But he does so wistfully. If only he'd had time before the war for another year of training . . . he might have been a surgeon.

When Fred nods and asks him to be head of medicine, Bart turns him down; he doesn't want O'Brien, one of his first roommates, who is heading medicine now and doing a fine job, to be ousted. But Fred and

Bart have been friends for an even longer time, and Fred understands. He decides to put Bart in charge of gas casualties instead and begins to map out plans. Bart is to be responsible for five tents in which gas casualties are treated. In the meantime, Bart is happy at the prospect of working in a medical ward—*and finally working at all,* he thinks.

He reads extensively about chemical warfare, gas wounds, treatment, and equipment, attends a lecture on penicillin, which he's heard is the new miracle drug, gives a gas-mask drill to nurses. He jeeps into Bristol to consult with experienced physicians there.

In Fort Knox, he already completed a thirty-two-hour course in Defense Against Chemical Attack and was certified to "perform the duties of UNIT GAS OFFICER." But by the time nearly two years later he's assigned to "gas gangrene school," as he calls it, he fears he's forgotten all he learned. So he drives to Shrivenham, two-and-a-half hours from Tortworth, eight miles from the nearest town, to Chemical Warfare School.

He depicts the place as "a huge camp used as American Military schools," and his definitive assessment is that "This place stinks. The cottage has nothing in it but 6 empty wooden cots. The small fireplace tries to warm the room in vain. There are no clubs and buildings are miles apart. The classroom is in an unheated garage where the exhaled breath causes a fog screen before you and the instructor, the bake-bean supper was in an unheated wooden mess hall. I feel like I'm in a large open air penitentiary." For the next eight days he studies gas munitions and personal decontamination, sees displays of flame throwers, high explosives, and phosphorus incendiaries used in pillbox attacks, and in the evenings, arranges a few ping-pong games. In classes he pulls rank and sits next to the only stove. It's little consolation that, though half the class fails the exam, he receives the only perfect score.

When he returns to Tortworth, he fashions a gas chamber out of a pyramidal tent and runs his men through it. In his classes on gas detection, he has fun blowing up bottles of real gas by using detonating caps, a skill for which he's now earned a new nickname: Blaster Passanante. But he's still waiting to do what he came for, and blowing up bottles with detonator caps isn't it.

ALL THE BRAND-NEW medical and surgical equipment they need for a move has been rolling in since January. *The big move,* Bart hopes.

The enlisted men have even practiced putting up the hospital tents and equipment in blackout. His ward has a nameplate on his desk. *The operating rooms look truly beautiful,* he thinks, and he hears that their model hospital is so good that big shots from all over England are coming to see it. An Army hospital inspector has offered one of the most gratifying compliments ever given by an inspector, proclaiming the hospital the "best manned, best trained, best equipped and put-together hospital he had seen yet." The excitement is mitigated only by Bart's noting that the type of hospital they have also sports a big red cross in the center, which is too easy to use as a target for dive bombers. Not to mention the fact that the compliment means, he tells Bertie, that they "may be dodging bombs and machine-gun bullets on the first wave." But he adds, "Oh well—I guess it's better that way."

It's shortly after the first week of April when the rumors of movement start worming their way around Tortworth Court. But there are other indications: waterproofing material is being applied to jeep and truck engines, new gas masks are delivered. And Bart hears from a reliable source that "all plans are ready," but even without this intelligence, within two weeks it's clear—all passes to Bristol have been mysteriously cancelled.

Two days later, the colonel receives an alert order, but experience has taught Bart that it will be at least a month before anything significant happens, and he finds himself impatient. Welch informs him that he's revised his plan for the invasion and invites Bart to be a surgeon on an operating team wherever they'll be next. Although taken aback at the abrupt change of assignment, Bart is pleased (as long as he can be assured a hefty amount of work). But an onslaught of sudden, severe headaches makes him anxious. He tries not to worry about what these indicate about his eyes, or his brain—or what the invasion will mean for doctors who will have to operate on the wounded in tents under fire.

He begins to spend more time mulling over the mercurial predictions—his and those of the powers that be—about when the war will end. During his first week at Tortworth he predicted that "Germany will be beaten by a better Army and Air Force with a powerful Navy only after a big fight at her gates early next fall. Of course, I'd like to see it end within a month but it would be a big surprise to me and a very delightful one I must say." Bertie has speculated that the invasion date will be April 1, about two weeks before her birthday, but within three weeks of that prediction, Churchill and Roosevelt suggest that the war in Europe will not be over this year. At the end of April, after another of Bertie's birthdays passes in his absence and with no invasion in sight, Bart says, "Darling I think I'll promise to be home on your next birthday—if only that it makes you and me feel better. But I really do believe it this time." He begins a new volume of his diary with his own prediction: "I prophesy the end of the war in the next book and then home—I hope. God how I hope so."

It's mid-May before the newly waterproofed ward boxes are packed and stenciled. "The air is filled with impending movement. I can feel it again," he pens. His sleep is interrupted at 2:15 a.m. when a raider drops six bombs nearby. Its beastly racket rockets his mind back to Sicily—and to portents of what is soon to come.

CHAPTER 31

THE MURKY SPECTER OF CHANGE

Sadness and lonesomeness do funny things and can be dangerous.

IN MAY the days are uncannily long in England—hours and hours of rainy-gray skies, the late light a novelty that makes the days seem endless. In spite of the distracting activities Bart devises for himself, mostly what he does is think. And worry. And it's not just about what he imagines will come on the fields of France and who knows where else. It's also about Bertie. Perhaps it's the sense the looming invasion brings that if—*when*, it must be *when*—they win the war, he will return to her and they will have to reconstruct their life. When she sends him photos of the two of them together in happier times, he responds, "Gosh it's been such a long time that looking at the pictures is like looking at the pictures of two other people—who are to be greatly envied." He wonders if he'll be a bashful bridegroom when he returns.

"Darling, please don't be sad about us," he writes. "Just feel it in your heart, as I do, and keep it there. Then wrap it up and just pick at it only once in a while and smile gritting your teeth. Let's make up our minds that this separation, so horrible to us, must last a great while longer and let's not allow it to change us. Sadness and lonesomeness do funny things and can be dangerous."

But she can't help herself—not only sinking into sadness but chewing on the what-if's. A month before the invasion she asks him anxiously if he has changed during the year and five months since she has seen him. He assures her that he has not lost weight, that his calves and biceps still bulge, that he always scrounges up enough to eat to placate his capacious appetite. "The only change in me, I believe, is an increased sparsity in hair and a more fully developed sense of humor which has been a good weapon against the monotony of heartless existence. The only thing that bothers me just at present is that my new boots refuse to be broken in and pinch the hell out of me."

Another source of apprehension surfaced for both of them earlier that spring. It was piqued when Bertie mentioned in passing that some of the interns at Barnes brought her candy and he found himself fueled by a jealousy that's been threatening to ignite for weeks. He dreams that he unexpectedly comes home and walks in on a conversation Bertie and her office girl friends are having. They are extolling the assets of her *new* boyfriend, and as soon as she spies Bart, she shushes them.

Abruptly the murky specter of change, which has been hovering ghost-like between them, materializes as a clear and menacing vision. The first inkling of this threat begins soon after he is settled at Tortworth. She admits to having been drunk "twice in a space of three days." He is shocked. She never used to drink when she was with him. She has a history of Crohn's disease, and it is dangerous for her to drink alcohol. What bothers him even more is that, one of the times she was inebriated, she was at a banquet where there were men as well as women. And then, he learns that Bertie has been invited to the interns' picnic, and he can almost feel his blood pressure spike. As he reads her letter, his mood plunges; he stares at the fireplace in the dark for hours and finally, feeling depressed, far away, and helpless, concludes that she has indeed changed. When he responds, he closes with "I haven't changed a bit. You still are the one that makes this war endurable. You still are my prize. Please let me keep you on the pedestal where you always have been."

Bertie has been feeling jealousy pangs of her own. The day after the thirtieth birthday party he hosted for himself, Bart confessed that he took a nurse with him since many of the other guys also invited nurses to join them. "She knows how married I am," he assured Bertie the next day, "and likes how much I love my wife. Everyone knows Bertie and is envious of her. Please don't mind my 'date.' Please: stay the way you are, do as you have done and think as you have while we were together. Please." But when he read her response, he was puzzled, remorseful, and a little frightened.

She will save the letter she sent him about this and keep it with all his letters until the day she dies.

If and when in the future comes a similar occasion, I think it would be better for you to let me know beforehand of any 'date' arrangements you might make. For reasons I'm sure you will understand I would prefer not to think of you alone when you are not. I do realize the likelihood of impromptu occasions, but of course your party was not one & rather a long planned & "reservation made" affair. The point is rather small, I grant, and while I would under any circumstances think of you with particular affection & longing on your birthday, I do like to have things straight when, as in this instance, it is possible for you to do so.

One thing more—I release myself from my promise to you not to drink more than one even on special occasions. I was doing it for just such a reason & it's too good an 'out' to give up. Inasmuch as I must reserve some form of outlet for what causes me unhappiness.

I think I'm right and you're wrong. After the peace has come and you are home we will build us a new happy life as I said—not take up our old happy life as you say. I feel more strongly as the months roll past, that this war gives me an unwanted vacation from life—from you. I feel that we will know its effect for as long as we live, but that we are helpless to fight it. Life goes on for you and me—but not for us. I have no doubt but that we can do our rebuilding in a lasting manner on perhaps an even better foundation, for our love will have been tried + found true, + we will be wiser + perhaps stronger for the grief we have endured. I would accept no price for either the memories of our remarkable harmony of soul + spirit, nor the future that lies before us. You are the miracle of life to me. For you to be happy is the only wish of my life. My love for you is a burning, consuming, perpetual flame that throws off light and warmth with no abatement—a maniacal, frenzied love—but under it a steady and gentle permanent thing of beauty.

But it isn't until five weeks after he writes her about taking the nurse to his party and three weeks after she writes her response that he receives it. Bart's heart is thudding against his ribs when he composes his response: "Your letter, although full of love and tenderness, leaves me with the feeling that I have done a great wrong. I didn't, honey. If you knew what was in my mind during that date you would laugh. It was definitely all you that evening and any evening. I lay awake that night thinking and thinking and hoping I could cry so I could relieve the horrible heaviness in my heart. Don't you think I knew you were shedding a tear or two? Why am I afraid? I'm afraid that you will also have dates just because I did—and when I am unhappy you will tell me how innocuous your date was. That's no good sweetheart—I'd rather not come home. Jesus Christ—I was happy and I'm writing myself into a helpless state of unhappiness."

By the third week in May, the air seems to have cleared a little. He notes that he has lived only half of his married life with her. "Don't you think life owes us something for that?" he writes.

At the same time, Bertie is writing words that will alarm him again soon. Their letters cross in the mail. Cleaning the attic, she's found three letters addressed to him from three women she doesn't know. Bart explains each letter in clear, outline form: they are all grateful patients, and he can't even recall the name of one of them. He is horrified that she thinks he's been untrue to her in any way. He's pleaded with her not to be despondent—and now *this* from her: "Any fidelity you show me is not dictated by moral scruples whatever but rather a general satisfaction w/ your choice of a mate—& perhaps a little fear that any side-stepping on your part will result in similar activities for me. I shall complete the job of molding my behavior after yours."

The intensity of the imminent invasion ramping up by the hour, he begs: "Darling—don't, please don't torture me with the feeling that I displease you—<u>not</u> <u>right</u> <u>now</u>—it's the wrong time. I'd like to carry with me something better. One of these letters, some day, will be the last I'll get for a long time—or longer. I'm not being dramatic, sweetheart. It's just the truth."

CHAPTER 32
HERE WE GO

We've got to invade soon or I'll go nuts.

"GEE WHIZ—this is a war of nerves. We've got to invade soon or I'll go nuts," Bart writes mid-May. Within two weeks the 91st is restricted to camp except for two or three hours at a time. To take charge and focus his mind on the controllable, Bart begins packing and taking stock of his personal belongings. He knows he can keep only what he can carry himself—and who knows for how long. Since censors won't let him send home his photo album, he determines to lug it with him.

While Bart is centering his energies on what he can control, Bertie focuses on what she has no control over but on what is most important—whether the Allies win the war, whether her husband returns to her. She pores over the newspapers, tracing maps, reading as much as she can so that she can estimate where he is, where he will be, so that she can picture him safe.

He gently reminds her that he can't reveal any specifics and suggests that it's probably unwise to articulate her own, usually correct, conjectures in writing. "Lest I forget darling, and I shall repeat it later maybe, I want to warn you that some day perhaps soon, perhaps much later (who knows) you may suddenly not hear from me for weeks or more. You are to realize then that it is impossible to write and that you should not worry—not too much." He entreats her to send him the picture he took of her in her white nightgown the morning after they were married.

On June 3, frustrated with waiting for the word to go, Bart buses into Bristol to retrieve his Kodachromes. Harry meets him for lunch, but instead of returning home with Harry, Bart lingers for a movie, then catches the 4 p.m. bus to Thornfield to hitch back to Wotton-under-Edge from there.

When he crosses the threshold of Tortworth Court, he stops still, his mouth gaping, his eyes staring at empty rooms, at everyone busying about in march uniform. Panicked, he asks about his belongings and finds out they've been packed willy-nilly, most of everything he owns having been poured into his bedding roll by his roommates, chucked into some truck or other, and already hauled to the train platform. They'd had his name flashed on the screen of the Odeon Theater, but Bart was at the other movie house in Bristol and, of course, oblivious. Now he feels stupid.

He shucks on his officers' blouse and boots and joins the others in playing bridge and waiting. When they finally get to bed at 1 a.m., the windows are rumbling. *Distant bombing,* he thinks. He jots off one last note to Bertie, asking her to keep her chin up.

Finally, after a befuddling series of false starts, on June 5 the 91st Evacuation Hospital men and women don their helmets and march to Charfield, catch a train to Eastleigh, and truck to Hursley Camp, five miles from the staging area in Southampton, where soon a ship will carry them into the battle's core. Allied forces have already swept German minefields from the English Channel. In occupied France, resistance workers have cut communication and transportation ties. Bogus radio broadcasts—and soon, dummy paratroopers floating down—are already duping the Germans into thinking the attack is to be targeted at Pas-de-Calais instead of the Normandy beaches. Eleven thousand aircraft are gunning up for action. And 5,000 ships chopping through the waves are bound for the continent.

All day and night a seemingly endless procession of planes: squadron after squadron drone by, and two huge two- and four-motored planes tow what must be 100 or more gliders south. When Bart hears that Allied paratroopers have landed at the mouth of the Seine, he runs to the radio. And, again, waits. At 9:30 they receive their first official news that the Allies have landed on the north coast of France. The first inkling that with a great deal of grit, guts, ammunition, and luck, the world would be won back, and all the people in it catapulted back to sanity and peace. "June 6. This morning the Invasion the whole world expected, began," he records.

They're still waiting for orders the next day when they finally get a briefing: Fred informs him that the 91st is to be on the beaches D+4. He lists the name of the transport, the name of the beach, the divisions they will support, and the enemy strength just a few miles away. Bart can't help noting that ought to be about the time of a German counter-offensive. Fred's disconcerting concluding words ring in his ears: "Soon as we hit the beach, spread out, get under cover and wait until I find out what to do next."

At least Bart knows more now, knows that he'll be sleeping in his clothes this night and for many nights to follow, knows he'll carry a sleeping bag over his shoulders—and a 45–50-pound duffle bag, gas mask, belt with canteen, musette bag (about 15–20 pounds), life preserver, and steel helmet. And knows the password on the beaches that will help him get by, maybe even save his life, if he is challenged. "There's a lot of nonchalance this evening—but I wonder," he scribbles in his final diary entry in England. "Needless to say, this is it."

Mustering the rhetoric he needs, he painstakingly composes what will be his last letter from England, maybe, for all he knows, his last letter entirely:

Dearest heart:

Once again I have opportunity to write. I may, or may not be able to write again in the next day or two—or perhaps much longer. At any rate please do not worry at all—promise. It's hard as hell to write a letter just now darling—so please understand.

And today is "D" day. The invasion everyone has been waiting for has started. We had all the information quite early—as a matter of fact it kept me awake all night. I'm proud of us, darling—it's a big thing—a great show. I'm grateful for sitting in one of the first row seats.

Somehow, I've become fatalistic about the whole thing. I'm not as scared as I thought I was going to be.

Don't forget that I love you with all my heart—chin up high, please.

Request: Please send rabbit's foot.

Husb. Bart

On June 8 they finally board the liberty ship that will bring them to the war. As the loading of trucks and A-T guns and godknows what else clanks and crashes on, he and Harry stake their claim in the crowd for a place to sleep in the hold. They're too tired to let the noise bother them, though. The 91st is to be the first evacuation hospital on French soil, and Bart is thrilled.

When one day later they finally pull up the anchor and their convoy speeds into the turbulent channel, Bart is busy jotting down notes to type later, constructing memories, all his instincts trained on the future.

"Here we go," he writes.

"Here we go, Honey," he says, enveloping my seven-year-old hand as we step out into the damp St. Louis sunlight. "Here we go," he says as he revs the motor in the black Ford on our way to a Saturday matinee to gasp at John Wayne's grit as he hefts a rifle and fires bullets into those treacherous boulders and Technicolor-blue skies—or to the Barnum and Bailey big top, to draw in our breath at the trapeze artists on the quivering wire, or to the hospital lawn, where he lifts me as high as he can so that I can see in the window the already disappearing image of my grandfather Alex, who is waving to me and who will die a handful of days later. Here we go.

CHAPTER 33

THE TWENTY-FIRST CENTURY—
AND THE EIGHTEENTH

As GARY AND I wound down country roads and circled roundabouts in the west of England, I tapped my foot in anticipation. Sun particularly pale for July. Wheat fields a dusty gold, haystacks in neat rectangles. White sheep in green meadows. The Snooty Fox Inn. Neatly trimmed hedges. Quintessentially English. But I was distracted by the transcribed diaries bulging my backpack between my feet and an untidy pile of photocopies (snapshots and slides from 1943 to 1944) sliding down my lap. As our rented Renault Megane sped along hairpins above manicured fields in geometric shapes, curving hedgerows, and sweeping vistas, I leaned forward in my seat.

At the crest of a wooded hill, nine letters on a plain white sign: "Tortworth." Soon we were passing under the arch of the stately gates that Bart photographed—the gates that must have seemed like the entrance to paradise to a twenty-nine-year-old man who had lived for the last eleven months in tents in cow pastures in Morocco, in a racetrack in Algeria, and in a bombed-out hospital in Sicily. As Bart had done over seventy years before, I gaped at the Victorian mansion in front of me, still called Tortworth Court but now converted into a hotel. A tour bus was parked outside. I tried not to let it ruin my vision of my father's first astonished entrance. Inside, as we angled up a long staircase to a dark wood interior balcony, we followed a line of gilt-framed copies of portraits of aristocrats. We had requested a room in the "old part," hoping that somehow we would be housed in the same wing as my father, but all the interiors had been rebuilt since a fire in 1991. Still, the outside of the place looked much the same as it did in his photos and descriptions.

The estate, built in the mid-nineteenth century, has a history befitting a key place in a world war, a tradition of power. It tops the highest hill above the Severn valley. The grand-sounding names of the owners and builders of the estate paraded through the photocopied, stapled-together sheets of paper the concierge gave us: Throckmorton, Ducie, barons, and a succession of earls and countesses. The records of land ownership date to the Norman Conquest.

The manor also has a connection to medicine dating from before the American medical corps took it over. Just over 130 years before the Americans arrived, the owners of the house supported the vaccine pioneer Edward Jenner, who lived in the nearby village of Berkeley. The wife of the earl, by having herself inoculated against smallpox, attracted Royal attention to Dr. Jenner's innovations. Two weeks after Bart arrived in England, he pedaled into an icy wind to Jenner's hut, the site of the very first vaccination, and paid homage.

We passed under the arch of wisteria and laburnum, which I recognized from one of his photos, though Bart's, in winter, was just a bare metal framework. The grounds were shaded with green from enveloping branches and limbs. I was not surprised that he thought the trees we were seeing now were strange. They *are* strange. The estate encompasses an arboretum with 300 acres of trees, some of them ancient. The Earl of Ducie planted hundreds more beginning about 100 years before Bart took such delight in exploring the grounds. There are trees native to Persia, to China, and even to the Atlas Mountains of Morocco, of the sort that Bart might have seen from the open freight car he rode into Algeria. Apparently some of the trees that awed Bart were destroyed by gasoline spills from military vehicles concealed among them.

After dinner in what used to be the library, we headed out into the sunset. We drove north, back down the valley to the towns whose names Bart had so carefully recorded. We wanted to visit the pubs Bart and his cronies frequented, to which Bart sometimes hiked overland through fields twice a day in the fog or rain.

The Huntsman was two-story and stucco, painted with white and red trim, a string of lights on the eaves. A video game or slot machine took up a corner. The chairs at the tables were mismatched. I tried to see in it the place it once was, swarming with the servicemen and their cigarettes and ribbons as pictured in Bart's slides. I could imagine the polished wood piano Bart loved to cut up on. I leaned on the bar to chat with the current owners, Kaye Thomas and her husband Jim. They were affable and eager to be helpful. They told me that once in a while an older man or woman comes in and remembers the Americans singing and playing the piano. *Playing the piano?* I was thrilled. If I squinted I could almost see my father, a bit tipsy and showing off, his fingers scampering up and down the black-and-whites, glancing about to see who was paying attention.

With Kaye and Jim we spent a companionable hour or so trying to re-imagine their place the way it was before a fire destroyed the interior. But as we found the other inns on our list, I was increasingly beset by a raw feeling of loss. The Berkeley Vale Hotel, where Bart walked to eat when he couldn't stomach Tortworth fare, was now boarded up and defaced with graffiti. The Tower was now an ordinary-looking, Indian-run hotel. The Ship's Inn in Alveston, now a Days Inn but with flower boxes adorning the windows and weathered timbers, was the only pub that seemed to have preserved some of its wartime charm: alcoves, exposed brick archways. It was the place where Bart threw a thirtieth birthday for himself, where Harry read out loud the poem he wrote as a gift to Bart, narrating the saga of the 91st and their months as friends and peppered by such idiosyncratic doggerel as:

And then came Port Lyautey, and Bedside Manor was born,
And the Snack Bar, what a joy it was until that fateful morn;
The damn thing set the tent on fire, it gave us all a fright,
We cleaned up the mess, reopened the bar and "business as usual" that
     night.

A twenty-something waiter informed us, proudly, that quite a few people had visited there inquiring about the war, and he darted into a back room to pull out some "old pictures"—but those turned out to be from 1961. I was frustrated, yearning for links between the generations, a bridge that would close the gap of the decades between my father's experience of England and ours. A key perhaps to finding out what part those months played in Bart's life, in the kind of man he became, the father a little girl in a gingham jumper might scan the street for every day. The Zangara connection seemed so haloed in emotion, so perfectly poised to continue cascading down into the next generations—I wanted something like that.

That night, in our room with its heraldic furnishings, its fan blowing hot air over my head toward the oak beams above, I again shuffled through my photocopies. In one photo, which I was almost certain was taken at Tortworth, Bart is looking more than a little two-sheets-to-the-wind. He appears to be sitting between a table and a desk on which a goose-necked lamp, a clock, and a large box (possibly a radio) rest in back of him. A jerry-rigged wire extends up and back out of the frame of the picture and casts an eerie shadow. The windows are blacked out. He's tilting back in his chair, his dark hair pompadoured away from his forehead, his eyebrows arching over half-lidded eyes. On a makeshift pedestal on the table in front of him sits a nearly empty wine glass. The liquid is pale. Fruit juice and alcohol? There's a slightly fuller glass in front of him, and to his side, next to an empty bottle, is another glass, empty.

Another photo shows his wooden cot with thin mattress wedged in a corner. A small footlocker serves as a tabletop, on which stands a gaping camera case, a neatly stacked sheaf of papers, and the framed photo of Bertie with her white, ruffled collar, which contrasts artistically with her raven-glossy hair. Her lips are full, lustrous, on the cusp of a smile.

Before we struck out for the countryside the next morning—china blue sky, not a wisp of cloud—I asked that our coffee be brought outside to the veranda, where we could be alone. We overlooked the neat maze of gardens quietly, almost reverently, and suddenly it struck me that I'd been staring at a tree on the park lawn, a Japanese maple, the same kind my father had planted next to the swimming pool.

And although my gaze was fixed and straight ahead, I was *seeing* the star-pointed leaves and elegant limbs of that other tree, thousands of miles and more than a quarter of a century away. I am in the heart of America, at the house I grew up in. It's an August day, and, as I always did every summer, I am about to catch a plane to take me back to my home in Idaho. I am in the kitchen and about to hug my father goodbye when he holds up his index finger and says, "Wait, I have something I want you to take back with you." He disappears out the back door, and when he returns, he is cradling in his palm the bottom half of an ice cream carton full of dirt, through which, sticking up in the center, is a green shoot the size of his ring finger.

"This is from your tree," he says, looking slightly away, almost shy. *My tree?* I wonder. Of course—the tree in the swimming pool area, under or around which I'd spent almost every summer of my life; the delicate tree that sheltered me from the blistering sun; the tree with the sharp-pointed leaves that I saw as silhouettes when I looked straight into the sky. The Japanese maple. From the place where I'd sat by the pool and read and written—and talked, or not talked—with him. My tree.

On two planes from eastern Missouri to western Idaho, I carried the maple shoot in the ice cream carton, its loose soil dribbling out when the container dipped in my hand. I pushed the open carton under the seats, carefully arching the pliant stem so as not to snap it. I carried it as I paced around the Minneapolis airport for four hours between flights. I carried it on my lap in the car for the final ninety miles of my journey back to my home of nearly a quarter of a century. As soon as I arrived, I placed the seedling on a sided cookie sheet and watered it, and every afternoon for a week, I brought it outside to sun on the purple-painted chair on the deck outside our bedroom.

The shoot grew rapidly, and over several years I bedded it in a series of increasingly bigger pots. One day the leaves were dotted with little buds; soon, the buds transformed themselves into furled leaves. When the little leaves unfurled, I was about to rejoice, but then I looked more closely. These new leaves were nothing like the rusty red of the Japanese maple; they were definitely green, and broader, less serrated. I stood still, my arms at my side, my shoulders sagging. My father had planted the wrong seed, given me the wrong tree. It wasn't my tree at all.

But I continued to nurture it, moved it around the yard, following the sun, as my father had when he moved my lounge by the pool and sat with me. As the tree matured from a spindly sapling into a solid stalk with shooting limbs, I planted it on the side of our house, setting around it a miniature fence to protect it. One June a surprise snow-storm bore down on its early summer leaves, bent its branches back-ward, and cracked its slender trunk in two. One late February night, a hit-and-run car mowed it down, flattening its little fence to the ground. Both times I wept and mourned. But both times the tree grew back, one time regenerating from the single branch that had been sprouting next to the trunk. On the surface of things, each time Bart's maple was resurrected, I felt assured of its permanence, its shield against the terror of absence. I had a plaque made that read "Bart Passanante's Maple from St. Louis, MO," and Gary dug a rectangular hole under the tree to set the sign in concrete. With each resurrection, for me it always returned as the Japanese maple, with its lacey rust-colored leaves and its muscular trunk, just as lovely as the one we used to sit under together by the pool.

As GARY AND I pulled out to follow the roads Bart traveled on his forty-mile bike excursion, I saluted Tortworth Court and squirmed around in my seat to keep the manor in view as long as possible.

Driving Bart's route in reverse, we followed roads lined with Queen Anne's lace toward the edge of the Cotswolds. Most of what I knew about the English countryside I had learned from reading the nineteenth-century British novels that were jammed into the bookshelves of my parents' house. What did I expect to find now? Perhaps evidence of the England I once claimed as my own, the place where I spent my girlhood: Chevy Chase, in the newly bulldozed suburb where my parents built their modest dream house, the neighborhood some canny St. Louis developer constructed to replicate the Americans' fantasy of Olde England. The entrance to Chevy Chase was heralded by two stone towers, each with a small gothic-looking window, highly mysterious to a diminutive child with a capacious imagination. The sign was painted with prancing horses pulling a carriage, spurred by a coachman in a top hat. A matching stone wall rimmed an elliptical bird sanctuary, which our living room picture window faced, and delineated the maze of curving streets sporting English names—Kings Lynn, Aylesbury, Enfield, Rye Lane. It was on these streets that my father taught me how to ride a bike. Soon I was zooming alone down the slope of Aylesbury and rounding the arc into Kings Lynn—on my right, the stone walls cupping the bird sanctuary; on my left, my red brick house with its three scalloped-leafed oaks forming a triangle in the front yard. Now I wonder if it might have been on this particular day-long bicycle journey that my father, unwittingly or not, envisioned the life he would create for the three daughters he was yet to conceive, his life with them in the house he would live in for the rest of his years, even as his memory tumbled toward its final frenzy.

At Dursley, with its half-timbered houses and spruced-up village center, we drove to Berkeley Heath to visit Edward Jenner's hut and paid homage, as Bart had done, to Jenner's grave. But in town, where Panache Unisex hair dressers advertised waxing, the reality of twenty-first-century England colored our looking. Indeed, the farther up the river we drove, the less quaint-English and the more commercial-industrial we got. In Sharpness we followed the drab Severn Estuary. We navigated our way past a slag heap, scrap metal piled as tall as a house marring the view of the river, an unintentional symbol of the *real* England, which was far from the Victorian postcard I'd been conditioned to see. Like Bart, the glimpse we got across the estuary was nothing like Richard Llewellyn's, and, a little dispirited, we started back.

On our way, I dashed one final time into the Huntsman, this time by myself since Gary's patience for pub-hopping and hearing me pose the same questions over and over was wearing a tad thin. After I said a grateful goodbye and returned to the car, he was poking a pencil nib at a map he'd balanced on the steering wheel.

"You're not gonna believe this," he said, then trailed off, absorbed in the map. "I was looking again at Dad's bike route, and we're only twenty minutes away."

"Away from *what*?" But I was already picturing Bart peering far across the Severn to Wales, searching for that elusive northern bridge.

"From Tintern Abbey!" Gary paused for effect. "There's a bridge not far from here." Nib jabbed, nearly piercing paper.

"Oh my god!" I said. It was almost a whoop. I buckled my seatbelt.

As we crossed the suspension bridge into those green valleys of Wales, my pulse quickened. We followed the Wye, the river Wordsworth memorializes in his famous poem written not far from the abbey. I was almost certain Bart had read the poem, but I suspected that, in 1944, he had no clue as he was meandering on his bike how close the long-ago immortalized abbey was to his own path. The road narrowed, and suddenly, around a sharp corner, the towering ruins of the abbey flashed into view.

Soon Gary and I were on sacred literary ground. We ambled around among the remains of the abbey's auspicious stone columns and walls, and, on the grassy ground, the ornamental corbels that had once decorated the enormous pillars. We loved seeing, framed by the empty windows and arches and spaces between walls, the sylvan hills where Wordsworth rambled that other July over two hundred years before. I wanted to see this place as Bart would have seen it. How he would have thrilled at the serendipity. I could see and hear him now: his jaw dropping as mine had, his excitement tempered with reverence, as mine was, and proclaiming, "Tintern Abbey. Imagine that."

Gary and I rested on a ledge in the slender shadow of a stone wall. Under our roofless paradise of ruins, we munched on the sparse lunch we'd squirreled away in our backpack from our last Tortworth breakfast. Then he opened the folded card-stock copy of the poem, which we'd purchased in the gift shop, and began to read.

As he unfurled Wordsworth's experience for us both, my mind spun in a way it never had, in any class, or any library, before. In the way a poet's *conviction* can be trusted as much as his eloquence, I began seeing our journey, Gary's and mine, in a more far-reaching light. I considered the simple narrative of the poem: as the poet strolls with his beloved younger sister Dorothy along the path above the Wye, gazing down on what was left of the abbey, he is offering himself lyrical solace for the passing of time. He considers the delightful excursion he took along the river alone five years earlier, the reality of his aging, his nostalgia about past pleasures that can never be literally relived. But he is taking comfort in his ability to see and feel again the pleasures of his youth through his younger sister's eyes: the same pleasures can be his through her—and, in his writing, ours—forever.

Bart, too, only two years older than the poet was when he wrote the poem, and bemoaning the seemingly sudden thinning of his hair, was feeling the pressures of aging. He confesses that he took his bike trip over all those hills for Bertie "so that I may convince you of my youth." He, too, was reflecting on the "dizzy raptures" of earlier days. His memories of joy with his wife had accompanied him from Morocco to Algeria to Tunisia to Sicily and now to England, and would travel inside him, a primal part of him like a kernel at the heart of a nut, longer than either of them could have anticipated. When Gary read the line "through a long absence," I stopped him, asked him to read it again.

In the heart of these beauteous ruins so distant from home, I heard a poet more than two centuries dead whisper something I perhaps had already known: we cannot possibly recreate the past. We, Gary and I, could not recreate Bart's life, not even a microscopic fragment of it. But we could take pleasure in his meticulous recording of his memories, no matter how disturbing, how wrenching.

"Oh! yet a little while / May I behold in thee what I once was," Gary read, then paused to look at me and smile. And I knew he knew that in trying to reconstruct Bart's years before I knew him, I was creating a memory of him in my own light, by necessity filtered through thought and imagination, as Wordsworth had recreated his own memory. We had journeyed over a continent and an ocean to safeguard and confirm that through memory nothing can be lost.

It struck me that Bart must have had at least an inkling, even if he didn't recognize it as such, that in his eloquent descriptions in his diaries and letters he was creating "life and food for future years," as Wordsworth does. We can give voice to what we know and what we can imagine, the poet reminds us; and someone we love can carry that voice into the future. I want to believe that, in Bart's case, that voice is mine.

FRANCE

June 10, 1944 to September 28, 1944

CHAPTER 34

NORMANDY

I never dreamed I would ever sit on the stage when I hoped for a front seat.

THE MOVEMENTS of the 91st in France can be tracked on a website. The unit's path was relatively straightforward (though if you squint at these sites circled on a map, you might conjure up the image of a snake beginning to coil but then changing its mind and slithering away), and you can read a clear progression of places and dates online. But *what happened* there was anything but straightforward.

Bart's war odyssey in France begins on June 10, 1944, as he scans its shores from the deck of the SS *Thomas Wolfe*. The ship bobbing on the choppy sea, he catches his first glimpses of the show he's been waiting for. But the drama of the next two-and-a-half months is staged on the ground, on relatively few square miles, the bulk of them in fields not all that far from the shore. His unit will shadow a front defined largely by the course of the First United States Army and the reactions and counteroffensives of the Wehrmacht. The 91st lands on Utah Beach four days after the first Allied landings. Bart will feel proud all his life that his hospital unit was the first at Utah to see the French coastline, and now his chest is swelling as he draws in his breath and his boat pulls in among the hundreds of others. On all sides of them beyond the horizon, ships and ships and ships, barrage balloons teth-

ered to each one, cruisers and battleships on one side of them firing at
the beach designated for the 91st. Squadrons of bombers are roaring
inland, the leaden clouds darkened with Allied fighter planes carving
circles in the sky, their drones incessant in his ears. Warships shell the
shore—a ball of flame, smoke, a harrowing pause, a cloud of smoke
inland—then the blast. An anchorless fear sails up from intestines to
throat that soon they must disembark and there is no port in sight.

Finally, nearly twenty hours after they left England, they climb
down ropes on the ship's side onto landing barges that deliver them to
makeshift docks. They slog inland from the narrow bombarded beachhead. Feet blistered from trudging up rutted roads, shoulders burning
from lugging their requisite fifty pounds of personal equipment, they
search for a place to sleep that's at least reputed to be cleared of mines.
They are walking toward the front, but as far as Bart is able to ascertain, they are already there. They pass a battered town, smashed tanks,
a field of broken gliders, bodies maimed and dead, felled paratroopers
who want to tell their gory tales. Some of the parachute silk on the
ground is drenched with blood. They finally bivouac two miles inland
in a cow pasture close to Ste.-Marie-du-Mont.

If you look at a map, you'll see that for the next 110 days they are
in France, they will shift positions nine times. You can follow their
route in the patchwork of farmlands in Normandy and the plains farther east to eight additional sites, most of which you will not have
heard of, near Boutteville, Pont l'Abbé, La Cambe, Marigny, Brécey,
Senonches, Guyancourt, La Capelle. You can put your finger on the
towns they visit along the way, towns that, by the time Bart sees them,
have been blasted into shards, rubble, and ash. Including their medical
installation near Paris, they will set up hospitals swiftly, efficiently, in
tents on fields at five of these sites, and treat more wounds and perform more operations than any of the doctors could have imagined.

If you were reading a summary of the work of the 91st online of
their days in France, or a slick-paged history book intent on covering the entire war in a finite number of pages, you might find these
numbers to feed your own imagination. Here the 91st admitted 8,214
patients to their hospitals. And in their 75 days of official hospital
operation, they performed surgery as follows: in Boutteville, 635; Pont
L'Abbé, 1,826; Marigny, 875; Brécey, 798; Guyancourt, 340. The numbers may speak for themselves but don't tell the whole story, and it's
what they do not tell that you'll remember.

Bart's *personal* odyssey in France follows new interior terrain, maneuvering through a sphere of pandemonium and ruin. He is at his most articulate, most precise, as he tries not to be overwhelmed, tries to keep focused on the thousands of patients waiting in piles like discarded laundry on the lawn to pass under his scrutiny and his scalpel. How does he live through this? He plugs his ears with surgical cotton and pops Nembutals or washes them down with homemade gin to block out the racket when the luxury of an hour or two of sleep presents itself, when he does not have a bloodied body in front of his face. He concentrates on the minutiae, the absolute necessity of work—the diagnosing and dressing, the stitching and sewing, the needles and knives. He dreams of Bertie, her white freckled arms, her trailing, black hair. And he writes. He writes as if his words are the only steadfast weapon against the force of this onslaught.

CHAPTER 35

STE.-MARIE-DU-MONT, BOUTTEVILLE,
THE FIRST EIGHTEEN DAYS

It's a stinkin' mess.

AT STE.-MARIE-DU-MONT, he and Harry dig a foxhole together and pitch a tent nearly over their ditch. Just after dusk the Germans fly over and trigger the large anti-aircraft batteries. At the eerie scream of the descending bombs, Harry and Bart drop into their ditch and hug the ground. One bomb lands only 100–200 yards away. *What an ungodly explosion!* A plane strafes the road next to where they are parked. Another plane bursts into flames.

After half an hour, they climb out of their ditch, and for the fourth successive night, Bart goes to bed with all his clothes on—even his impregnated coveralls. A few minutes later, he dives once again into the foxhole. In the middle of the night, the *whoomp* of shells again interrupts his sleep. Huge flashes light up their beach. The next morning after the hellish noise finally fades, Bart learns that their rival, the 128th Evacuation Hospital, officially beat them onto French ground by a couple of hours while the 91st, awaiting the delayed stevedores, was still gawking at the show off the shore.

Within a day and an evening, they ride inland and set up their first hospital near Boutteville, four miles south of Ste.-Mère-Église, where, the night before the armada sailed from the shores of England, American paratroopers glided down to help clear the way for liberation. Some of the boys of the 91st venture out into the fields just a few yards from the fighting to pick up parachutes left by the first troops. Bart scoops up a scrap to use as a scarf.

Their tents, only three miles from the front, straddle a hill next to a farmhouse, with no camouflage, the painted red crosses their only hope at protection. *It's probably a dandy military objective,* Bart figures. For two nights they've been witnessing the Allies' costly battles on the way to Carenton to link the territory they gained on the beachheads at Utah and Omaha and create a defensive line against German counterattacks before they pressed inland. The Allies are encountering their first struggles with the French *bocage,* the formidable hedgerows. Bordering the roads and fields of Normandy and separating one field from another, the hedgerows are tangles of thornbushes and undergrowth rooted into impenetrable embankments. They grow so thick and tall that they can easily be used to prohibit not only physical progress but communication between combat units. German battalions, already familiar with the terrain, hide behind them and wait to surprise the Allies with their 88s, machine guns, and mortars.

When the doctors and nurses open the doors of the hospital tents, hundreds of wounded soldiers are already waiting. The first twenty-four hours bring them 475 severely wounded, all needing surgery. Through-and-through holes in chests and abdomens, shattered limbs, some with full-blown gas gangrene, all manner of injuries from shell fragments—buttocks, genitals, legs, arms, face, brain. Some burns. Amputations are rampant. The damage is manifold, and nearly half the operations take more than an hour. *The German 88 mm gun is doing its work,* Bart thinks. Their wooden bullets are causing massive destruction, too. Two of the worst wounds Bart has ever seen stun him—an 88 has burst before two boys and maimed their faces so that nothing but their tongues are visible. This is the closest he's ever been to being nauseated in medicine. They have six operating tables going at once, but they have to stop intermittently to wait until the linen and instruments are ready again to perform more operations.

The mass of the severely wounded that continues to stream in launches them into chaos. And not all the equipment and officers have arrived. Some of the vehicles that carried equipment across the channel were submerged in seawater, and the vehicles had to be taken ashore, the equipment dried and cleaned. There are so many patients they have to call in two auxiliary surgery teams—and wait twenty-four hours for them to arrive.

Bart can't sleep the first night, not at all. The gunfire is infernal; the artillery barrages, intense. Just to the side of them a 105 Howitzer shakes the earth again and again. Close-sounding sniper bullets whine. He hates the night and he believes he will always hate it—that is, if he lives through this. But he can't help thinking about the poor infantry men and paratroopers—it must be horrible up there in the thick of it. It gets dark at midnight, and they wait for the enemy planes to make their final dives before heading home.

The next night is worse—the worst he could ever have imagined. Not in a nightmare did he ever feel so pressed. It's an inferno. It seems that every gun in the world opened up. Flares, smoke, and spectral lights ornate an arc in the horizon before them. Blasts shake the operating room tent, and every dive seems intended for them. Though they do their best to appear unconcerned, they automatically cringe and clench their teeth. The anti-aircraft barrages are just as loud and close as anything else. Working in helmets, they pull in their necks while feeling their way from ward to ward, hoping the falling fragments will miss them just this once.

Every night German raiders zoom directly over the surgical tent. While standing at the OR table Bart grits his teeth, still certain the next one will be it. One night planes dive-bomb and drop eerie flares all night long, and huge guns let go at them, and he is so frightened that, between patients, he ducks out of the tent to watch the fireworks outdoors. It helps to see what's going on. When he isn't on the surgery nightshift and can look up and listen to the whistle of the bombs and see the direction of the tracers, he isn't nervous at all. But in surgery he has to stay inside the flimsy tent and try to focus on the open body in front of him until it's ready for him to leave it, while some insidious demon whispers to him that each explosion is meant for him, that the next one will be his last.

After an endless week of these nightly terrors, he tells Welch he wants to work days instead of nights though he knows he would then have to give up surgery. He tells Welch he's had enough of surgery. Welch offers him the Preoperative Section as sole head and says Bart can supervise it during the day. Bart will work twelve-hour days examining, diagnosing, X-raying, medicating, dressing, and lining up patients for the OR. Welch still wants him to do some surgery, too, especially when there's a backlog.

He will write Bertie about this, but not for four months. "O. K. so I was scared," he will confess eventually. "Yes I was and I don't mind admitting it. It's a dreadfully helpless feeling, dolly."

Somewhere along the lineup of these horrifying nights, his bedding roll arrives, and he moves into a ward tent so he doesn't have to sleep in the open. It's beastly cold in there, but he can sleep in layers and a wool cap. They eat what passes for meals whenever they can grab a couple cans of food. They don't know a thing except what goes on in front of them. As far as Bart can see, the Allies aren't moving an inch, and if anyone should ask him, he'd say that the 91st is too damned close to the front.

They are supposed to be a 400-bed hospital, but between 600 and 700 patients crowd the tents; some wait on the grass. Since the 91st is a 90 percent surgical hospital handling fresh trauma cases, the majority of these cases have to go through Bart and the shock ward. There are so many patients that they have to quit admitting for a few days while they try to catch up. They use every person they can. Even the chaplain scrubs in. Flak falls in droves about them and their tents. Bart's clothes are mottled with blood at all times. Supplies can't land on the beaches, and they run out of penicillin. It's days before it can be dropped from the air. Snipers shoot a hole through one of their tents. Air strikes continue to dive low over their tents at night, and any moment feels like this one is it.

He sees nearly all the types of injuries he's read about and then some. They're grateful for the blood that has been shipped or flown over, refrigerated, and ready to give. Sometimes they have to do away with correct surgical principles—but when life and death are balanced so precariously, a gown, a scrub longer than a minute, or proper asepsis do not seem very important.

Wounded French civilians and German prisoners wait their turn in the OR, but there are so many American boys in such bad shape that it's hard to put the enemy before them. "We can only try to be humanitarian," Bart writes. But increasingly the patients tell them that they have been given first aid by the Germans on the battlefield and left there. One of his patients was captured and taken to a German hospital where, he says, he got as good treatment as anybody else. So now the medical staff begins to reciprocate. Still, he wonders what people back home would say if they knew their blood was being used on Germans.

He hears there's a landing strip nearby now. That means they can now evacuate patients by air. But that also means that the nights will be holy hell. And it doesn't appear to him that the Allies are doing all that well, though he guesses that's because he can *still see* the front from where he's standing. Progress also seems slow according to the radio and maps. The Allies are holding such a small piece of land, it seems that just one enemy breakthrough would catch them right in the middle.

Even when the bombing and ack-ack sound farther away and they stop receiving new patients, the cacophony of battle from Cherbourg rumbles in the distance, and the nearby artillery and bombing still jolt them nearly every night. Barrage balloons containing bombs break loose from their moorings. One drops about 100 yards from Bart's tent, and he braces himself, but the bomb doesn't explode. Sleep seems impossible. Evacuations are stalled because of rough seas, so the patients—150 one day, 65 another—once again overflow the hospital's capacity to take care of them. He knows he can't stay focused on the intricate minutiae of muscles and organs and veins without sleep. He hasn't had time for even a bird-bath, and it's been twelve days since he changed his underwear.

One day he helps out in Tuhy's ward, the chest and abdomen ward full of colostomies, bladders, and bloody chests. "It's a stinkin' mess," he writes. But artillery fire sounds farther and farther away. There's a new moon in a clear, starry night and, finally, after two weeks in Normandy, not one burst of ack-ack.

Bart uses this lull to explore the neighborhood—he's spotted some crashed gliders in the field next to theirs—but knows there are snipers and, possibly, land mines about. Bart and Shields walk over to the 128th to look over their OR. They talk to German prisoners. The POWs are garrulous, and ecstatic that they are out of the war. They enjoy the food, cigarettes, and the work, and they damn Hitler at the drop of a hat.

"And so it goes," Bart writes. "First the Italians and now the Germans." He also types some of the diary notes he took en route and starts another sketch. At a meeting he learns some bad news: Fred Lahourcade is leaving to command the 45th Field Hospital. Everyone will miss him, but Bart, who has been a friend of his since months before they left for Africa, is especially sorry to have to say goodbye.

They also get good news: over two weeks of operation, Bart's unit has cared for more than 2,000 casualties. And the Allies have taken Cherbourg and the Cotentin peninsula. That means that tomorrow the 91st will be someplace else again.

CHAPTER 36
PONT L'ABBÉ

I never dreamt of such destruction.

On June 28, the 91st hauls their tents and equipment and already exhausted bodies and trucks ten miles west to the shattered town of Pont l'Abbé to back up the front line. They are farther up the front than any installation except the British Aid stations and now in position behind the new front that expects to push in a day or two, southward. As they move into bivouac, the mine sweepers are just leaving and the bulldozers are clearing out the Germans' anti-landing uprights, the stakes they drove into the ground to slash through gliders attempting to land.

Bart starts to dig his foxhole, collect his belongings, and pitch his pup tent, but the artillery gunfire, even in the light of afternoon, is so loud—so close—that it's giving him the jitters. He knows that tonight it will be terrifying. He plans to dig his hole deeper tomorrow.

Shortly after midnight he hears a sound he's never heard before—a whirring whistle, then a splintering blast. The din seems to land in the surrounding fields, and it strikes him that they are caught in the middle of an artillery duel. He doesn't wait until morning to deepen his foxhole, and soon Harry joins him in digging. Bart remains alone in his hole throughout the night, thinking, smoking, and wondering. The shells shriek across the skies until dawn. "What a hell of a place to put the hospital," he writes when the morning light lifts the terror from his gut, at least for the time being.

Still, he remains jittery all day—sleepless, tired, and worried. His appetite has fallen off. He needs to get used to this very soon or he knows he'll be a physical wreck. What if he never gets used to the noise, the whistle and blast, the racket of machine guns, the hellish gunfire? He moves into Harry's wall tent. Now they can share a trench, and Bart can sleep on a cot. The other officers and nurses are now housed five to a pyramidal tent. To avoid being drenched by the relentless rains, he helps Harry put up his pup tent over the slit trench. In the dim daylight, as the guns thunder not far away, they set up and equip a second pre-op tent, which Bart will supervise from noon until midnight. They all expect a big push to begin the day after tomorrow. And they've learned that they are farther up the front than any installation except the British Aid stations. It's not safe to leave the area.

As they wait for patients, tanks jounce over the roads. Allied planes plunge toward them; blasts move nearer. He spends nights climbing in and out of his foxhole. One night his sleep is interrupted by a visiting major who is brought in DOA, shot through the neck by a trigger-happy sentry at their area boundary. In his pockets Bart finds a bottle of mustard and a bottle of tobasco sauce. "*C'est le guerre,*" he says. Bart, Harry, and Welch stay up to drain the Wehrmacht cognac the CO gave each tent of officers.

It's becoming clear that over the weeks in the *bocage* the Allies are losing troops by the thousands. German-engineered floods drown Allied glider pilots, passengers, and paratroopers, and Allied tanks bog down in the swampy soil. Stormy weather grounds their planes. In spite of all this, meter by meter, for the remainder of Bart's days in Pont l'Abbé, the Americans will press onward to St. Lô, the sleepy town they know is their gateway to chasing the enemy out of France for good.

The onset of the big drive begins just south of Carenton, less than twelve miles from the 91st. Bart peels back the flap of the tent and watches the battle front. All hell is breaking loose. *It's like the movies,* he thinks, a constant roar of every type of gun backed up and accentuated by their neighbors—four or five batteries of big cannon. The flashes light the sky in rapid intermittent bursts, confluent with myriads of others. He can't possibly conceive of anybody living through such a barrage.

Within a few hours they start receiving casualties, at least the less serious ones, those who don't need more time to be dragged or gurneyed from the battlefield. Bart grimaces at wounds of the left big toe, which are so obviously self-inflicted. But soon he no longer has time to be disgusted, or to think. Ambulance after ambulance, the bodies roll in, over 400 in a single day.

They request yet another auxiliary surgical team—this one with their own portable operating room. A gas treatment battalion across the field is taking minor cases, but still there's a backlog of over 200. "I distinctly hate this part of France," Bart comments. During the next days, Bart's twelve-hour shifts last thirteen and fourteen hours. He knows that the longer the patients have to wait for the OR, the greater their chances are of getting gas gangrene. That knowledge weighs on him, and there's nothing he can do. Most patients have more than one wound, often five or six. *It's a madhouse,* he thinks. He treats for shock, evaluates abdominal cases, studies X-rays, changes dressings, checks penicillin doses, gives assurance, and examines each new case as soon as an older one goes out. And his is only one of four pre-op tents. A patient tells him that his medical unit, also marked by enormous bright red crosses, has been bombed and strafed. So the next morning at 4:30 when a-a guns fire up and an enemy plane buzzes the hospital, Bart dives into his foxhole.

After ten days of the push, the artillery racket fades, and Bart figures the front must have moved or scattered at least ten miles away. There's still no quiet. The generators hum and throb twenty-four hours. And even now he can't keep up with the steady inflow.

But by mid-July, the news is looking up. Gunfire is beginning to seem like a nightmare of the past, and only distant flashes illuminate the blackness of a starless and moonless night. And patients just dribble in. By the time the hospital is shut down, they will have treated over 2,700 of them. The invasion is clearly a success, but the war's progress has been painstakingly snail-like, much too slow for Bart.

On July 18, Colonel Beeler informs them that they will now rest for a while and then move to Omaha Beach and get in on the next big push. They are to take their prisoners with them. The POWs have worked well with the officers, and they are so frightened that they'll be left behind that they are tearful.

The day before they are to leave Pont l'Abbé, George, on the pretext of acquiring a PA system, inveigles a command car to drive Bart up the Cotentin peninsula. The thirty-two miles over torn roads are dusty, the traffic dense. Their destination is Cherbourg with its decimated concrete pillboxes, its fort on a rocky hill overlooking the city. It has not been as mangled as other towns. Several ships are docked in the harbor, the docks have been revamped and fixed, and some supplies are coming in now, and soon, Bart is confident, the harbor will bulge with incoming troops. On the way to Cherbourg, the pitted roads have taken them by Montbourg, Valognes, and Ste.-Marie-du-Mont—towns that made them shudder. "Montbourg is a mass of rubble," Bart writes. "And Valognes is a crumbling ruins. I never dreamt of such destruction."

On the road back to camp, as the miles that are now in Allied hands spread out before him, he feels more and more certain that although the liberated territory appears to be small on the map, it's really quite a chunk and that the Allies are firmly established. And that the worst for him is over.

CHAPTER 37

LA CAMBE

We certainly are enjoying our rest but I don't think we'll be laughing much longer.

THE MEN AND women of the 91st as well as about forty POWs cross the Vire River and convoy near First Army Headquarters, beyond Isigny and four miles inland from Omaha Beach. They bivouac in a field bounded by hedgerows, just a stone's throw from La Cambe, its toppled housetops in view. Their orders are not to set up a hospital, but to rest. The scuttlebutt is that the Army intends to place their by now well-seasoned hospital strategically near the next big push of the First Army. Only eighteen miles away is St.-Lô, which has just fallen to the Americans. At least what is left of it: skeletal walls, bombed out windows, scorched timbers sprawling across the streets. An anti-aircraft gun is poised just yards from Bart's tent.

Five days after they arrive Bart sees what he believes is the spectacle of his life: over a thousand bombers and their escorts soaring toward the front. But nearly nightly air raids blast on, and some of the planes return crippled. One night, when a 90 mm shell whistles past their tent, all four tent-mates (Meyer, Riday, Beranek, and he) hit the floor simultaneously. During an air raid early one morning, a plane roars too close, and flak spits down among the tents. Another night there are three—the men agree that they are the worst they've ever had—and they spend a good deal of time hugging the earth in a nearby ditch. Two bombs land so close that their teeth rattle. The searchlights can't find the planes in the cloudy skies, and the terrific ack-ack for miles misses every time. When Patton's heavy-armored, newly formed Third Army lands a few miles away, the ground trembles until dawn.

Although Bart grumbles about drenching rain and slow, empty days with no mail, he's happy to have time for showers, sleep, movies, reading, and even a few hands of poker. The tent-mates steal a little bread from the mess tent, and he shares his can of beef with them. For exercise he runs down the lumpy field in a soccer game with the German prisoners. He reconnoiters, looking for a suitable place to sketch, a view to watercolor. His painting captures some of the nurses' tents and a flimsy-looking farmer's fence in the foreground, in the back, rooftops and chimneys, trees and grasses, and, in the distance, in the center of the viewer's perspective, a church, its tower rising from its perch on a hill.

He paints an idyllic picture of this break to Bertie: "This evening after supper I lugged my overfilled belly about the grassy field chasing and hitting a baseball with Harry. This afternoon I spent in the gentle draft of a pyramidal tent with the sides rolled up and radio phonograph going, reading R-digest and finishing H. Allen Smith's book. Last nite I catalogued my prints in my album which in itself will tell the whole story of my travels (Say, I have travelled a lot, haven't I?). We certainly are enjoying our rest but I don't think we'll be laughing much longer."

Always, he keeps an ear tuned to the radio, where he takes heart at the news of Hitler's attempted assassination and of Hitler's outraged demand that the populace give him a vote of confidence. And by the time the 91st is ready to leave, the news is good: the Allies have taken Coutances and are moving forward, there's been a significant breakthrough near St.-Lô, and the Russians are creeping up on Warsaw. Bart bets Harry their unit will be in Paris by the end of August.

CHAPTER 38

MARIGNY AND BRÉCEY

We sure liberated the hell out of those towns.

ELEVEN DAYS AFTER they began their rest in La Cambe, their trucks make their way past slopes strewn with bodies, shell holes, bomb craters, and charred tanks on their way to Marigny, between Coutances and St.-Lô. "We sure liberated the hell out of those towns," Bart remarks. Their area is stippled with the dead. The heads of some have been blown off, and all are bloated and stink. Flak falls on their tents from their own ack-ack flung at enemy planes. They, along with the nearby 96th, are the nearest hospital to the front. In the first thirty hours alone, they admit 562 patients, and again Bart takes on surgery, too.

After eleven days in Marigny, the 91st drives into Brécey, the crashing of tanks with bazookas, of rocket-firing fighter bombers and assault tanks echoing behind them. The battle fourteen miles away around Mortain is flaring to its dramatic conclusion. On a plateau between Avranches and Brécey, once again astride an exposed hill, they set up their hospital. But Bart is distracted by searching frantically for his musette bag, which contains not only his camera and a couple hundred dollars but his diary. The story that will someday be Bertie's, the details of his life, his now-twenty months in her absence. The story she will learn if he himself is there—or not.

Later that first evening, his nerves escalating from the racket in the skies that he can't see, Bart takes a break between operations to venture outside. Dogfights rage a couple miles away. Tracers streak horizontally along the skyline. A plane catches on fire, plummets in a column of black smoke, and bursts into a massive ball of flame leaping from the earth. Bart grabs his stomach and is sick. He guesses he's not tough enough for sights like that. He still doesn't know whether the still-circling victor is their plane or their enemy's. Ack-ack bangs out and splatters willy-nilly. Bombs drop down. Cannon fire and enemy shells boom. Terrific explosions vibrate the ground. He pictures some poor French civilian stepping onto a mine.

He doesn't locate his lost bag with his camera and diary until the next morning. He decides to forego Harry's wall tent on the hospital grounds to live with the officers in the adjoining field. He needs to get away from the constant drone of the generators and the complex plac-ing of personal equipment when it's time to move. He's determined not to lose his diary in another move.

And then the Luftwaffe raid. It's about 2:45 in the morning when the sky lights up with planes dropping colored target flares. It's like daylight. Everybody gets up expecting the worst. They stand behind the hedge-mound in front of their tents and look over the valley toward Brécey and the front, about four miles away. Then the bomb-ers roar over their heads. Bart gets his camera to take colored pictures and make himself believe he isn't scared stiff, but the lens fogs with the moist, cold morning air. Bombs scream down in groups of two or three, and then colossal flashes and a blast pushed up like a silk bag of eiderdown. He grits his teeth, but apparently the planes aren't interested in him and his companions. He was more apprehensive than scared, he tells himself when he finally crawls into his bedding roll. But he knows—and can see—how close they are to where the Germans are trying to break through in their direction. *What a spot.*

Soon enough, though, more good news. There are about twenty enemy divisions in their area. But the American forces are advancing on Argentan in the south; British and Canadian forces are poised to reach Falaise from the north and have already launched their offensive. The plan is to drive the Germans back and trap them in what comes to be called the Falaise Pocket. He can't know it then, but the Battle of the Falaise Pocket, which will last for ten days, for nearly all the time the 91st is close, would become the decisive battle of Normandy. It will push the Germans back toward their own border. And winning it will enable the Allies to move forward with little resistance toward the Seine and beyond. It seems to be happening fast now, this war. He's got a hunch there'll be another invasion in southern France soon, and it's only a matter of days before the radio proves him right. They're working in the heat now, but he loves the sun soaking into his face when he finds time to take a break. Welch, now a Lieutenant Colonel, still calls on Bart to perform surgery, sometimes on French civilians or injured German POWs.

One morning while sitting in the Red Cross tent, Bart notices a group of eight POWs listening to the news broadcast. The broadcast, he learns, is Polish, as are the prisoners. He's surprised that so many Polish and Russians are mixed in with their Nazi supermen. The guard explains that when the Nazis capture these "non-Aryan" Allies, they force them into military duty for their enemy—one Pole for every two Germans and one Russian for every *squad* of Germans. Bart just shakes his head. There's a move to exchange German prisoners for Americans, and their POWs are dispirited: they do not want to return. A few are even crying. The 91st now has orders not to fraternize with the POWs.

Bart is eager for the English broadcast, eager for news about the entrapping of the Nazi army in the Falaise-Mortain gap and the Allied armored's advance toward Paris. All he knows is from an air pilot whose inflamed appendix Bart diagnosed. He told Bart that the Nazis are pulling out most of their troops and equipment from the Falaise Gap, but they are being bombed unmercifully in their retreat. And there are rumors: crushed artillery parts and lifeless bodies littering the road, vehicles smashed and smoldering, corpses of cows and horses bloated in the heat.

After eight days in Brécey, and over 1,300 admissions, they stop receiving patients. Bart is invited by the CO and some women from the Red Cross to accompany them in the command car to Mont St. Michel, the fortified islet the Nazis used as a shelter until its recent liberation. Bart spirals up the cobblestone streets to the monastery built on a rock jutting out into the sea. A beautiful sight—especially since some of the restaurants and hotels and souvenir shops lining the streets are now reopening. Every time his truck enters another ash-and-glass littered, shard-heaped shell of a town, he closes his eyes to shut out the devastation.

By the next day the Allied armored columns are within thirty miles of Paris. In the skies, he soon gawks at a pretty sight, squadron after squadron of troop-carrier planes and some gliders slowly parading by toward Paris and the Seine.

Indeed, the war seems to have moved away from them, and now the medical staff is resting. But as much as he has longed for a sojourn at another rest area, Bart worries. He guesses that the 91st has lost its usual priority. What if the Army has forgotten about them? He takes walks, picks blackberries. He plays ball with enlisted men, goes target-shooting down the valley. And he waits—to finish this war, and to see at last the city he's read so much about in history and art books. "This is a calm before another storm," he tells Bertie. "Look for the storm and we'll be there—soon I imagine—"

Finally the news he's been waiting for comes: Paris has been liberated by the French forces of the interior, and the Nazis have at last been ousted from their four-year stay. So his two-month-old prophecy has come true.

Three days later, the officers scramble into the backs of trucks. They are to drive about 100 miles, leaving behind the decimated towns of Mortain and Barenton and continuing east of Falaise, east of Argentan and that terrifying pocket of blast and fire. As they press on inland across rolling hills and flat land laden with apple trees and harvested wheat fields, the townspeople run out to cheer. That night, when the convoy stops on a broad swath of land just outside Senonches, he and Harry lay out their sleeping bags under a tree. And though Bart knows the fireworks will start again soon enough, by late afternoon the next day they will be on the outskirts of Paris!

CHAPTER 39

SOMEWHERE IN FRANCE

How calloused and unmoved we have become. Front line surgeons—ho hum.

OVER THOSE ELEVEN weeks the 91st followed the front lines in Normandy—nearly one-fourth of an entire year—Bart wrote fewer letters than in any other place overseas. The casualties in field after field, piled on the ground or groaning on gurneys, the endless, complicated work, the lack of sleep crucial to wield a scalpel with an unswerving hand—all gnawed away at what might have been his writing time. And the conundrum of sifting through what he could and could not say conspired against him.

It was eight days since his last letter from Tortworth before he could snatch a few minutes in France to write his wife. But even before that, he had already launched his resolve to buffer her, as much as possible, from apprehension and terror. He composed his first letter from France in Boutteville, but since Bertie did not and *could not* know where he was, the return address is simply *Somewhere in France.*

Dearest Love:
    I haven't much time to write a lot even though I could tell you a bookful.
    I am very busy and we all look to our work which has become very important.

I thought you might like to know that I am O. K. so you won't worry. You might as well show this letter to my mother so she won't worry either.

We hope some day soon to get letters from home.

Thanks a hell of a lot for keeping that chin up for me—I've needed it.

I must rest now—there isn't much time to sleep. Soon, I hope, we get more time and assistance.

I love you very much and I think of you always.

Husb.

Bart

In almost all these letters his language about what he sees and hears, only some of which he understands, is cautious, protective. He tempers his rhetoric. He hedges. He edits. He emends. All this beyond the demands of the censors, whose job is to insist that the people fighting the war not expose information that could lead to knowledge of military campaigns. Instead of crafting elaborate descriptions of battles and wounds as Bart records in his diary, he merely refers in the letters to "other intense activity," "new experiences," "noise," "disturbances," "huge activities," "fireworks over the valley," and even further mitigates the details that are terrifying him by adding a lighthearted spin in a phrase or two, as in "nuisances with flares and stuff."

Whereas in the past his letters have contained more emotional, more colorful, more ebullient writing, his letters from France are more carefully controlled. The focus on his work, he tells her, helps him ignore the noise, the trembling tent, the pandemonium. He assures her that a deep trench is directly in back of the wall tent he shares with Harry, that he has the luxury of a nice, warm bath in a helmet half full of water. He tells her how the beastly cold makes him don seven layers of clothing, how even a wool cap can't keep the marrow from chilling. How he longs for fresh meat and eggs. How he hasn't spent a penny in twenty-three days but will send some money to her so she can spend it for him. That he's been saving some money for Berlin!

He reminds her to cross her fingers occasionally, coaxes her to keep her chin up. Letter after letter, his refrain: chin up, chin up, chin up, chin up. He develops and sends her a photo of himself in Boutteville that depicts him smiling, lying on the grass in back of the tents, propped up on one arm, and a nurse fiddling with her stocking in the background. The legend on the back says, *Yup, I could still smile.* But what he records in his diary that day centers on snipers, crashed gliders, and land mines. When he mentions his side trips to Mountberg and Valognes and divulges that he saw "a mass of rubble and devastating destruction," he tempers these phrases with: "Of course the good side of it is the immense teamwork and energy that goes on to rebuild for military purposes. One becomes awful proud of Uncle Sam at seeing the impossible rise before one's eyes. We are here to stay—and how!"

He is forthcoming with details of his medical experience, enumerates the ways in which Welch has encouraged and promoted his work, offered him interesting surgery cases, taken his advice, and acted quickly on Bart's diagnoses. How Bart is the only person Welch asks what work he prefers to do. It's befuddling to Bart how Welch, who has what seems like an infinite stream of harsh words for almost everyone else, is so accommodating—even generous—to Bart himself. How confident he is in Bart's diagnoses, in his medical instincts. How far Bart has come since he was a raw intern, even since he started working with the 91st. Although Bart gives Bertie the particulars of some of the operations he performs, he's generally silent about the war wounds that have made him sick to his stomach. The closest he comes to describing a specific wound to repair surgically is a reference to "multiple holes in the gut."

As much as he can be, he is philosophical. He follows the dramatic line he wrote her from Pont l'Abbé—"I never dreamed I would ever sit on the stage when I hoped for a front seat"—with the more moderated and even uplifting: "It's surprising how one becomes accustomed to the general situation. One becomes fatalistic. The war is coming along grand in our favor but it's not as rapid as we would like."

He discusses the minutiae of his quotidian life. "It may sound paradoxical to you but we do have the luxury of hot showers (portable, you know) and that's also funny. As a matter of fact there was much laughter in the shower today about it. The idea was that the folks back home just couldn't believe our situation if they heard that 'we just finished with a nice hot shower.' They must believe in a modern, luxurious, immense, over-equipped U.S. Army—I'm proud of it."

He also mentions the innovations he's encountered, particularly penicillin and Kodachromes, both introduced to the world just a few years before the war began. Although Welch seems skeptical about cause and effect, the 91st and other military medical units are using penicillin (when they can keep it in supply) as their chief weapon against gas gangrene and other infections and are saving thousands of lives. And his Kodachromes' bright colors make the photos he sends to Bertie all the more lifelike, more *real*. He's amazed at the speed of development processes these days. "In this letter," he says, "you are getting a picture of me taken yesterday, printed this morning and sent this evening. Can you match that?"

He praises the Americans and the Army as well as their unit, not only to be upbeat, but perhaps in an effort to give her the sort of confidence he may well be ambivalent about himself. From Boutteville he tells her he's proud that they—his unit, the Americans, the Allies, Justice and Righteousness themselves—are doing as well as they are. He repeats "proud" more than once. And after about eight weeks in Normandy, he says, "Fighting has become stiffer but it's no use—nothing will stop our greatly encouraged troops now. They are fighting with home and their loved ones in sight—and that's quite an incentive." And shortly after Paris is liberated: "The armies are doing more than anyone dreamed possible two months ago. (Don't tell anyone, but I expected it.)"

He masks much of what he's feeling in humor: "Wotta ya think of them 'ere flying bombs? Nahsty things I think reahilly. Don't let it worry you. You've got your favorite husband in thar to fight for you." And during a lull in the fighting: "I just had a delightful experience. Though it's just an hour before lunch I braved the scorning glances of the kitchen personnel and brazenly pulled out a steaming-hot pork chop from the griddle and devoured it with fiendish glee."

Sometimes he does complain, and even confess: he confesses that he needs rest and sleep badly, that his feet and back ache when he has to bend over the operating table. That he's jittery as a bedbug, that he can see himself jumping right out of his trousers at every door that slams when he gets home. But he comforts her by reporting how quickly they all forget the disturbances of the night before. "How calloused and unmoved we have become," he adds. "Front line surgeons—ho hum." Occasionally, he's straightforward, matter-of-fact, then pulls himself back from the penumbra of self-pity: "I hate ack-ack. I hate search lights. I hate tracer bullets and most heartily dislike falling flak and unburst a-a shells. But tonite we have a movie and we can't let anything interfere with our rest, convenience, and entertainment." Several times, as if all he could tell her might upset her, he just plain admits that he's run out of things to say.

Always, he assures her that he has a long story to tell and that he will make certain she receives, one way or another, the photos he's so neatly organized in his album, his sketches and paintings, and his munificent words. With all these she will know his story. "It won't be long now," he promises. "All you have to do is wait just a little while longer. Watch the headlines, sweetheart—and uncover the right side of the bed for me."

His love letters are as poignant and peppered with humor as ever: "I miss you horribly but I shouldn't think the day is too far in the distance when you can drag me away to the mountains for purposes of violent love with which I am in favor (with which). Today, they tell me, is Sunday. It feels like Tuesday or Friday. The only important thing is that it's 1944. In 1945 you and I will be the only important thing. In 1945 you and I will be together again. Wait just a little longer darling." And "Darling: This month has certainly passed madly away and in a hurry. Next June I'm going to gently fondle every hour—breathe in each minute and exhale it long and slowly and shall caress each day and take it to bed with me and you (If I'm home, and I'm quite sure I will be.)" During the weeks-long stretches in which he doesn't hear from her, he is stricken. "I am starving for news of you," he says. But he might as well as scream those words into the smoke-hazed air.

More and more he is plagued by the sting and alienation of missing out on so much of their life together, so much of their family's life. In La Cambe he's alarmed to learn that his mother had an operation. Although he's confident Bertie is taking good care of her in her usual unselfish way, still, he frets. Since he's been gone, Marvin, now fourteen, has grown taller than Bertie—and is shaving! And Rosie will be entering college and, maybe soon, launching her singing career. And to think of the babies he hasn't even seen—his nephew Anthony Bart, already seven months old and with teeth! Their new niece Joanie, who is said to look so much like Bertie. And Rosemae's daughter Diana already three years old.

While he's in Brécey, Bertie writes several lines that stun and sting him. And suddenly their tender *pas de deux* swerves into an ungainly do-si-do. She speaks frankly about her thoughts on sex and desire, and she speculates about how she might react to other men. He tries to control his panic and entreats her to take her mind off it. But as he has less and less work to distract him, and as the Allies forge into Germany and the battles move increasingly farther away, his future with his bride seizes his brain. "I wonder how I'll act when they tell me that it's all over. . . . Darling I wanna come home. It's been such a long time now, hasn't it? Will you recognize me? Will you think me changed? Will I remember how you like me to act in bed?"

He can't stop himself from expressing anxiety. It's even getting hard to remember her physically now. All he remembers, he tells her, is how lovely, how heavenly being with her was. In spite of all these worries, only once in France does he bare his heart completely about the war and about the effect of his long absence from her. And by then, Normandy literally behind him, he is in Guyancourt, idle and simply waiting to help end the war and return.

CHAPTER 40

ST. LOUIS, BERTIE'S LETTERS IMAGINED

A FEW MONTHS after my mother died, I flew back to St. Louis to close up the apartment she'd lived in during the four years between my father's death and hers. At the end of the few days I spent there, sleeping on the floor on sofa cushions and sorting through papers and books and photographs and knickknacks and keepsakes to mete out the myriad brutal judgments about which fragments of family history, which ephemeral testaments to our having lived and loved together, would be designated for strangers, which would be stuffed into garbage bins in the garage and abandoned. By the end of the last day, I felt as if my belly had been switchbladed open, my intestines wrenched from my skin. I'd saved one pile of things by the door to hand-carry home to Idaho. That pile was the only thing remaining in the empty apartment: four blue three-ring binders, bulging with pieces of paper. The contents of the binders were meticulously organized to read backward in time, and a bit frayed from the constraints of their three-hole punches, but I knew they were all there: the letters my parents wrote during what would be their 951-day separation. My mother, an extraordinary caretaker in every sense, had tended them well. The letters would be new to all of us: Bertie and Bart's daughters, granddaughters, sons-in-law.

Bertie had declared that no one was to read them until she died, and even though she kept them in plain sight on her night-table shelf for years, no one had ever opened the binders but her.

Three years later, I was kicking myself internally. The four blue three-ring binders of letters had been stacked in the corner of my cluttered study, and I had yet to read all of them. The unfathomably deep wound from having lost both my parents was still that raw; the impossibility of a world without them, that inconceivable. And when, anxiety rising not at what I'd find but at what I'd *feel*, I finally leafed through all 1,359 pages—sheaves of paper inked, penciled, typed, the compact V-mails, the tissue-thin, translucent sheets—I was swept away by what I was beginning to realize was the most astonishing fact of these letters, one that in many ways defined this collection. Hundreds must have vanished.

I immediately called my sister Jeannie. "What happened to Mom's letters to Dad?" I asked. For a second or two, she said nothing. "You know. From the war," I prodded. "I have all of his here in those binders, but at first I could find only one of her letters, the first one she wrote him. Then I saw that there were a few from the last two months of their time apart. But that's *all*."

"Remember those two white boxes on the top shelf in the basement?" she said. "I think those were her letters." I would have seen them on my way down the basement stairs, the only entrance to the garage, every day of my St. Louis life. But I swooped through my memory storehouse and bounced back empty.

"One day I came home and noticed they'd disappeared," she continued. I was still trying to picture the boxes when she added, "I'm not sure how I know this, but . . ." and when she finished her sentence I could find no words to respond. But her answer had fired my imagination, and I could now see what happened—if only as though through the lens of a kaleidoscope, the tinted sections sliding over each other with the grace of bodies making love.

This is how I have imagined the fate of Bertie's letters. One day, decades after the war, when Bart and Bertie are alone in their dream house and the thought of the letters she made love to him in has been troubling her—what will happen to them?—they catch each other's gaze over the glass top of the ironwork table. "We don't need to talk any more, do we?" he says. She smiles, shakes her head, and reaches for his hand. For some months they have been squaring off with the pressing certitude of their mortality. He has already begun, when he can remember to do so, to write the names of things on strips of surgical tape and adhere them to their backs so that he recognizes what they are: *camera, tackle box, medical bag, oil painting set.* They have finally allowed the news that his memory is abandoning him to filter through and settle in. They both comprehend the incomprehensible: that his mind is massacring his memories with the speed and force of an automatic assault weapon; that his synapses are collapsing, neurotransmitters too weary to travel. That he, meticulous as he has always been in his work as the archivist of his life, in recounting it with the precise details of which he has been such a careful custodian—*he,* against his will, is letting it slip away. Then what will be left of their story?

They lift down those white boxes to read the letters together one last time. Then he pulls her tight to his chest so that she cannot see the tears he's fighting back, as he did uncountable years before when he had to leave her on the dock in New Brunswick. And yes, though it's difficult to make love when your mortality is waiting for you so impatiently, they make love. It's different now from the way it was before, when they were young and yearned for each other with the force of trees urging to leaf. Or when they ached for each other so intently after their long absence from each other during the war. Afterward, each cradling a white box, they walk outside to the high-backed barbeque pit he'd built, red brick by red brick. The scents of lilac and magnolia drift around them and sweep them back to that day scores of years before when his forsythia-colored clothes, her bark-black hair drew them toward each other. Even before Bertie (or is it Bart?) strikes the match, they know it's a funeral of sorts, and there are tears. They stand side by side at the pit, wrap their arms around each other's waists. As the ashes rise and flutter toward the violet sunset behind the spirea, Bertie and Bart slide into their own versions of the memories they have just, together, offered up to the amorphous mysteries of the past. They are grateful to have consecrated every letter, every page, every word to only each other. Forever.

Bart's confirmation at age 14 while living with Mike Accardi in St. Louis.

After a year of saving money for a belated wedding trip, Bart and Bertie honeymoon in Florida in 1941.

In Port Lyautey Bart writes one of the 1,365 pages of letters he will send to Bertie while overseas.

Bertie in 1943, the photo Bart always kept facing him when he was in his room or tent.

Bart sketches in north Africa. In spring 1943, he writes Bertie, "They [the watercolors and sketches] were done for you. Keep them, dear and when I return we'll go over them together."

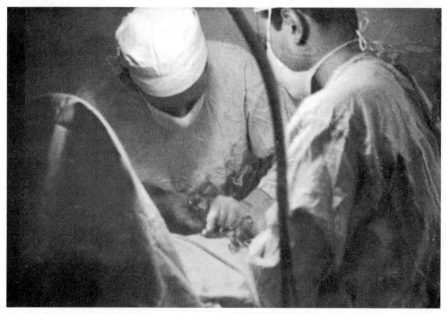

Bart performs surgery in Palermo, summer 1943, with Tom Fox.

Harry Meyer (left), George Riday (center), and Bart at Tortworth Court near Bristol, England, training for the Allied invasion of Europe.

Normandy, June 1944. Shortly after landing on Utah Beach, while bivouacking in Boutteville where he performed surgery in tents under fire, Bart reassures Bertie by having his picture taken and writing on the back, "Yup, I could still smile."

Bart painted this watercolor during the winter of 1944 near Valkenburg, Holland, while the guns on the front lines boomed behind him and an anti-aircraft outfit shot down a drone.

Bart flashes the Victory sign in March 1945 as the unit trucks through Mönchengladbach, Germany, on its way to cross the Rhine.

Practicing the "Warsaw Concerto" in Wolfenbüttel, Germany, in June 1945. Bart played pianos wherever he could find them in Europe.

Married 60 years, Bertie and Bart in 2000, a few months before he died. (Photograph by Regina Corrado.)

CHAPTER 41

NORMANDY, THE BATTLE FOR
MEMORY, THE TWENTY-FIRST CENTURY

IN NORMANDY, we began as tourists, Gary and I. We swept around and through the Mémorial de Caen with its moving depictions of horror and triumph, the beaches where the ramps of the Allied landing crafts lucky enough to dodge the mines slammed into the sand to spill out thousands of soldiers, the pillboxes and bunkers from which the Germans gunned down troops even before they could secure a foothold on shore, and the remaining barbed wire and rusty anti-tank Czech hedgehogs dotting the land. We followed a trail of towns and statues and plaques and monuments and gravestones that narrate the story of the three bloody months of the Battle for Normandy. I was overwhelmed by images and fragments of information. Yet those I could summon from memory—from Bart's memory—served as the main matrix for all the information and emotions we would process during the days we spent in France.

Our more idiosyncratic personal tour was inclusive, bold. We'd launch it from where Bart launched his: Utah Beach, Ste.-Marie-du-Mont, Boutteville, Ste.-Mère-Église. Then we'd hit Pont l'Abbé, La Cambe and Omaha Beach, Marigny, Brécey, then on to the more distant Senonches, Guyancourt, Paris, and La Capelle. But although we hunted down the places Bart so carefully identified, we encountered snags. Over the decades several of these towns had already been swallowed by suburbs or bulldozed and rebuilt, or not rebuilt at all. And then, beyond these boundaries, we were looking for fields. The fields where the hospitals were set up were unnamed except by their proximity to towns, and they were also unmarked, one looking pretty much like the next.

As Gary chauffeured, I rested my camera on my knees from time to time to scrawl out notes. Hedgerows constricted the narrow roads, the same hedgerows that had bordered some of the hospital fields. Hedgerows, which now seemed a metaphor for the impermeable tangles Bart's memory would become mired in. As our shaky little Opel lurched through the maze, I tried to capture this latter-day Normandy in camera shots. But there was something both pathetic and prophetic in my wild snapping out the car window as Gary steered over bumps and careened around roundabouts. In one corner or another of nearly all of my shots, I managed to include the car mirror on the passenger side—and in it my own reflection.

On the way to Ste.-Mère-Église, we zipped by stone houses with American, Canadian, and British flags perpetually at half-mast. Souvenir shops lined sidewalks: flags and postcards, plastic paratroopers. Everywhere paratroopers. We rubbernecked up, anticipating what we would see, and there he was: the illustrious effigy of the American soldier suspended from the steeple, his parachute spread out above him and to the side, like wings. In Ste.-Marie-du-Mont we noted the postwar stone houses with satellite dishes and countless text-heavy signs plastered onto the facades of buildings. I could picture the gunsmoke-hazed confusion on these streets those first days—Germans surprised by the presence of Americans, Americans surprised to have landed so close to the coast. Yet I felt cheated. In both towns history was being commercialized, reframed, and, therefore, reconstituted. It was a while before the irony dawned on me. Wasn't this what I was doing as I pared and pasted and rewrote and imagined and tried to breathe life into my father's story?

Late in the day we wandered into the small, almost scruffy-looking museum on Utah Beach. Inside, the presentation of history is a faded one, chipping away with the paint. We were nearly alone as we toured the grounds, which were studded with tank defense mechanisms, mostly left by the Germans. Some looked like lopsided crosses, half-buried in the sand.

We asked a few employees if they knew where the American doctors set up their hospital during the war. Finally someone uttered a name and pointed to the back room. The man who emerged looked, strangely, German, with his blond hair and lake-blue eyes. He was much too young to have fought in the war. His grandfather perhaps? Gary and I translated the sentences in the diary in which my father describes the position of the hospital. "Three miles from the front," I added. The young man thought he knew where the hospital had been. Near Brécourt, the manor where Lieutenant Dick Winters and para-troopers of the 101st Airborne Division captured four German howitzers in a battle popularized in the HBO television series *Band of Brothers*. The man found us another map to add to our storehouse, marked it with red, explained and re-explained. He waved away our apologies for our awkward French, and when I gratefully shook his hand, our eyes, for a second or two, locked.

Following Bart's path inland along the Way of Liberty, Gary and I charted the maps together, collating the young man's and the one formed of Bart's words. I read the words out loud: "atop a hill, next to a farmhouse, without camouflage, but our red crosses are up." Boutteville. We mounted hill after hill, scanning the landscape for a farmhouse and finding more than one. I began to feel obsessed with knowing which place was the exact spot where my father awaited his first patient on the continent. I imagined that my need for perfection in this venture was like the surgeon's need for meticulous adherence to protocol. Wire stretched across the bramble-bordered field we suspected might have been Bart's. I pictured the tents mushrooming up, as Bart had described them. Still . . . maybe we found the exact field, maybe we didn't. I tried to hold disappointment at bay.

We found no landmarks for the hospitals; all evidence was in the memory we had carried with us in the form of pictures and words from 1944. I was beginning to doubt my own memory, my ability to take in and synthesize detail upon detail. The sun had paled and dipped below the hedgerows and fields. The day was wearing on, and with it the sense that we had enough time to do what we came to do. I felt I was drowning in maps and directions and guidebooks, photocopies and brochures, history books and pamphlets, and photographs and the images now etched in my cranium from musty albums—and at every turn in the narrow road, I searched, senselessly, for my father's face.

The next day, as our Opel sped toward Pont l'Abbé, I repeated Bart's phrase in my head almost like a mantra: *shattered town, shattered town.* Hedgerows shielded us from corn fields. The husks still looked young, not quite formed, but the full, pendulous tassels were almost voluptuous. It was hot, and I thought about my father's appetite for sun, about how cold he was during his three-week stay here. Arriving, I felt a sense of relief. In a perverse way, I almost wanted to see the place shattered, but instead it was hum-drum. I'd like to say that it had a "more real" feel to it—it's a site that's not set up just for tourists—but actually it had no feel at all. We stopped, poked around. Most houses were a drab sand color, though one or two had bright blue shutters.

Gary and I angled up the peninsula on the road George and Bart followed to Cherbourg. In Valognes, over-cheery baskets of pink blooms suspended from modern street lights. Blue-painted curlicues on wrought-iron balcony railings. White-washed shutters. Everything looking new. But of course. One of Bart's slides of Valognes that day projected an image I could not stop seeing. It looked like the backdrop in a surreal play, a sci-fi film, the apocalypse. What was left of a town: the buildings mere remnants, like the blades of fractured saws. The skies gray as if to match the rubble. And, somehow, a thin-limbed fir tree, a perfect V, in dead center. "I never dreamt of such destruction," I quoted Bart in a murmur.

Drizzle thickened the air as we strode the rows of graves at the American Cemetery poised on a bluff overlooking Omaha Beach. The cemetery is simultaneously self-contained and expansive, alabaster crosses and Stars of David in rows straight and slanted as if toward infinity. I read some of the names out loud: Jones, Roosevelt, McNair, Sheffler. . . . Now, the white headstones are the only light in the gray air.

Down the hill, we settled into the moist sand where on D-Day thousands of American soldiers landed and, bombarded from the cliffs, stumbled over mangled bodies to gain a tiny scrap of ground or waded toward shore in churning water up to their chins toward a beach riddled with mines. We gazed around us at the calm waters, the neat path of beach pebbles around this part of the coastline, the clean dun-colored sand—no longer bloody and strewn with chunks of human flesh, shredded skin, or fragments of bone. Then we lifted our miniature bottles of Calvados, the brandy that put this coast on the map long before the Allies did, and clinked in celebration of Bart, Harry, George, the doctors, the nurses, the paramedics, the pilots, the paratroopers, the engineers, Ike, and the thousands of heroes dead.

As we walked slowly back to the car, an urn from the cemetery captured my gaze, its poignant bas-relief of a naked warrior, sword upright, on a wild-eyed horse and leaning back into the arms of an angel, who is lifting him up, one hand slid under his ribs, the other draped over his shoulder, easing him up from his mount.

Leaving the cemetery, veering inland, Gary and I, suddenly drained, sniped at each other about directions. He swerved into an ordinary-looking town, the rain puddling near the curbs. I was chilled, preoccupied. Just like my father, I thought, who, if the sun were not as fierce as it was in full, blistering summer in St. Louis, would wrap his arms around himself and shiver.

"This is La Cambe," Gary declared. The place where the doctors and nurses rested after nearly six punishing weeks in Normandy.

When Bart describes walking into La Cambe for the first time, he remarks that there was "Nothing there but broken up buildings and a lot of through traffic for our vehicles which kick up a great deal of dust." Now I felt a penetrating dampness. My attention was caught by a church on a hill, and I wriggled around to get a better view. And there it was—the church in the watercolor. The painting I had learned about only two days before we departed for France. I'd never seen it before, and I'd been startled to see it framed and on the wall of a house of a close St. Louis friend we were visiting. She told us Bertie had given it to her a few years before. Now, in the car, I stretched back for the laptop and poked at it until the photograph I'd taken of this watercolor filled the screen. The color made La Cambe look like a sunny town, and the church on the hill looked not merely picturesque but in some ways righteous, another survivor.

I was determined to find the particular place in which my father had watercolored the better part of a century ago. But no matter how I manipulated the laptop screen so that the image of the painting on it would align with the angle of the stone church I was looking at from some distance, art and church refused to do so. So our guess was more an act of faith than a certainty. We decided we'd pinpointed exactly the place (now graced with a post-war house constructed to appear pre-war) where Bart would have set up his collapsible easel. He would have tromped away from the fray of tents and nurses and equipment and other doctors to paint, which, during those turbulent weeks, must have served for him as a variation on meditation.

Nettles scratched my only partially covered legs. My obsessions were grinding away at my rationality. I didn't have to stand in the exact spot my father did, did I? Why is it that for decades we ignore our parents and then we want to know everything about them? What I was discovering was that I now wanted to connect to them, to *be* with them. To be the sort of time traveler that others, including skeptics like myself, could believe in. Every detail is fascinating; every one a gemstone. When I force myself to choose among them, those I leave behind beget a sort of grief. When I try to arrange the rocky details in my head, to assemble them and project them into sensible outcroppings of the brain or scattershot scenes borne of the imagination to reenvision and recreate my father's life, it is those abandoned that block my resolve. Yet they refuse to be destroyed. Everywhere: traces of a life I never lived but hunger for. Everywhere: the mechanism, the spirit, of memory. Memory most fragile, most elusive, and most malleable.

AS WE MADE our way back to our car, we spotted, appearing like a specter swathed in mist in the empty streets, balancing shopping bags in each hand, a diminutive elderly woman in a long coat. It occurred to me that she was about the same age my father would have been now. She smiled warmly, almost as if she recognized us.

Gary stopped suddenly as we were about to pass her and said in his clunky but serviceable French, "Pardon me, Madame. But were you here in the war?"

She stopped. "Yes," she said in French, a question in her tone.

"Can you please tell us where the American hospital was set up?" Gary asked.

"My father was a doctor here," I chimed in.

"Here? In La Cambe?" She pointed to the ground, and her eyes lit up.

"Do you know English?" I asked, rifling in my pack for photocopies of the diary and the painting of the church looming on the hill she was facing. She answered no, she was sorry. "Here," I said, finally, extracting the proper page and pointing to the word "La Cambe" in my father's loopy script.

"La Cambe," she said out loud, nodding. She lay her bags carefully on the damp, cracked sidewalk.

"My father wrote this in 1944," I continued, stumbling a bit with the translation. I showed her the date of his entry. "This is his diary. He was here during the invasion, a doctor, and he wrote about La Cambe." Her eyes brightened with recognition.

"Do you remember where the hospitals were set up?" Gary asked again. "My wife's father wrote about a field."

She nodded and pointed behind us, to the fields we had just traipsed around. I fought an urge to keep talking about the diaries, to translate each word for her, but more than that, I suddenly wanted to be part of her life and to imagine her a part of my father's. Perhaps when he was painting the church, she was inside, praying at a pew. Or perhaps . . .

"Well, *merci beaucoup*," Gary was saying, taking a step back, signaling me it was time to move on. But she tapped my arm. Her hands were weightless and spidery, and I imagined them smooth through my coat.

"When I was a young girl during the war, I was wounded." She spoke slowly, to help us understand each French word. "That was before my husband and I were married, and he was away fighting. I wasn't in La Cambe, but near here. I was wounded, and the Americans gave me penicillin." She shaped her right hand into a syringe, her thumb as plunger, which she mime-injected into her left arm above the elbow.

My breath stopped. I stood dumbly, picturing my dashing father helping the young woman version of this sprightly lady. My eyes swam.

She continued. "When I was a young girl, I was asked if the Germans were in the right, and while the town was occupied, I said yes, the Germans are in the right. But as soon as we were liberated, I said, no, they are brigands!" She chortled, mischievous. Then repeated, more volubly, "*Brigands!*" We all laughed. An odd feeling surfaced and exploded its sweet fuel inside me. I recognized it as being in love. I was in love with this gentle lady. Yes, I was.

"May we take your picture?" Gary asked, already cocking open the camera. She and I posed for him, the click coupling us forever.

We thanked her and thanked her again and were about to walk away when she asked, "May I kiss you?" I dropped my bag, not at all carefully, and embraced her. We kissed, French-fashion, on one cheek at a time, and, our raincoats rubbing together, we hugged each other tight.

It wasn't until Gary and I whizzed by the Carentan Hotel de Ville about half an hour later that I realized I'd forgotten to ask her name. And in the way that I missed my father in the months before he died, even while I was with him and holding his hand, when his mind had already been spirited away by Alzheimer's disease, I missed her already.

CHAPTER 42

HELD FOR GREATER THINGS

Hope this show stops soon—it's beginning to tell on me.

IT'S STILL DRIZZLING, remnants of the preceding night's rain that has left them wet and chilled, when the 91st parks near the village of Guyancourt, only two miles from Versailles, and the townspeople gather around them. They bring flowers, tomatoes, and eggs—and they all smile. *They are indeed happy to have les Americaines,* Bart thinks.

They set up the hospital on flat, grassy land near a forest, so near Paris it's hard for Bart to believe. "This is the spot for us and where I'd like to stay for the duration," he writes. Even before he starts work, he chances a ride into Versailles with George—the place the Nazis passed through on their drive to claim the city of Paris, black smoke billowing in their wake from their burning of oil and gasoline plants along the way. The palace where they unfurled the swastika flag, then hoisted it high. Now, just over four years later, Bart and George window-shop and then see for the first time the splendid palace Bart has read so much about but never dreamed he'd have an opportunity to see. And what a beautiful town!

There is still a great roar overhead, and from the length of time it has continued he presumes the Germans are about to catch hell again somewhere. Still, he feels relatively safe here and hasn't had a sleepless night in days. He thinks it would feel strange to hear the scream of descending bombs and that horrific anti-aircraft again. He hopes he's heard the last of them. They're no good for his alimentary tract.

Bart and George return from Versailles to rumors that Patton has reached the German border. Indeed, the day they open their fifth and last hospital in France, August 30, the last German troops are retreating across the Seine, and the First Army is now only thirty miles from Belgium. It certainly looks like the Allies are coming in for the kill. Bart summarizes the situation for Bertie: "The British have a few scores to settle in the Calais area, Patton's mouth is watering for Berlin to show his skillful generalship, Bradly is showing what a Missourian can do, the 7th A is running the South making certain ends meet, the French Army is working wonders and the Russians won't be stopped. That is an analysis which makes me believe that soon I can be in the arms of the most wonderful and most loved girl in the world." And for the weeks Bart is waiting on the outskirts of Paris, the war does seem to be elsewhere, with Allied and Russian gains in Verdun, Dieppe, Rouen, Antwerp, Abbeville, Brussels, Finland, Estonia, and Bucharest.

Not much work comes in, and within five days of settling in, Bart digs out his greens and polishes his brass and boots—he's found a ride to the city he's dreamed about since he first read about it. "Today I went to Paris!" he exclaims in his diary. "Once again I saw civilization—beautiful women, beautiful clothes and a beautiful city." Although most restaurants are closed because food is in short supply, he and George lunch at the Café des Sports on roast beef, baked beans, and even sauterne. They toast the liberation. They are tourists, taking in l'Opéra Garnier, Notre Dame, the Louvre, the Arc de Triomphe, Eiffel Tower, the Seine! From the Café de la Paix, Bart can see, between the opera's columns, the gilded busts of some of the composers whose piano music he mastered as a young boy. On the street his eyes follow women riding bicycles, who hold their hair down and let their skirts fly in the breeze, exposing shapely limbs. He buys lingerie and perfume for his wife at the Galeries Lafayette.

Over his four weeks camped outside Guyancourt, he will take four jaunts to Paris and six to Versailles. His letters and diary burst with his impressions of this immersion into this land of urbanity and refinement, this long-delayed, much anticipated personal introduction to European culture. Who would have thought the child who'd tagged along with petty criminals to taverns and brothels, the boy who bootlegged whiskey, would be promenading around the manicured lawns and labyrinthine gardens at the palace of Louis XIV? Or gape at the flying buttresses of the cathedral that Victor Hugo described so compellingly in his haunting novel? He has so much to say (and right now so much time to say it in) that he begins to write in a tinier manuscript. He's already filled half of this volume of his diary and still has so much to record, so much to remember.

He's in Guyancourt barely a week when casualties taper off and the temperatures drop so low that, unless he huddles close to the woodstove he's had installed in the ward, his fingers feel too numb to write. The ward is empty, and there is no work. He would rather work than sit there and freeze. In fact, there are so few patients, sometimes only four all day, that he doesn't understand why the unit is stationed there. A few bombers are still flying over Paris, but no one talks about them. An increasing percentage of their patients are Nazi "supermen" left behind by the fleeing Wehrmacht, who now seem amazed at being out-Blitzed, out-maneuvered, and stunned by the machinery of destruction the Americans can throw at them at will.

For the first weeks of September there's no word from Bertie. He tells himself that the APO is moving with the front, farther and farther away from them, but still . . . He tries to console himself with drinking alcohol and fruit juice, printing and enlarging film in the photographic tent, watercoloring a farmhouse. What he is doing above all else, though, is aching for his wife's understanding, her solace, her shining presence. And so, one night he summons up his heart-on-his-sleeve straightforwardness and exposes the truth.

My darling: Maybe I shouldn't write tonite. But I will. I feel that I want to talk to my wife who was always a pal. I'd like to cry on her soft shoulders. In short, my dolly, tonite I feel blue, low and miserable. Darling, how long am I going to grit my teeth. Perhaps I've been gay and spirited in my letters.

Do you know how I really feel? Do you know that since I said goodbye to you with tears in my eyes and choked throat I have been eating my heart out with longing. I try not to be by myself. I try to laugh and be a likeable guy. But sometime I feel like screaming and crying. My sturdy manliness has been reduced to sheer infancy. My emotions have been so confused that my heart pounds heavily at ordinary thoughts. I know it's an unwritten law among us away from home to polish up the paper with morale-lifting nonsense. Tonite I'm breaking that law. I need you and there's all that's to it.

I had a lovely hour of wonderful reading in the many juicy and very dear letters you sent. But when I put the letters down I looked into the mirror and remembered that I was 28 when I left you and now soon I'll be 31. I've been away far away for a long time. It's such a helpless feeling—I guess one just grits his teeth—that's all.

The next day, September 17, the radio blares out an air-borne invasion by Allied troops in Holland. Bart writes, "Do you remember me telling you that I didn't want to come home until I thought I had done something worthwhile and was in on the invasion? O. K. I've had it. Now I want to come home. I hope this show stops soon—it's beginning to tell on me." He asks her, once more—he hopes for the last time—to keep her chin up.

He's becoming increasingly antsy. He wants—*he needs, they all need*—to get this show on the road and bring it to conclusion fast. As far as he and his buddies are concerned, it seems like they've been forgotten. Or could it be that such a weather-beaten, battle-scarred, veteran organization as theirs is being held for greater things? In the meantime Bart and Harry have decided to do something that will make them forget about their qualms and impatience for some time.

CHAPTER 43
AFTER THE LIBERATION

Absurd.

IT IS A chilly fall day in Paris. Bart and Harry order their driver to
head directly to an imposing gray building with Romanesque arches
and stained glass windows. Bart slants his head to view the uppermost
window rosettes, which are circled by smaller circles, each encompass-
ing a six-pointed star, the Star of David. This is the Grande Synagogue
de la Victoire, the largest synagogue in Paris. Until less than a month
before, the windows were boarded up and posted with signs that
read "*Verboten—Juif*" in a collaboration of languages, both German
and French. Today, September 18, 1944, is the second day of Rosh
Hashana, the Jewish New Year, the time for fresh beginnings, for making a noise unto the Lord and leaving the past behind. For more than
two years synagogues have been silent. No worshippers rose for the
opening of the Holy Ark that housed the Torah's sacred scrolls, no
minion in Tallits recited poems accompanied by ancient melodies, no
apples were dipped in honey. And the polished spiral of the ram's horn
remained mute.

Uniformed U.S. troops and civilians jam the seats, the galleries, the
balcony, where the congregants, straining their necks to see, seem to
stretch to the high domed ceilings of the sanctuary. Bart's artist's eye

takes in the glow of the gilded bronze candelabra and silver chandelier, the Hebrew letters inscribed into the Ark. He pictures Bertie's father, Alexander—Shandor, the name his father-in-law left behind with his Czechoslovakian past when he traveled those myriad miles to become an American. Bart can almost hear this soft-spoken man, his Eastern European accent softening the edge of the Hebrew guttural as he leads the Kiddush blessing over the challah and the grape juice that served as wine on Shabbos every Friday at sundown. Or see him lighting the Chanukkah candles in his pewter menorah, the only thing his family brought with them when they journeyed to the land whose streets, they had heard, were paved with gold. And Bart can almost see him today, in St. Louis walking Marvie to shul, soon swaying in prayer with the other men. Praying that, finally, *this new year,* the world would receive the *mitzvah* of release from this stranglehold, the conclusion of this dreadful war that has shattered life after life.

Bart's eyes follow the Torah as it is tenderly paraded with dignity down the aisles, worshippers and celebrants reaching out to kiss it as it passes by. He senses something much grander, more significant than the worship of a single people or of a single religion or holy day; he senses gratitude, he senses liberation, a return to humanity. Victory.

Outside, the sidewalks and streets are a river of people, some jockeying for the sight and sound of what only months before they had considered impossible. Some balance on the remaining timbers charred by the flames of three years earlier, Yom Kippur, the Day of Atonement, when the Nazis seeded every synagogue in the city with incendiaries.

Bart and Harry edge out of the building, the throng carrying them down the steps and along the Rue de la Victoire. One civilian in the chaotic confetti of motion makes eye contact. The man greets Bart in English with a heavy accent. Whatever is going on in Bart's head must have flashed on his face. The man says, "I'm a Jew." Abruptly Bart has a vision: Bertie's black hair rippling down her bare back, wave after wave after wave.

The man is talking over the crowd, and Bart and Harry have to concentrate to take in the stories that tumble out of this stranger's mouth. The man was raised in Turkey, he lived for a time in Berlin, he married a French woman. The only thing that kept the man from being deported to a death camp was that his wife was a Gentile—and *that* protection would not have lasted many days longer. He describes the anti-Jewish laws in Paris, the laws thousands of people were subjected to by the Vichy government—perhaps he mentions the confiscation of, first, their radios and then their businesses and homes, the curfews, the banishment from public places, the wearing of the gold star of hope and protection as a yellow badge of danger and shame. And then the terrifying roundups, the days-long train transports, people prodded and packed into freight cars as if they were hogs on the way to slaughter. The deportations to camps, the bone-breaking labor and beatings, the shoveling into iced-over ground, the digging out of railroad tracks, the clearing of mine fields at the cost of a hand or a face. How the starved belly's contractions twisted even into the chest, the nausea bent the body in half and drove it to the ground. Perhaps the man mentions that it was the Vichy's suggestion to meet their quota of ridding the country of Jews by abducting children, delivering them to the camps, an inspiration that even the Nazis had not anticipated. Or that designated camps near Paris and around much of northeastern France became treacherous stepping stones to Auschwitz and annihilation. That, until just a few weeks before, he himself was enslaved in a concentration camp.

Later Bart will record the word "enslaved" in his diary. "Absurd," he will write Bertie, as if he cannot understand how all that he has just heard is possible in any world he knows. And though he's been immersed in war—*living* this war—for nearly two years, he is apparently shocked. Given his penchant for detail, it is odd that in neither his diary nor his letters does he explicitly identify even one of the stomach-churning series of abominations this man has proffered. As if he doesn't want to make any of it believable.

This is the first time Bart has met a person who has survived a concentration camp. It is his first firsthand account of the terror of tyranny, the reason the Americans crossed the ocean, the reason he, Bart, is there now, in Paris, at this synagogue. He has no way to know that within a few months he himself will bear witness to atrocities beyond even his imagination.

It was a chilly fall day in Paris, as it had been when Bart and Harry attended Rosh Hashanah services at the Synagogue de la Victoire. Now seventy years later, Gary and I rode two Metros from our apartment in the Marais and then wove our way on foot to the Rue de la Victoire.

We first spotted its façade, flanked by two more contemporary buildings, from the side. The Byzantine ornamental touches looked exotic; the round windows and arches were graceful, comforting, even ensconced in their gray stone walls. On our side of the street, a young tree, with sapling-slender branches, was still in leaf in spite of the November gusts. In front of the façade, paralleling the sidewalk, were several layers of barriers, no doubt a way to literally keep worshippers and tourists in line. Behind an ornate ironwork fence stood an anachronistic structure that resembled a phone booth.

Crossing the street, we tried to avoid eye contact with the uniformed man who was ensconced in the booth and glaring at us. He exited his enclosure and addressed us with authority. "*Attendez,*" he said as he strode toward us.

We turned to face him, and I grasped for the words I needed to enter. They blundered out in French, throwing out basic facts about my father and his connection with the synagogue. I was hoping I could charm him. I announced that we had traveled all the way from the American West, and that this would be the only time we would have to see this synagogue, which we must do *right then* because it was so marvelous and so famous and so important to my so very important book. But as I tripped over my syntax, I could see that I was failing. He was shaking his head. The synagogue was closed to visitors, he pronounced. "*Fermez.*"

Before I could make a nuisance of myself, or slink away, another uniformed man came strolling up with his walkie-talkie and his bulging holster. I repeated my story, only this time, instead of proclaiming or deploying arguments, I pleaded. After a few seconds of silence, the new guard asked for identification. Gary proffered his Harvard visiting scholar ID, and the guard said, "*Attendez,*" and carrying it into the building, left us looking blankly at each other. When the man returned, he handed back Gary's card and cocked his head toward some invisible point down the street. We thanked him profusely, though we had no idea whom or what to look for.

Around the corner we discovered . . . another guard booth. This guard was waiting for us, and before he could say no, I began to speak. This time, using as many of the French words as I could call up, I narrated. I described my father as he was seventy years before, the young doctor in love with his Jewish wife, the American who had lived for months in French fields under fire, doing his part to liberate all the French people and all the Jews of Europe. The young U.S. Army Major, traveling from bivouac to synagogue to celebrate the Jewish new year and the restoration of freedom. And somehow, as I stumbled through my account, I could see him now, my father the young liberator, and my words flowed in spite of the catch in my voice.

"OK," the guard said. In English.

I was still thanking him as Gary reached for my hand and led us toward the heavy doors. He turned the handle and—it seemed almost miraculous—the door opened wide. We entered without a hitch, as if liberated ourselves. After another ID and bag examination, another guard behind thick glass pointed us toward the metal detector, behind which waited a kind-looking man in an open-collared blue shirt and a suit jacket. He was short enough for me to see that his head was capped with a yarmulke. When he noticed that Gary's head wasn't covered, he ducked into a side office, handed the cap to Gary, and led us into the sanctuary.

Although the pews were empty, I could picture them jammed with people like Bart, marveling that religious freedom was once again possible, furious at having needed to fight such brutal opponents for it, grieving at the price of liberation. And I could just see my father straining to see over the heads of taller men, could see Harry as Bart described him, almost knocking over the Torah when it reached their aisle because he didn't realize it would come close so he could kiss it.

The sanctuary was luminous, the light as gorgeous and otherworldly as on a Rembrandt landscape. It emanated from the clusters of bulbs on the carved pillars and from the half-circle of candles under the twelve rose windows symbolizing the tribes of Israel, and suffused the room even to the pinnacle of the high canopy. Such soft splendor, such a sense of shelter here. Each treasure of this holy place—its Ark (which an armed militia had desecrated a year before Bart saw it) engraved with Hebrew letters, its arches and stars and carved columns, the wine-colored carpet woven with gold Stars of David—appeared to me, as I believe it did to my father, a metaphor for the exquisiteness of righteous victory.

Just months after Gary and I entered this space, Paris was smitten with three days of terror. The methodical, coordinated attacks that seemed almost impossible: black-masked gunmen fired their AK-47 rifles with the exactitude of a trained army, terrifying hostages, gunning down police officers, and targeting journalists at *Charlie Hebdo* magazine and Jews at a kosher market for massacre, emptying the world of some of its most brilliant satirical minds and entirely innocent people. The police closed the Rue de Rosiers, in the core of the historically Jewish neighborhood of the Marais, where Gary and I had rented an apartment.

For the first time since the Nazis forbade the Jews to worship, the synagogue was closed for Shabbat services. But in the wake of the carnage, the next day thousands of people joined together in the streets and congregated in the Grand Synagogue, just as they had in 1944. This time behind the pulpit stood not only the president of France and the country's chief rabbi, but the prime minister of Israel, his yarmulke visible to millions of onlookers from across the globe as he bowed over the microphones to remember the dead. And this time, as seven decades earlier, at the heart of the heart of the ceremony pulsed the sacred dream of freedom.

My husband and I left the Grand Synagogue de la Victoire with a treasure more exquisite than any carving or ornament. It was not a thing, one to be seen or touched. It was, instead, a shard of story, a gift from the man in the yarmulke, and we took this fragment home with us. This man, who had not offered his name or revealed to us his position in the synagogue, had given us the *mitzvah* of yet another connection. He had told us that he, too, before his family moved for many years to Lebanon for a fresh start, attended services in this synagogue just after the liberation—as a baby. I wondered if my father saw him, a swaddled bundle in his father's arms, as he glanced up to the candlelight in the gallery or across to one of the over-full pews. Somehow I think it is entirely possible.

THE LAST NIGHT Gary and I spent in Paris we found a table on the sidewalk outside at the Café de la Paix. We had just come from a velvet loge at the Opera Garnier across the street, eyes filling at the sight of Chagall's glorious painted ceilings, which the Nazis would have destroyed if their Jewish artist had painted them merely two decades earlier. The soft lights, the smooth marble statues, the cut-glass chandeliers—we were still in the glow of all this beauty, all this pleasure. It was a crisp evening, and we shivered a bit as we basked in the bubbles swimming up in our champagne flutes and marveled, as Bart had, at the opera's lit facade and its gilded busts of some of the composers whose music he played for me as young girl.

, We raised our glasses to Paris. We toasted the German general, Dietrich Von Choltitz, who was ordered to burn it to the ground, but in an arrangement with the Resistance, refused; we toasted Dom Perignon himself, the Benedictine monk in Reims, where the Wehrmacht surrendered to Ike. So much to honor and celebrate—the men and women who saved this glittering city from being decimated, who delivered generations from slavery and slaughter. My father's tender and stirring words. His safe return. His DNA in our daughters and our baby grandson. In the dark between us and the radiant opera house, the tortured shadows of a war zone flickered in front of me. But for now, as my father must have done that day so many years before we sat here, I felt at peace. We drained the flutes and spooned the remaining morsels of the elegant profiteroles between our lips. And unlike Bart, who, as he toasted the liberation in his fatigues and helmet at his sidewalk table—who knows, perhaps this very table—had already been parted from the love of his life for one year, eight months, and two weeks, we left reluctantly, hand in hand, in no hurry to be home.

HOLLAND

September 28, 1944 to March 1, 1945

CHAPTER 44
THE BIG PUSH IS UNDERWAY

More and more I can stand it less and less.

TEN DAYS AFTER Rosh Hashana and several false starts, Bart is in the cab of the personnel truck on his way, they've been told, to cross Belgium into Eupen, a German-annexed border town where the fighting is heavy. While Bart was packing his diary and keepsakes, the Allies' offensive Operation Market Garden, the largest airborne operation of the war, was creating havoc. Bart does not yet know it, but the failure of this operation has already derailed the Allies'—and his own—expectations of winning the war by Christmas. Still, in towns where any slab or splinter of a wall left standing is pocked with bullets and shrapnel, the people blow kisses, toss them apples and grapes.

Their last night in France, they stop near La Capelle, where sixty-five trucks park bumper to bumper only 100 miles from the front. *In the open.* Bart can hardly believe it. American planes soar past all night, blinking their lights. Before dawn when sleep overtakes him at last, excitement and fear are warring within him. By evening the next day, they find themselves rattling over the narrow cobblestone streets of a border town not in Germany but in Holland—Valkenburg, about twenty miles from the front.

In May of 1940, Germany invaded Holland and in a surprise air blitz leveled the heart of Rotterdam, killing hundreds of civilians. The Dutch, with their scant battalions and outdated aircraft and artillery, were forced to surrender. As the 91st pulls in, Holland has endured Nazi occupation for four years and four months. While Bart was filling his empty time in Guyancourt, Allied troops liberated Maastricht and a smattering of other Dutch towns. Two weeks later Allied tanks and trucks rolled under Valkenburg's stone arches, and, after some intense fighting, pushed the Germans back across their border.

By the time Bart and the other officers were ordered to move, the Allies controlled a narrow pocket of thirty miles extending from Eindhoven to Grave. In Valkenburg they are poised to cross the border into Germany, the town of Aachen only thirteen miles away. Capturing Aachen would mean that the Allies had finally taken a city in Germany.

Bart's truck passes houses and hotels with skeletal and half-collapsed roofs, their windows and walls blasted away. Teeming peaks of rubble, some ground to powder, have been swept to the sides of the roads. They drive up a hill and park in back of a mammoth, E-shaped building. The building—a former Jesuit monastery, which the Nazis commandeered even before the war to establish one of their infamous boarding schools for young boys and train them to be leaders in the Third Reich—is now abandoned. This is to be the unit's hospital and living quarters. Bart will stay with Harry and Sedam in adjoining rooms with a washstand and kerosene stove for heating water for shaving. Downstairs there's a mural, drawn in colored chalk by one of the former Nazi students of this school. The Dutch words at the bottom read: "To the East We Will Ride." *The misinformed bastards were taught that they would overrun Russia,* Bart thinks. It's warm inside the building, and there are showers.

Exploring, he finds several libraries, an enormous kitchen, and two pianos. Though he suspects he'll be a bit rusty, he sets his sights on practicing on the baby grand. What luxury all this is after France's hard, too-often shuddering ground and those unnaturally lit skies shrouded with smoke. Now, again, Bart is head of the pre-op section, which has been running smoothly, he's proud to say, since he took over in Normandy. He will be able do surgery if he's needed. He surveys the hospital, which is set up on the first floor, and feels satisfied. His ward includes eighty cots in a large mess hall, and this time, he has an assistant and a nurse. Besides, it shouldn't be long now.

Two days later, buzz bombs shake the building, and Bart crosses his fingers and wills himself to sleep. He's heard that another big push is expected in a matter of days, and he focuses on that. Two days later, all through the dazzlingly sunny morning, Allied bombers streak over their roof. By evening, smoke blackens the skies, patients are rolling in, and indeed the big push is underway.

In fact, what will become known as the Battle of Aachen has begun. The blasts rattle their windows for nearly three weeks. Bart watches the blaze from the observatory. The hospital roads are strafed; some of the American tanks are too bulky to squeeze down all the debris-congested streets, but their soldiers scrabble and bombard the Germans with artillery shells in the cold and mud; the Germans fiercely defend their *Westwall,* their extensive line of bunkers, pillboxes and forts, minefields, tank traps, and tunnels that safeguards the western border of their country and encloses Aachen. Artillery rumbles drum-like all day, and the 77th Evacuation Hospital Unit, less than twenty miles away, is shelled and bombed. The war is in their backyard again, and there's nothing Bart can do but watch and wait for more patients.

Throughout the next months of the long autumn, one Allied push follows another, but in surges and bursts, a haunting rhythm: the noise and the light, the ambulances speeding in all day and all night, the litters jamming the corridors, some slack time, and then, it all starts again. Bart can mark the beginning of the new cycle just by looking at the sky. But the patients appear only erratically, and the wasted time plagues him, as it plagues most of the doctors and nurses. He has time to think, which isn't necessarily a healthy activity as far as he's concerned. This idle time, he tells Bertie, is "a culture medium for the bacteria *Rumorus.*"

Sure enough, a few days later Harry crosses the threshold into Bart's room and tells him *sotto voce* that there's a semi-official rumor flapping about that the First Army is destined for the South Pacific and that the 91st will have to be transferred to the Ninth Army to escape going with them. The idea of the South Pacific after all this—all this work, all these years of his life—sinks leaden into his chest. "This is where I begin not liking it very much," he writes. He goes to the piano and bangs out the crescendos and fortissimos of the "Warsaw Concerto" with the force of a charging bull, eyes trained on the red cape of the enemy.

He celebrates his and Bertie's fourth wedding anniversary by breaking open a bottle of Scotch, alone. He writes his bride, as he has done for the past two years of their separation. "Well, darling, it wasn't this cold on that memorable day. It was sunny and warm and the next day we bought kitchenware at a dime store. Today the wind is forcing the cold through the cracks in the window. My hands are cold and I am blue. I am tired spiritually. I think I've taken a long beating."

That day the Americans invade the Philippines; the next day Aachen is won. The day after that the 91st officially becomes part of the Ninth U.S. Army. Bart might be elated if the windows didn't still quake as the months sputter on. And if the fierce battles in the impenetrable Hürtgen forest, its firs scarred by machine-gun blasts, its trails seeded with thousands of mines, were not still raging less than thirty miles away. And if the Germans' ferocious resistance at their border hadn't set the war back, he surmises, by at least half a year. The last time he heard Churchill's inspiring stutter on the radio, he used the word "hope." He *"hopes"* the war will end in 1945.

As October blusters into November, a couple of 90 mm anti-aircraft guns are set up close to their building. Bart has not ventured beyond the grounds for nearly a month. Even after the officers receive permission to go to town, the thunder and blaze of mortar and artillery are still too close, and the cold bites into Bart's fingers, even in gloves. The windows shatter so frequently that the hallways are nothing but glass-splattered draft traps.

The first robot plane they see flies low, directly over the hospital, a ball of flame spread across the black sky, smoke streaming out of its hump tail, with its foreign-sounding, chilling drone. He writes Bertie rather sheepishly: "I hope I haven't given you the impression that I'm yellow. Only when I hear, as last night, a constant drone overhead, knowing full well that our planes were put away for the night—well I kinda get a funny feeling at the end of my spine." And now the new rumors, fed by German propaganda, center on the terrifying V-2.

Still, he likes to watch the show. Toward the end of November he sometimes runs up to the observatory for a closer view. The big American guns flash on the horizon. As two enemy planes sail through the Allied lines with the flak following them all the way, his eyes follow a thousand tracers, balls of smoke, and starlight bursts. Or he blacks out his room and leans as far as he dares out the window to take in the drama.

For a time, work is again chaotic. One day in mid-November they admit 414. Bart scrambles around in wards crammed with shivering, mud-caked soldiers, jabbing cigarettes between their lips, using a knife to scrape away dirty uniforms, pouring blood and plasma into bodies, taking time to examine wounds carefully enough to prioritize amputations, lacerations, shrapnel damage, and a host of other injuries for surgery. And then, another lull.

The 91st is planning a dance, but the very idea of it spikes his bile. The guys rib him about it, but he can't help feeling that something is terribly wrong about a dance in this place, so close to where their soldiers are living day and night in foxholes and being slaughtered. He feels like a sentimental fool, but he can't help it. Listening to the wounded American boys, he wells up with empathy, pride, and the particular kind of patriotism that perhaps the newest generation of Americans can feel most keenly.

As increasing numbers of prisoners of war enter his ward—*a good sign that everything is going well,* he thinks—he also finds himself talking with the enemy. More often, the enemy is just a boy, albeit a brainwashed and hateful boy, and after Bart hears these boys recite the poison they've been fed, his emotions escalate into something more than simple fury.

Then he broods about how, when the war is finally over, the whole world will have changed. What exactly will he do? How will he relearn the things he needs to know to make a life with Bertie? He knows that, despite all his experience these last two years, he's forgotten a great deal about medicine and may have to start from the beginning. But the irony!—he'll be virtually just another intern then, on an intern's wages and with an intern's endless hours. Bertie may not know how much this will demand from both of them, and he's half-afraid.

And when Bertie again confesses that she is apprehensive that he will be different from the way he was, that *they* will be different from each other, her anxieties trigger his, which come shooting up. He does his best to reassure her—and himself—but this is another worry he doesn't need. She wonders if, given his experience of so much of the world, he will be a snob when he returns.

In retrospect I feel aged and wiser. But darling I haven't changed. I still feel like a high school boy and I want to play. The most I've lost in myself has been regular exercise and hair. I've gained weight and a more ready smile. Do you really think our ideas will be divergent just because I have become a traveler and because we have been apart for years? Hell no.

But his mind can't help revisiting that moment the ship moved out of the harbor, as if out of life itself, maybe to return—and maybe not. One night he writes,

I'm so lonesome for you. More and more I can stand it less and less. All I want is my own sweet wife—in a two by four room with a "don't disturb" sign on the door. I never realized a heart could be so heavy with longing and lonesomeness. I play games with myself. The name of it is "See how clearly you can throw an image in your mind of the woman you love better than life." The second part of it is "See how long you can keep that up without going crazy."

He mutters plaintively in his sleep, and one afternoon he arises from a nap in the ward with his cheeks wet from tears.

I dreamed I had come home. I met you for the first time in over two years. You were very nice and kind—but obviously different. You didn't hug me tight. You didn't kiss me with all yourself like you used to. And then you said something about things changing with time and that the sooner we knew about the loss of our love, the better.

The nurse who shakes him awake doesn't laugh at him. She says he was repeating "Honey, honey" over and over again in the most agonized tones she'd ever heard. "My God!" he writes. "Should I have to bear such nightmares too?"

"Three years ago today," he tells Bertie soon after that,

I was lying on my bunk in Ft. Leonard Wood, half asleep when the radio brought the news of war. It seems that a whole life time has gone by since then. It is a strange thought that brings to mind a place where lights are on at night outdoors, that a plane over head is nothing more than a mail carrier, that a noise is not a cannon, ack-ack or a bomb explosion, that rumors are extinct, that going to a civilian's house for a meal is not a treat and a holiday, that a fresh egg is not kept in the family safe, that there is such a thing as privacy and that day or night, one can be with the woman he loves. Aren't there any more army doctors and soldiers to take our place for a while? I've got my share of the glory, work, sweat and lonesomeness in three campaigns. I wanted to get in on the big thing—I did. Now let someone else get some glory and stuff.

CHAPTER 45

THE LANDSCAPE, THE PORTRAIT, AND THE TUNNELS

How much do I owe you?

AND THEN AMID this loneliness and angst, something extraordinary happens: he meets Charles Eyck. Only recently has Bart ventured from the hospital. He walks into Valkenburg, examines the rubble from the bombed-out walls of buildings, then strolls down the main street. Perhaps it is while he's peeking in the windows of a shop or café that the young Dr. Passanante, in the reflection of the glass, spies the pleasant-looking man with wavy hair flapping in the wind at angles from his head and a large sketch pad tucked under his arm. They catch each other's eye. Bart has heard rumors of a man of some reputation who is painting portraits of the Americans, and he stops to shake his hand. And between the time when they first spot each other and when the oils have dried on the portrait Eyck will paint of Bart, they become, just as Bart and Zangara had, friends.

When I say friends, I mean of a particular sort—because their time together is fleeting and because no words are spoken. Eyck is deaf, as deaf as Bart will become before his own story concludes. They agree to meet soon. In a tea shop the next day the artist removes his scarf and coat, takes out his paints, centers a sketch pad onto the table, and applies pigment to canvas while Bart watches the metamorphosis of dabs and sweeps into a Dutch landscape. He notes the grace of the wrist as the brush bobs and arcs, the certainty of the strokes. They talk, in their way, Eyck with one hand slanting a pencil toward paper, the other hand slicking back his unruly hair over his receding, slightly shiny scalp. And when Bart scoots back his chair to leave, Eyck hands him the painting carefully, keeping it horizontal so that the wet paint-shapes don't smack against Bart's coat. He gestures that the painting is a gift.

During the two weeks he and Eyck meet off and on while he paints Bart's portrait, they communicate by pencil. Since Eyck studied in Italy, Bart writes in Italian, and Eyck answers in a mishmash of English, American, French, Dutch, and German. Bart tells him about Bertie—syllables and phrases in various languages rush back and forth on paper—and can see from the way Eyck's lips curve up in his shy smile that he likes Bertie. Bart is grateful. The next time they meet, Eyck brings a wooden box, one he's made for the landscape so that Bart can send it to Bertie. He's even addressed the box. Before he leaves, he promises to make a container for the portrait, too.

That night, Bart digs around in one of the desks the Nazis abandoned when they bolted from the advancing Allies and finds a Christmas postcard, a drab picture of a Dutch landscape with a windmill. The adrenaline keeps him up past midnight, sketching the scene in watercolors, trying to paint it the way he saw Eyck sketching his portrait in oils. Frost is collecting in the corners of the windows, and he pulls his bed closer to the radiator. Tonight, instead of dwelling on his loneliness, his hunger for Bertie, or on the robot bombs that redden the horizon and blast close enough to shake the winter-hardened earth, he turns his mind to art. He resolves to learn techniques that will enable him to improve his painting. He'll take an art class—he'll take more than one. He asks Bertie to make sure he keeps this promise to himself. And he jots down a suggestion for his birthday present: an easel, lots of paints, brushes, canvas, and a palette.

In just a few weeks he strides out of town, stopping to ask directions now and then, and finally, three miles away, there it is—the windmill he's been hoping to find since his first day in Holland. He snaps a few colored pictures, then lays his helmet onto the snow-brushed ground, and somehow blocking out the booming from the front lines, with cold fingers he renders a rough sketch, poring over every line and shade until the sleet threatens to smear his paper.

When Bart meets Eyck in the tea shop for the last time, the artist is waiting for Bart at a corner table, the completed portrait in the box he has made for it on his lap. He lifts it out of the box, and Bart inspects it, admires it. The portrait has been painted on linen. He thinks Bertie will like it, too. Later, Bertie will say that the portrait makes her Italian husband look Dutch, but she will keep it with her always, in a spot on the wall of her living room where everyone who enters their house can admire it.

Bart turns to Eyck and scribbles in Italian, something like, "How much do I owe you for your excellent work?" As Bart bends his head to take out his wallet, Eyck lays his hand gently on Bart's arm. Eyck's gaze penetrates from behind his round, black glasses, which make his eyes look owlish and wise, and he shakes his head. He lifts the pencil. "Send me a souvenir from America," Eyck writes. "The Americans come 3,000 miles to help me, and I'm only a ten-minute walk from here. I'd like to work out the other 2,998 miles."

THE FUTURE WILL celebrate Charles Eyck as an expressionist painter. In Maastricht, a little over eight miles from Valkenburg, a lush-lawned park hugging the River Meuse will be named after him. In another century, Bart's eldest daughter and son-in-law will stroll in that park, their arms touching all the way up from the tips of their fingers, the river irradiated a saturated sapphire under the marigold sun, recalling the pure and pulsating hues of the painter's post-war work, which is showcased in the nearby museum. Inspired by the then-budding artist, the windmill Bart sketched outside near the front and later painted will be framed and become the sole adornment on his second daughter Judy's bedroom wall in California. Eyck's first gift to Bart and Bertie, the dashed-off Dutch scenery, will be lost, perhaps with Zangara's in Bart and Bertie's frequently flooded basement. But Bart's portrait, signed by Charles Eyck, will hang for more than half a century over the fireplace. And after that it will preside over the framed family photographs at the head of his daughter's staircase in Idaho and wait for the next generation to step up as its stewards.

IN EARLY DECEMBER two other diversions find berths in Bart's unsettling world. One is a budding friendship with a charming couple named Wirtz. Jules and Mickey have an eleven-month-old baby daughter, Drieka, with wispy hair the color of egg yolks, and they invite Bart to what he thinks is a dollhouse of sorts, with entire walls adorned in oils, watercolors, and etchings. George met them first—Bart will not remember how—and introduced them to Harry, who introduced them to Bart. The chaplain no doubt thought he was doing all of them a favor, and besides, he liked to think of the three of them as a triumvirate, a term he would use to describe him and his two best friends well into his nineties. The Wirtzes' house is cozy, and some of the woodcuts were made by Jules himself.

That first night, Harry brings Bart along for an evening of bridge playing. Bart is grateful: for the way he can talk about art with Jules, for the way Jules is interested in Bart's own dabbling in line and color, for the way the vivacious Mickey dotes on him, serving tea and apple fritters. He loves the way that she, who speaks only a few words of English, stays so engaged in the conversation, even in his extended anecdotes, prodding her husband for instant translations as if she were a little child. When it's close to 11 and their car is on its way to pick them up, Bart and Harry rise to leave. Jules turns and walks to his desk, then returns with an etching, which he places in Bart's hand, who neatly wraps his fingers around it. When he and Harry are putting on their coats at the door, Jules makes them promise that they will come whenever they want, that they will make the Wirtz home theirs. It is the first evening Bart has spent in an actual home in two years. In the weeks that follow, the Wirtzes invite Bart to their house many times. Sometimes the maid prepares mushrooms on toast. They play chess and bridge, they mull over the military situation, and, for a few hours at a time, it's almost like having a normal life again.

About the same time the Wirtzes come into Bart's life, Colonel Hayes sends Bart a message inviting him to his office for a drink before lunch. Bart's pulse races, not because this is a surprise—it isn't, Harry has been talking to the colonel and has kept Bart apprised—but because it concerns something Bart has been wanting to do ever since he and Harry smoothed the creases in their folded map and figured out just where the hell they were. Or at least since Bart got wind of the rumors about the underground tunnels. Harry has confided to him that Colonel Hayes knows Bart is interested in art, and a seed of hope germinates.

By the time he enters Colonel Hayes's office, four others—an RAC nurse, the executive officer Colonel Beeler, Waggoner, and Harry—are already there. There's someone else, too, a tall, clean-cut gentleman, a Mr. van Poppel, whose pewter-hued hair and mustache make him look more dignified than stern. He is the curator of the collection of the world-famous paintings, the Dutch masters, that have been sequestered from the bombing and are stored and tended below the surface of the earth in a maze of tunnels under a small mountain in Maastricht. With a sweep of his hand, Colonel Hayes invites them all to join him and Mr. van Poppel at his table for lunch.

What a delightful lunch companion Mr. van Poppel is. He's in the art business and traveled to the Dutch East Indies and America before he was commissioned to curate the paintings. He speaks fluent English, and Bart is enthralled talking with him about music and art. And, of course, war. Maastricht has been liberated not quite three months. Van Poppel has had to endure the years-long reign of terror by the German SS, in fear for not only his family but his solemn charge, the artworks.

When the conversation turns to the tunnels, van Poppel reports proudly that during the occupation only two German generals were allowed in the vault that houses the art. And when he leans in toward Bart and describes the clever contrivances he's devised to keep the paintings intact in their temporary home under the earth, Bart very nearly, at least for those minutes, forgets about the dreary weather, the drone of low-flying planes, the mines planted around the town outside the hospital grounds. The more van Poppel sketches in his tales of the paintings, the more Bart longs to go to Maastricht and see for himself.

Perhaps it's the colonel who asks the vital question—Colonel Hayes, always the diplomat, always searching for means to compensate the men and women under his command for the sacrifices of these years of their life in more humane ways. But I like to think that it was Bart who impressed and charmed the curator so acutely that he elicited the answer they were all so eager to have. Whatever the dynamics, van Poppel consents to eschewing the rules and allowing four of them, chosen on the basis of their love for art, to take a tour. Just before he pushes back his chair and dons his coat and scarf to brave the damp, van Poppel invites Bart to his home to see his East Indies woodcuts.

At his first glimpse of the van Poppel house two days later, Bart's eyes widen. Lavish Chinese chests, teakwood panels, Balinese wood carvings, East Indian dolls, walls rendered sumptuous with oils and etchings—*if only Bertie could see all this,* he thinks. He has a hard time concentrating on the present. But when he and the two nurses who have been invited to accompany him, Miss Mitchell and Miss Schaffer, climb into the car to make their way to the tunnels, van Poppel starts to spool out what Bart knows is still history in the making. It was the Germans who brought the art here, the Germans who were protecting it in order to steal it. As part of the Atlantic Wall, they constructed a defensive corridor to surround what became known as the Vault in Sint Pietersberg hill. Bart makes a mental note that the 780 artworks were crated and trucked up the mountain and buried in the belly of the tunnels only nine months before he arrived in Casablanca two years before.

Their guide unlocks the iron gates, then unbolts and lugs open the thick, metal door, corroded the color of the algae Bart noted on the warmed water in Africa, and they thread their way in the dark— along the passageways of this former marlstone mine, negotiating the ground's abrupt pockets and bypassing the serpentine coils, the convex quarry walls, the graffiti that recounts the charcoaled, etched, and chiseled record of centuries of other refugees from wars and cold, the brick ovens built for bread to sustain people under siege after siege, the corridor where Napoleon eased his horse—at last, to the belly, the sanctum sanctorum. At that entrance—more iron, more green, another bolt—Bart and the nurses gather around van Poppel, who offers information. The humidity and temperature have to be precisely measured and controlled so that the treasures do not crack or buckle or fade. The lesser-valued paintings are carefully crated and lined against the walls. Some of the large paintings, including Rembrandt's *Night Watch,* are rolled between wax paper in a windlass of some sort, which is turned 45° every week to prevent sagging. Some of the racks are on rolls that can be pulled out from the crevices of the tunnel. The 200 or so portraits that are visible are lined up on chicken-wire frames that come together, with ample spaces between, in the form of leaves of a book. As van Poppel draws apart these leaves ceremoniously one by one— Ruisdael, Rubens, Vermeer, Hals, Wasserman, Steen, and even El Greco and Monet—Bart gawks at the exquisite workmanship of the master painters.

And then, he stands perfectly still. Van Poppel is uncovering a painting Bart remembers well. It's Rembrandt's *Titus,* a portrait of the artist's son—the boy with the blonde-streaked curls in the rust-colored

beret like the underside of the broad leaves of the magnolia that Bart
will plant in the front yard, the boy's cheeks pinked like the blush of
the unfurled buds of the crabapple trees. Something new stirs. He asks
the curator to pause a moment, and it's not just because the painting
is familiar. In the moment the painting is held before his eyes in that
dark tunnel, it appears soaked in light and a vivid sense of the possible.

WHEN, THE BETTER PART of a century later, my husband and I
entered the tunnels, we swung our gas lanterns to illuminate the hol-
lows and swells in the cave floor. It's as if we'd sprung from a myth: a
journey, a battle, a secret, a treasure, a quest; there's even a labyrinth.
"Ariadne!" Gary exclaimed. "Dante!" I responded. Never mind that
our guide had orange-pink hair, or that we had first scaled the wrong
side of the hill with the wrong entrance and had arrived at the sum-
mit of Sint Pietersberg huffing and befuddled from having sprinted up
steep slopes on dirt paths. We, too, had merged with this modern-day
mythology. We, too, had threaded our way and, even in the absence of
battle, watched our guide heft that algae-colored iron door. We, too,
entered the sanctum sanctorum. We, too, emerged whole and restored.

I feel certain that in spite of his dreary drive back, the frightening
flashes in the black, for Bart there came a sense of renewal, a fleeting
feeling of peace. Within ten days German paratroopers will clutter the
foggy skies over Maastricht. Perhaps some of them drop to the layers
of dirt branching over the tunnels and shielding the art from the harm
of humans. Bart's stomach will churn at the swarming of fireballs, the
ever-nearer crash of bombs. The ferocious German counterattack that
would become infamous as the Battle of the Bulge will explode into
history within fifty miles of his ward and his bedroom, and the coldest
winter in nearly 100 years will launch a protracted battle of its own.
And even as Bart works to save the lives of those paratroopers, the
strident story of the war will stretch out in all its chaos, all its waste,
beyond all his hopes.

CHAPTER 46

ANYTHING FOR A LAUGH

My teeth are clenched and my chin is up, but these prostheses are heavy.

AFTER BART'S VISIT to the tunnels, and before he has even an inkling of the imminent battle that will change his life once again, time seems to crawl toward Christmas. It's his third away from home, and all he feels is disgust. Instead of patching up casualties and saving lives, he finds himself painting a mural for the Red Cross to complement the myriad Christmas decorations. He roams around the building, cleans and reorganizes the cupboard spaces, takes inventory, or just sits, thinking about how stupid he looks. He shakes his head at the remodeled recreation room with the new bar, at the pleasures of roast chicken and ice cream at dinner. "Is there a war on?" he asks.

The day the Battle of the Bulge begins, Bart is decorating a Christmas tree in his ward and photographing the nurses, ward boys, and even patients, all of whom are helping. But that night, the booming keeps him awake, his pulse throbbing, belly tense, until dawn. And then every night, all night, the thunder and clatter from enemy planes and anti-aircraft guns is terrific. But soon it's apparent that, though German paratroopers were dropped eight miles from them, the 91st is not receiving the casualties that must be piling up so near. "I don't know what the score is but I can't imagine keeping an important hospital like ours idle while things are going on," he laments.

As the din and his anxiety ramp up, he longs for Bertie to help him feel better. But how to do so without worrying her, or without his words being scissored out of his letters? So, once again, he relies on vague rhetoric. His code to her varies on any given day. He says, "Apparently we are having some reverses and we find ourselves in a peculiar situation." Or, after news of the counterattack becomes public, "The counter attack is something of which we are not fond." Or, "Your husband and a few others are sweating out the German breakthrough. I feel like I'm at a football game, sitting on the ten-yard line hollerin', Hold that line, hold that line."

In spite of the gunfire and bombs, the Wirtzes insist he and Harry join them for Christmas Eve, a celebration they've been planning for days. The table in the tiny room is laid with a tablecloth, napkins, candles, and evergreen. At each plate is a menu, *the product of Jules's artistic temperament,* Bart thinks. Jules regales them with many tales of how he nearly got caught offending the Nazis. The anti-Nazi jokes he bandied about and the radio he listened to with spotters as his guards, well placed down the street, worried Mickey often. Bart is inspired by this rebelliousness but increasingly anxious the more he comes to like and admire Jules.

Another night at the Wirtzes', when the cacophony and fireworks begin even before the wintry sun stops streaking the sky and Harry and Bart can no longer keep a civil conversation going without worrying about a new influx of patients, they grab their coats and walk out into the lit-up night. As they zigzag their way back to the hospital, trying not to let the booms jar them into terror, soldiers jump out from a shadowed corner, jab guns into their ribs, and bark for identification. This happens three times within half a mile. After that, Bart decides not to go out for a while.

The advent of 1944 is heralded by the pinging sound of ricocheting bullets from a plane strafing the hospital and ambulances.

When Bart learns that Warsaw has been liberated, he performs the "Warsaw Concerto" for a small gathering of officers. He does so with the ceremony befitting the occasion. His arpeggios, after so many weeks of practice, after so much waiting for this event, are almost flawless. But when he pounds out the final trills and chords, in spite of the applause and accolades, he feels no sense of liberation, no sense of celebration. He cannot muster the fervor of his optimism of August and September that the war will end soon.

A few days later he writes Bertie: "If it weren't for the hope-filling news of the Russian breakthrough taking Warsaw, Cracow and Lodz I would be tempted to lock myself in my room—if we owned a key. You say that you'll probably be neurotic by the time I get home. Well, get an extra set of paper-doll cutting equipment, darling—for me. I think I too am going nuts. My teeth are clenched and my chin is up, but these prostheses are heavy."

BY THE TIME January drifts toward February, as the German salient is being rapidly obliterated and the unit is still receiving only occasional casualties, Bart wonders about his state of mind. "I must be nuts!" he writes. "Today I went up in an airplane—the first time in my life. I say 'nuts' because of all the times to go up in a plane for a first experience, this is the silliest ever. I flew along the front lines, watched the artillery and saw the smashed towns of which Aachen is an example. Later, after landing, I got worried. Supposing, thought I with a little green about my gills, that a Jerry plane would have been around. We were in an L5 (a reconnaissance plane), a two-seater with the great speed of about 100 mph. The pilot said that under the circumstances he would come down and duck among the trees—wotta treat! Lt. Pickles has for the past month, threatened to take me up, knowing how I dislike it, and finally today he sent a jeep over to pick me up. I suddenly decided that I'd fly—probably the product of complete and utter boredom. Even on a loop and barrel-roll your crazy husband refused to get sick or frightened."

And then there springs up what seems to be a craze for theatricals. A group of particularly bored guys have organized a show (not the kind that Bart had been hoping to watch, not the kind that, at least since Normandy, he *has* been watching). There are many directors, and they've written some original songs. The show, which they're calling *Anything for a Laugh,* will be comprised of skits, gags, and tricks. And they've written six parts for Bart, to cash in on his deadpan poker face. *It is so ludicrous that it just may go over,* he thinks. "Fine War!" he writes again. "Life at the Ninety First goes on in 'Fine War' style."

The show goes over with a bang. The evening's performance climaxes with a racket of applause, shouts, and whistles as well as a standing ovation. And Bart's a star; he's told he stole the show. News of their success spreads, and Bart begrudgingly agrees to repeat his skit for a combat exhaustion center in a town a few miles away. He wishes he could say no, but he doesn't want to let anyone down. As the troupe edges nearer to the front lines at night, his stomach tightens, and all the laughs they get are from members of the cast. His blue mood is exacerbated by the words of the commanding officer of the Ninth Army Medical Corps, their head man, who told them bluntly they'd be in tents again, in the mud and rain, up closer to the front soon. At least the Russians have crossed the German border.

Since after a short-lived influx of patients their current cases consist of backaches, knee conditions, hemorrhoids, chronic abdominal pains, and in-grown toenails, and the show is over, he decides to accept the adjutant's offer to take seventeen enlisted men to Paris for a few days. *I must look lonesome and in need of fun,* he thinks, but he's happy to be able to do this for them and knows the trip will, at the very least, distract him. He stays in the Grand Hotel across the street from the Louvre, just down the block from the opera. The room is so cold that his breath vaporizes the mirror as he shaves.

He notes the changes in Paris since only a few months before. Now Paris seems like an R and R camp. He rides his first subway—now free to Allied troops! Movie theaters are free to the troops, too. He takes in the follies, drinks champagne. Before his leave ends, he cajoles the Red Cross into letting him have sandwiches for the enlisted men on the twelve-hour trip back to Valkenburg. On the way back after navigating around detours caused by crushed roads and floods from the swollen Marne and Meuse, he tells Bertie to forget about his coming home before the war ends.

BY FEBRUARY, bombs are battering German cities, Dresden is fire-bombed for days on end, and the Reds, as they close in on Berlin, have penetrated into Germany as far as Frankfurt on the Oder, demanding that the Nazis surrender immediately.

Bart has no idea where all the casualties this mess must be making are being shipped off to for treatment, but in the slack time while he waits for patients he considers his future—and to do that, he looks back into his years of practice. It's no surprise, of course, that the more time he spends with patients with any ailment, the more he learns, and the more satisfaction his work gives him. But now, after these years of riding the vicissitudes of his medical performance, after these months of overseeing the pre-op ward, interspersed sporadically with lessons and practice in surgery, his vision of his future is coming into focus. His and Bertie's, of course—always, always, with Bertie at the core—but he knows they will need more than each other to be fully happy and thrive. In spite of his crises of confidence, his setbacks, and his sense of being hollowed out without her, medicine has been providing him a series of milestones beyond the more impersonal, more distant ones—the battles, the troop movements, or even the marks he's inked on the map that designate all the places he's traveled.

He's been envisaging the sweep of his progress. He remembers how as early as fall he noticed he was gaining a reputation for being a fine surgical diagnostician. He pictures the night he heard that little boy whimpering, the night two of the surgeons refused to believe the spleen was the source of the little boy's problem, the night Bart examined him a second time, then hurried over to Welch in surgery and made his case for operating. The spleen torn in two pieces. Surgery successful. Welch might as well have tossed bouquets he looked so pleased. Bart smiles at how, after that, the cases the surgeons threw his way began to multiply.

The images flow to a few months later, when, in Welch's absence, Pearson was acting chief surgeon and Bart was the only one of the doctors to diagnose a patient with peritonitis, always fatal unless operated on. He was pretty sure he also knew the source, too, and that gangrene had probably already set in. Perhaps it was the commanding tone he summoned to persuade Pearson to operate—or perhaps, by then, Pearson had learned to respect Bart's opinion enough to doubt his own diagnosis—but when Bart insisted, Pearson operated. A crowd collected, as if waiting for a showdown. Bart hung back, away from the table, his heart pulsing. He didn't dare look, but soon the telling words "suction" and "there it is" and "I'll be damned" shot through the silence. The boy lived, and for days afterward Bart felt like he was living in glory.

Perhaps the turning point for Bart's resolution about his future didn't come until more recently, when Bertie told him she bought him a volume of *Best and Taylor Physiology,* the new book with thousands of facts he knows he'll need for reference when he takes his exams, starting with the fascinations of the cell and building up to tissues and—well, his mind spins just thinking of all those bits of information he needs to absorb. He'll use the book to refresh his memory when he returns, to prepare for his career. And—he can see it now—he'll be a surgeon. It will take work, more work than he's ever done, but he vows to start now. He'll need Bertie's help as he's never needed it before, but he *will* take the American Board of Surgery exam someday, as soon as he's ready.

Ok? he asks Bertie. *Ok?* But he knows what her answer will be.

On February 23 his ward suddenly fills up, and by the end of the first day of receiving casualties, he's cleared 131 cases through either surgery or treatment and evacuation. *A record,* he's happy to say, *a fat, juicy record.* His patients are brimming with stories: how the Germans flooded the little stream of the Roer; how in a smokescreen the Americans, in spite of enemy barrages of machine guns and mortars, ran across the Roer on countless foot and pontoon bridges built by combat engineers. *A breakthrough,* Bart thinks. And now, finally, the Allies are on their way to the Rhine, and he hasn't heard a German plane in weeks. He imagines that spring will be the time of the showdown at last.

That night he writes: "I hope this is it, darling. If it is, the war should be over before your birthday. I'm willing to work night and day to that end." If the war ends by April 12, he might be home by June. He begins to count the full moons that will brighten the nights and shrink into shadow before he can see her beautiful face again.

Finally, on March 1 they get word that they will move the following day someplace across the Roer River, closer to the Rhine. Apparently everything is moving. Once again the 91st launches into the usual hustle-and-bustle and rush. But that's fine with Bart. Bertie's birthday is less than two months away, and there is need for certain haste.

CHAPTER 47

NANCY DREW AND THE HARDY BOY, THE TWENTY-FIRST CENTURY

THE GPS IN our rented cornflower blue Smartcar directed Gary and me into Valkenburg through the perfect stone arches heralding the city, arches the photographs we'd been poring over depicted as crumbled from explosives but were now restored to perfection. It was a mid-September morning, sixty-eight years and one day after Valkenburg was liberated from the Nazis, and sixty-eight years and ten days after Bart rumbled through those ruined gates in the cab of a truck. We parked by the train station, a 1944 photo of which Gary had just posted on Facebook to herald our journey. It was very early in the morning, and we were trying to avoid the traffic, detours, and blocked roads we had been warned to expect from the world-championship cycling races obstructing the thoroughfares of Limburg this week. At the station, though, alone, we strolled around in back to the tracks so that we could photograph the same view Bart's picture preserved of the imposing building up the hill. Although it was partially obscured, the dome of its observatory curved over the treetops and told us that this was where Bart spent five months: his residence, his hospital, his home, his work.

Before we headed up the hill, we ordered croissants and cappuccino at the chic-looking café in front of the station. It was nippy even in the direct sun, and we were the only customers. No matter how chilled, I wanted to be outside, to peer down toward town and see more of what Bart saw. The waiter, a friendly young man named Philippe, gave us warm responses in English to my series of questions about the Americans in Valkenburg and the building behind the station and up the hill. But he was too young to remember and knew little about the history of the building, and so he invited us to cross the street to the Hotel Tummers to talk to its owner, his father.

We were admiring the understated, fading elegance of the lobby when Mr. Tummers appeared. A soft-spoken gentleman with a thick cap of styled white hair, he directed a staff member to serve us coffee. Sipping from china cups, we chatted with him. He was interested in seeing the photographs we'd brought of Valkenburg just after its liberation. We all hovered around my laptop and watched our collected photos of Valkenburg, most of them Bart's, scroll by. Mr. Tummers described how, when his parents owned the hotel, he had worked in the kitchen during 1944 and 1945 when Bart was living up the hill. He recalled the Americans in town, and he recalled the Nazis before that, but he couldn't summon any specific memories. After the war, he told us, the building was turned into a Maharishi transcendental meditation center, and recently plans were brewing to develop it into a retirement center, but skepticism about the ability to modernize the facilities had scrapped the plan. Now, he said, the building was locked. I could feel my face crumple.

"I can't believe we can't even go inside," I said as Gary and I walked back across the street to the car about an hour later. I wanted to see this place, Bart's first warm place to sleep in months, the place where he made so many decisions about his future and imagined it more fully and clearly, though I knew these memories were shaded with bitterness, bouts of loneliness, and resentment.

"We'll see," Gary said. I knew better than to contradict him. We'd already had so many surprises on this journey.

We wound up the hill, and, as Mr. Tummers had predicted, the iron gates of the first entrance were shut and locked; they blocked the road. Undeterred, Gary swung up on a side road, and whaddaya know, drove through an open gate right to the building. We parked on the side and were surprised to see several other cars in front. A new-looking wing, with bright contemporary stained glass windows set into the brick walls, jutted out toward the place where the fleet of ambulances once waited to speed in and drive out evacuated patients.

We tried a door. Locked. I kept pulling on it as if I could loosen it. Gary tapped my shoulder and pointed to another door. Bingo—this one was secured open with a broom handle.

"Cheeky, plucky Yanks," Gary said, inside.

"Nancy Drew and the Hardy boys!" I retorted. "Boy," I corrected myself. "Only one." Gary smiled boyishly.

And for a while, we *were* all of those. The place, coated with dust, looked empty and dilapidated in spite of the muted voices that echoed from down the hall. We treaded stealthily down the corridors the other direction and tiptoed through the Gothic-arched hallways that were uncannily familiar from Bart's words and photographs—the ironwork on the staircases, the latticed windows, the tiled floors, and even the wallpaper, though wide flaps of it drooped. We crept past a poster of the Maharishi himself, past the cavernous-looking kitchen where Bruno, the night cook and Bart's pal and partner in kitchen crime, aided and abetted Bart's raids on the refrigerator to remove hot dogs and eggs and hunks of tenderloin and throw them into the grease pan or store them away in the pharmacy icebox for what he called leaner days.

We spiraled up the staircase; at each landing we peeked into all the adjoining rooms, glancing through windows to find the views from the photos, and the view that would show us that this was indeed Bart's room. On the top floor, on impulse I walked straight to a room in a row of adjoining rooms, stepped gingerly to the window, and scoured the yard.

Out the smudged glass I could see the place the garden might have been where Bart pilfered some early-October tomatoes a few days after he arrived, the firs that were flocked with ice in December, the field where he chucked snowballs at his friends, and the slopes that he sledded down in January to try to block out thoughts of battles and death and loneliness.

"I think this is it," I whispered.

Gary said, "Could be, could be."

When I was ready to turn from the window to leave, he was waiting for me in the hall. The voices seemed suddenly louder, more ominous. He gestured for me to follow him, and we sneaked down the several flights of stairs quickly. On the ground floor, we hurried to the door, but it was shut, the broom now standing alongside it. Our eyebrows shot up, and it was all I could do not to burst into laughter. If only Bart could have heard the story of our snooping in the hospital where he spent some of the most miserable days of his life, of our trying to cheat time and spy on—maybe even usurp—his past. I could see him (head shaking, dimple flashing) and hear him (his most incredulous tone) as if he were sneaking around with us. I could almost hear him exclaim: "You've *got* to be kidding!"

I took this image with me as we exited by a side door, sprinted to the car, gunned the motor, and fled. As we sped toward Germany, black clouds were gathering over Aachen and toward the Rhine.

CHAPTER 48

A PICTURE A KID SHOULDN'T SEE

WHEN THE KERNEL of the idea of following my father around Europe germinated, I had planned not to include Germany in my travels. After all, I reasoned, he was there only a few months until the war ended, and more than half the time he was stationed there was after Germany surrendered. It was only after reading the 465 pages of letters he wrote my mother those last ten grueling months of his war that I began to shift my perspective and in some ways, finally, to see myself fully in the mirror. I made my decision to visit Germany slowly, at first begrudgingly, then ambivalently.

Although I recall no direct admonishment while growing up to avoid Germans, nothing to denigrate them as an entire population and culture, and although my Jewish Hungarian grandmother spoke fluent German and was purported to have been educated for at least a year in Austria, insidious forces must have created a clearing of sorts, fallow ground for prejudice to take root within me. Most of the Jewish side of my European relatives had already immigrated to the United States when the Nazis launched their vicious mission to establish an Aryan race and "cleanse" the world of Jews and millions of other so-called degenerates. The only story I remember about my own family may have been the first one I'd heard about anyone's plight with the Nazis. My mother sat down with me in the alcove loveseat in the powder blue bedroom she shared with my father. Perhaps I asked a question about something I'd heard about Nazis? Or about our family in Europe? Her answer, as it often did, took the form of a dramatic narrative. In a hushed voice she recounted the story of how, when my grandmother's cousin discovered that his two sons, a doctor and a lawyer, had been forced into concentration camps, he committed suicide. There seemed to be such accounts circulating in the air in those days, beginning less than a decade after the end of the war, when I was in elementary school and most of my close friends were, like me, the scions of Jewish immigrants. I recall the sorrowful, or grave, or outraged voices of their parents when they spoke of family members who were not so fortunate as to have escaped.

One day, when I was shopping with my mother in a prominent St. Louis department store, I watched the sales clerk fold the slips and blouses my mother had bought me (I imagine this dark-eyed lady now with wisps of gunmetal-gray hair and a plain dress hanging from her shoulders) and studied the way she smoothed out wrinkles I could not see. She just kept smoothing, as if feeling the softness of the material soothed her. I saw my mother's face pale, and I looked at her quizzically, but she just shook her head ever so slightly, as if she almost didn't want me to notice, so I turned my head to the trinkets at the next counter.

That evening my mother opened the sliding door to my bedroom and sat on my canopy bed. "Do you remember the lady who folded our clothes for us?" she said. Yes, I did. "Did you notice the lady's arm?" I shrugged. "Just under her sleeve?" I began to sense that I'd disappointed my mother but had no clue why. Why should I have noticed someone's arm? All I recall is that question, not her answer. But, of course, I know the answer now.

This later vision also haunts me. I must have been ten or eleven. Hosting one of their many parties, my parents were about to cap the evening by projecting pictures onto the screen—images of their kids and of many of the family and friends who had gathered in their living room that night. The adults occupied the chairs and the sofas, and I, an insomniac who'd ventured downstairs to join them, sat cross-legged on the floor. The room was lit only by an eerie shaft of moonlight slanting in through the undraped picture window and by the glow of the blank screen. While my mother provided witty commentary, we watched a succession of images of my sisters and me turning cartwheels, tucking dolls into wooden cradles, pirouetting in vibrant red and blue leotards, gaping open our baby mouths and clamping down on Gerber carrots and peas proffered on tiny spoons by our doting European-born grandmothers. And suddenly a grainy, gray-and-white image appeared on the screen. Before the image could clarify in my mind, before anything about it made sense, one of my parents—I don't remember which—shut off the projector. An abrupt click.

"What was that, Daddy?" I asked into the silence.

"A picture I shouldn't have shown," he said cryptically.

"Why not?"

"A picture kids shouldn't see," he added. Then he turned to Bertie. "Honey, I had no idea it was in there." His voice sounded hangdog, regretful. Even in the dark I could see his anguish.

Decades later, when I was an adult and he brought up from the basement a box of war pictures to show me, I thumbed through the random photographs, some labeled, some not. I was about to close the lid when a particularly grainy one caught my eye. I thought I recognized it. Piles of disfigured bodies in a dark building, as eerily lit as our living room that evening years before.

No matter what the source, for many years I'd been harboring a secret, even from myself—a prejudice. It made me squirm.

GERMANY
March 2, 1945 to July 7, 1945

CHAPTER 49
DEEP IN THE HEART OF GERMANY

Cross your fingers just once more—the last time.

THE NINTH ARMY has already charged across the Roer River, and casualties have again filled the unit's hospital beds and their idle time for more than a week before the 91st packs up once again to follow the front. As the other men pile into trucks, Bart squeezes into George's car next to a Jesuit chaplain who has asked for a ride.

From his cushioned seat Bart crosses the Roer and weaves through ghost town after ghost town, staring at the masses of rubble through a sheet of sleet and snow. They bore through woods shredded by shells and bullets, tanks still smoking, farmland dented by craters. He sniffs the stench of death in the air. In Viersen a sign reads "Viersen welcomes you—with Heil Hitler," but "Hitler" is crossed out and "Roosevelt" (in American-looking letters) written in.

Eight miles west of Mönchengladbach, a cluster of imposing buildings, bold crosses slashed with red paint on the roofs, looms up in front of them: Hostert, the former Franciscan monastery the Allies have taken over from the Nazis. Within these walls the colonel gives Bart a couple of bottles of Moselle, which he swears have been, somehow, snatched from Herman Goering's private cellars. Bart plans to ship them to Daddy Rich. He's warmed by the notion of Bertie's Czech Jewish father owning and drinking Goering's wine.

Bart works at Hostert for a week. When the lights blink out, he examines wounds by lantern. Many of his patients are civilians, who, as they returned home or walked to their bicycles, say, had their legs or arms blown off by the mines the Germans set to stall the Allied advance. As far as Bart knows, this stony building was, until their unit arrived, a legitimate psychiatric hospital. But, as whispered by people who should know, people who had suddenly lost wives and husbands and children—children especially—it was more than that. Whispers would eventually tell another story: that the Nazis had converted the warm building Bart was so grateful for into a center to implement their extensive euthanasia program to rid the Aryan race of its "lives unworthy of life." Perhaps Bart is treating patients in the same rooms where over 100 mentally disabled and severely physically handicapped children mysteriously died, at least thirty of whom were murdered with a deathly dose of luminal. Now, the bulk of Bart's cases are severe injuries from German mines scattered about the area, nearly every patient an enemy.

One day, when he feels he can leave the patients, he and George spend a day touring in the chaplain's car and come within two miles of the Adolph Hitler Bridge at the Rhine. Bart longs to walk to the river, to stride right up its banks and shake a fist at Hitler's gang across it, but he's wary of stray shells, and he turns away disappointed. On the drive back, they see a mile-long procession of Germans, carrying their possessions or hoisting them over their shoulders or on carts. He glares at their silk stockings, their full faces and blooming complexions, and conjures up images of the starving and skeletal, the naked and the dead. *Shameless,* he calls the Germans. *Shameless.* He would like to see their expressions when they reach their homes and find instead a mountain of rubble.

"Within days the skies are overcast with bombers, fighters, C-49s, gliders," he writes Bertie. "What a lovely sight, honey—I'm sorry you couldn't see it. It made me feel so good and glad we are so great and that we are Americans—and that we can do anything—even win this war for a birthday present to my wife." For now, though, he's ready to move across the Rhine, even if he has to swim.

A few days after the Rhine invasion is launched, the 91st pulls out of Hostert, passes through Mönchengladbach (Bart in the back of a truck flashing the Victory sign), and finally steps onto the planks of pontoon bridges that take them across the Rhine. They establish their hospital in tents not far from its banks, near Voerde, in a drizzly, open field. The March wind threatens to blow down the tents, his tent has no stove, blasts shake the canvas, and the almost constant cannon fire from all directions keeps him in the ward nearly all the time he's not trying to sleep.

In the daytime, mud slushes onto his ankles and soaks his socks. In the nighttime, he writes Bertie from a wicker chair he moved into his tent from an abandoned house in town. One particularly damp night, he tells her about the most recent rumor: that within ninety days after hostilities cease, the 91st will be sent home. Ninety days? *Ninety days??* "What does one do in those 90 days," he writes. "Take 9 grains of Nembutal every 3 days? Or stay drunk?"

The next morning it's still raining, and he feels a new sort of discontent descend. He gives himself a pep talk: "Roll up your bedding roll, Bart, and wear that goddam dish-pan called a helmet again. No wonder my hair has worn thin." But it doesn't work. Welch notices that something is awry, asks if he wants to shift to surgery full-time. But as appealing as that prospect is becoming, Bart is concerned that they're too short on officers in the wards now to spare him. He can't help obsessing about the loss of those ninety days, and about the fact that he's missed the pleasure of Anthony Bart's infancy. *Just one more reason for hating Germany and every one of its people,* he thinks. "Yes, I could kill and feel just as I would swatting a fly or a mosquito." But at least casualties are light, the news grand, and before long, the booming increasingly distant.

With the onset of April, the armored columns have enveloped many pockets, and nervous searchlights are stabbing the skies. When it's time to climb into trucks again, the 91st takes the superhighway to Bad Salzuflen, which would take them to Hanover and Berlin if they kept going. They're so close to Berlin, Bart comments, that they "can't move further east without taking a drink of vodka." They pass truckload after truckload of prisoners in enormous cages being shuffled back from the front and miles of refugees streaming westward. Along the road they encounter several Germans brandishing white flags and anxious to surrender, but the officers in charge just point west and refuse to take them. Bart either bores his eyes into theirs, these so-called super-people, or turns the other way. He can't stand to look at them.

During their week in the spa town of Bad Salzuflen, Bart and the
other doctors and nurses treat over 700 soldiers, and on the surface
at least, he finds it peaceful there. It's nestled at the foot of forested
mountains, the town's healing waters gleaming in streams through the
astoundingly undisturbed heart of the Reich, the countryside there
having been spared from bombers and tanks. Bart appreciates the
beauty—the wooded paths, the lake, the well-groomed park. The hospital is set up in a spacious modern recreation building. They're quartered in hotels and rooming houses near the hospital, and Bart's room
comes with a featherbed and down pillows. Finally he can wash his
hair and body, the last opportunity for ablutions having been ten days
earlier. He hopes he's seen the last of cold, muddy fields. This ward
even has a grand piano.

The news whips around the building that an armored column from
the Ninth Army is now across the Elbe, less than seventy miles from
Berlin and only 100 miles from the Russians. And rumors are flitting
about that the 91st will soon be with them in Berlin. He'd promised
Bertie the gift of the end of the war for her birthday, but this will have
to serve as compensation. And even though the roller coaster continues with the death of FDR the next day, the serenity and the comfortable living of Bad Salzuflen do their part to restore him—as much as
any German town can, he supposes. "It has been a long voyage—" he
writes, "but the next stop is the destination. Cross your fingers just
once more—the last time."

CHAPTER 50
WITNESSING

Dearest: Read this story.

IN THE DARK the 91st Evacuation Hospital Unit trundles down narrow roads toward the Elbe River, where another open field awaits them, this time about twenty miles from the front line. They pull in so late that not all the officers' quarters have been set up, and Bart beds down in an ambulance.

Soon it becomes clear that their camp lies in the heart of a small salient surrounded by Germans. Salvos blasting from all directions, they are sealed off, with no trucks to beat a hasty exit, no ambulances to deliver patients. The men joke nervously. One morning German jets dive down and strafe the road. They're close enough for Bart to see how straight the edges of the planes' black crosses are. Bart and his comrades are holding their breath until the Russians break through to Berlin.

Within days Red Army tanks are indeed rolling into Germany's capital. Mussolini's bullet-riddled body is hanging by the heels. Hitler's dead flesh is rising from flame to ash in the Reich chancellery garden. The Allies have dropped leaflets detailing directions for German planes to take and altitudes to adopt in order to surrender. Plane after plane noses down to taxi onto Allied airfields. In the meantime the combat—

the bullets, the blood, the oozing wounds, the smoke and fear—continues, and the patient load multiplies. Bart believes hordes of Germans are fighting to be delivered into the hands of the Americans and away from the Russians waiting for them on the other side of the Elbe.

More quickly, it seems, than the transition from one spring month to another, a breathtaking sequence of events is unfurling that topples the twelve-year span of Hitler's Thousand Year Reich. As Bart says, "Events of the past few days have been magnificent. They've appeared in such rapid succession that they are hardly completely digested. But there's something about our reactions toward them that amazes me. Curiously enough, we are not very impressed. I guess there's such a thing as waiting for something so long that when it comes it cannot dent the hardened shell that time has produced. These startling news flashes should have had us dancing rapturously with glee. But they didn't."

How can they summon jubilation when, as the smoke clears, they find themselves still fretting about the unknown, the what-will-happen-to-them-now? When will they go home? Will they work in a civilian hospital in Germany? Ship out to the Pacific, where the smoke from the kamikaze attacks is still blackening the air? Or will they remain imprisoned in this field?

And then. And then, only a handful of days later, he writes the letter he has been longing to write for unfathomable numbers of months: "May 8, 1945. Darling. I love you. This is 'it,' as they say in the movies. You may now let go of your chins. We knew that the war was over yesterday morning but official confirmation did not come until late in the afternoon when it was proclaimed that today would be considered V. E. Day. There was not much rejoicing here. It has come so piecemeal-like that the flavor was taken out. I gave away most of my liquor, in a wave of good-neighborliness, to some enlisted men. Aren't you proud of me, honey—I finally winned the war."

He wants to feel a lilt, a sense of momentum about the rumor that has just resurfaced—that the 91st will have the honor of marching into Berlin to work for the Second Armored Division. But all he can do is slo-mo through the ritual of packing his diaries, letters, and medical books to prepare, once again, to move. Somewhere. The damp cold bites through to his bones; his only recourse is to use his canteen as a foot-warmer.

But all this was not what was on our minds nearly seven decades later as Gary, our daughter Emily, and I in our rented Volkswagen passed the sign for Wiepke and swept down the road to Gardelegen.

In town we stopped for directions. Emily had flown from Seattle to Germany to join us on our final journey. She has become, since her grandfather's death eleven years before, a researcher in her own right, though the stuff of her conclusions manifests itself more in numbers than in narrative. Like her grandfather, she is in the business of health, but she investigates public health policy and services. It struck me that the materials I had been interrogating here might not yield anything at all recognizable to her as results.

Not a tourist destination, Gardelegen is small with cobblestone streets and a smattering of half-timbered hotels. We entered one of them with elegant German pastries displayed on glass racks in a tower shape and with tables covered in white linen. But it was almost empty, and the gloom outside seemed to be seeping inside. Gary addressed a woman behind the counter with a worn face and a demeanor of authority. She was patient, but impassive, her expression blank. In response to my question, she jotted down three words in a traditional German script on a slip of paper torn from a small notepad and handed it to Gary. I looked at her face again, this time noting the black-tinted hair that puffed out softly, the handsome face that made her look younger than she likely was. What were she and her family doing the night of April 13, 1945, I wondered? When she glanced at the tower of pastries as if to signal that she needed to get back to work, Gary turned to leave, but I tugged on his sleeve. "Tell her more," I said. "Tell her my father was here during the war. Tell her he was an American doctor."

As Gary grappled with German (I recognized *Vater, Frau, hier während des Krieges, Arzt),* she looked toward me and nodded slowly. I suddenly heard myself saying, the words tumbling from my mouth, "Tell her that my father healed both Americans and Germans," and I caught her quizzical glance at me, as if she had understood the words in English. When he translated, she turned toward me, and the weight of the prejudice I had borne for so much of my life came rushing into my head, swirled around, and as I saw myself extending my hand and she took it and then held it a second or two, it lifted.

We were quiet as we drove toward the sign for *Mahn und Gedenkstatten*: the three words on the notepad. When we saw it and stopped, we got out of the car slowly, without speaking. We were already under the spell of what we knew we would see, and we found ourselves alone. This was the place that had enabled Bart and the other witnesses to crack the seal of censorship. This was the place where scores of stunned soldiers and doctors and officers wrote hundreds of dark words home to find their way to light. This was the place that would bring back that grainy slide.

The memorial was not enclosed, and even though a spit of rain fell on us in a cold field, I felt like I was entering a godforsaken chapel. We each drifted into our own meditations, where the sacred and the profane whirled together in the blasts of air flogging the clouds into sullied streaks. I felt I should be hearing in the gusts the howls of the dead. We followed the cement block path, where a procession of photographs with text in German told the story my father left us in words on paper, and where a bronze sculpture of a man so emaciated we could count his ribs stood erect, one hand opened, the other clasped into a fist, looking both imploring and resilient. The brick grain barn remained, but only in remnants—a rectangle of floor, a chunk of foundation, half a wall—as fragmented as details in letters and diaries, as fragmented as memories. A spray of blooms wilted over the low wall that framed the site where the grain barn used to be. Beyond a brick arch, once part of the wall of the original barn, the connected triangles of a contemporary steel statue rose into the air; a teddy bear holding a toy wooden boat sat in the crook of its base. Everything else out that archway seemed incongruous—twenty-first-century Germany with its electric-powered windmills, its young green trees, the whoosh of the cars along the autobahn.

Emily swiveled and headed toward the cemetery. We followed her through rows of white crosses, a few stars of David. She snapped pictures. Over an hour or more, we noted and in one way or another took in innumerable details in fragments—towheaded boys from the Hitler Youth Program shouldering machine guns, yellow and red triangles stitched to prison uniforms, mass graves. They were manifest as sketches in the cerebral cortex; in a chill from the volatile air; in words that leapt to meaning on a sign written in German; in the pattern of the bricks of the barn door arch; and in the photograph that reminded us of the single one Bart brought back and preserved—the black-and-white with the eerie light, the one in my hands now. We were doing what Bart did: though we could never be so close that the foul smoke from what happened here wafted into our nostrils, we were still witnessing.

Leaving Gardelegen, over the drone of the motor and the thumping of tires over ruts, I read out loud the words Bart penned in a pyramidal tent while the three-quarters moon shrouded the clouds over the fields we'd just left, the words that offered us all we had of his presence there. "Dearest: Read this story," he begins.

> About a month or so ago about 2,000 prisoners from the Eastern front including Poles, Hungarians, Jews, and Russians were marched toward Hanover. These prisoners knew not why they were prisoners. Some were in politics—some were just dispossessed. Anyway, only but about half of them got near Hanover. Last week the guards of this herd found Hanover taken by the Yanks so they herded the flock into Gardelegen. Last Friday night (April 13) these prisoners were jammed into a big barn just outside of Gardelegen—

Here my voice halted, choked, I knew what was coming. I waited before continuing.

> —a big barn in which inflammable material and straw covered the flooring thickly and there they (all 800–1000) were cremated <u>alive</u>. The first attempt at igniting the flooring was unsuccessful but later the Wehrmacht threw in burning oil and phosphorus grenades and the thing shot up in flames. About 50 made a break for it and all 50 were mowed down with machine guns. Do you believe it? It's hard to believe it, I know. It's not human, is it?
>
> Well, darling, do believe it, for today I saw hundreds of burnt, charred bodies, lying two to three deep—skulls burnt open, long bones eaten by flames—bodies in horribly grotesque positions—faces burnt open, guts dried—some bodies lying pitifully near air holes—horrible expressions on mummy-like faces where they were still vaguely recognizable—and some of the bodies were still smoldering. I saw it, darling—it made me nauseated. It sickened me mentally and physically. The stench was horrible. And I think General Simpson is right. He opened the gates of censorship. We are able to take pictures, name the town, say what we saw and keep writing and saying it to those back home. God—what a horrible thing. I took some pictures but I was glad to get away. I walked in a dream. How could a thing like that be pos-

sible. Yet there it was—in 1945. When the Yanks broke through two days ago, they found them. A few were alive, were hospitalized and the story was known.

My trip to Gardelegen was a very short one—every German has his white flag out—and is smiling and waving these days. But how incongruous such a show of humanity is with what I saw today.

I long to come home. I had enough, darling. I want to bury my head in your lap forever.

CHAPTER 51

THE FRAGRANCE OF ROSES

The war is still over, and I'm still here.

BART'S SOJOURN in Wolfenbüttel might best be described in binaries. As lovely as the town is with its velvety, shaded lawns and three-story houses, notwithstanding the plush armchairs, the paintings and fine fabric drapes, Bart's frustration spikes and threatens to spin out of control. He's ashamed to be paid for this easy living, and this dreadful waiting is agony. *Agony.* There's no useful work to do, and though the war is over and freedom has won, he feels as if he's in prison and will go mad if he doesn't see Bertie soon. The promise of marching into Berlin is still being dangled like a carrot on a wobbly stick. Now that they're part of the Second Armored Division, the 91st officers have been told that, in a week or two, they'll be given the honor of parading with that division into Berlin. He can just see it, gleaming like a prize. And yet. They've seen that dangling carrot before. Then there's the shadow settling over the unit that they might be ordered to the Pacific now that the war in Europe is over.

It may be that his frustration with the American Army has exacerbated his rancor at the German people. But most likely what has toppled him over the ledge from rancor into hate is Gardelegen. When he looks around him, when he sips wine from cut crystal and sinks into upholstered chairs, all untouched by war, all he can see in his mind is a mound of charred bodies. It's all he can do to summon his humor and ask Bertie to send that chin suspensory they've been joking about for years. He also tells her that he's read in the *Stars and Stripes* that "eggs in U.S. are getting scarce. The last straw. I die. I shall poison myself."

But during the long hours when he cannot summon that humor, the bile rises from his stomach to his throat and he can feel the bitterness as if it were churning throughout his body. The first anniversary of their landing on Normandy, D-Day+4, June 10, is especially painful. As proud as he was of the unit that day, he resents the Army. Why would they not be told what will happen to them now? Why would they have a month or two of duty after all this?—after the minutes and hours and days of their lives they have already given freely?

A darkness permeates his letters, especially when he mentions the German people. This particular shade of black has been deepening since his last weeks in Holland, or even before. In Valkenburg, one of his patients was a German radio operator, shot down New Year's Eve, and although the doctors of the 91st treated the Germans well medically, they tacitly agreed not to speak with them. Perhaps it was because this soldier spoke such educated English that Bart, while evaluating his wound, found himself pulled into conversation with him. Relating this encounter to Bertie, he admits, "I could have slapped to death a 16-year-old P. O. W. yesterday." The soldier told him that if he had a chance to escape and resume his fight for the Fatherland, he would do so. Bart just shook his head, kept his eye on the seared flesh, which zigzagged up the soldier's thigh, and opened another box of gauze bandages. The soldier—*a boy,* Bart reminded himself—droned on, his chin stiff, his shoulders back in pretentious Wehrmacht fashion, his tone suave, self-satisfied. The pubescent waver in his voice betrayed his military hero veneer and made it look ridiculous. Bart blushed with fury.

"We promise a long war for you, for all of you Americans," the boy-soldier retorted, spitting out the word "Americans" through teeth clenched against his pain. "And in England and Russia," he managed to articulate, then added, "You must expect many surprises." *Brainwashed,* Bart thought, reaching for a packet of safety pins. *Propaganda-fed.* "Will I be sent to America?" the soldier asked, and sounded—yes, Bart was sure—hopeful. As the doctor finished in silence, securing the bandage and scanning the wound site one final time, the soldier asked again, more emphatically, "Will I be sent to America?"

Bart felt like vomiting. Said nothing. He looked hard at his young patient's face. "No, my friend," he said finally. "You will be sent to Russia." The soldier blanched. That night Bart confessed to Bertie: "I sometimes wish I was not a doctor so that I could kill some vermin like him. It takes a strong will to keep from accidentally spilling a little cyanide in his wounds. But a doctor is a doctor. You didn't know you owned such a blood thirsty husband."

In a letter written two days before Bart entered Germany, he describes with something akin to wrath the sorry lot of sad-sack POWs then streaming in: "How I hate them—but medicine is medicine. One can't be affable to the dirty bastards. Many are kids and elderly men— but we're not fooled for a moment. They are Germans. Although I do the best I can for them, I secretly hope that they die. I'm sorry if you think me cruel and hard—but the German people should be totally destroyed, I think. They've messed up so many lives that any compassion I've ever had for them went by the roadside a long time ago."

If they'd given up shortly after D-Day it might have been a different story, he thinks.

Now, in pleasant, peaceful Wolfenbüttel, after the bachelor-button blue skies have been freed of drones and streaks of flame and orange pillars of smoke, he finds out that he can't buy photographic supplies "because the Germans need to get back on their feet." "It's a good thing I brought along my portable emesis basin," he tells Bertie. He's heard that one of the effects of the war for Germany will be starvation. "Yes, it is humanly sad," he says, "yet they asked for it, and no greater justice and punishment could be consciously meted out to them." And this: "The people who were dispossessed from these residences have filtered in to look after their beautiful gardens and plants. I don't blame them. Still I won't have them indoors even if the house does belong to them. These people were all 'members of the party'—Now they play the tune 'we were forced into it.' They have fear of the Americans, still—and that is borne of a guilty conscience. So I don't have pity for any of the bastards—whether they are old men, old women or kids. After all—they did condone Gardelegen and other crematories—directly or indirectly. They are strictly no good. They should all be killed off."

But in spite of his vitriol he finds himself asking a gardener if he can buy some of his radishes, lettuce, strawberries.

One of the nurses has presented him with what just might be a stopgap salvation to the hell he's been cast into: a small oil painting set, which she bought for him on her leave. Although he's had no experience with oils, no knowledge of how to mix the colors or what to put on the paper first, he's eager to try it out. He sits before an oil painting on the wall and spends an entire morning reproducing it. If he only had more canvas. He looks forward to painting in Berlin.

He hears that one organization after another outside his division is being granted leave, and knows that four or five of the enlisted men are going home every two weeks, but the officers of the 91st are passed over each time. The medical officers, it seems, have the curse of being "essential." *Essential for what?* he wonders. They still have a month or two of duty, yet they know nothing.

To rid himself of excess energy, he pounds out chords on the piano, even composes a melody or two for folks who bring him lyrics they've tried their hand at. At the Second Armored dance in town—champagne, sandwiches, music—he meets Marlene Dietrich. She's in Germany looking for her mother in Berlin. She has donned a borrowed nurse's uniform for the occasion (he suspects to show off her legs). She looks bored just sitting at that table with cigar-puffing generals surrounding her, and Bart asks her to dance. Although she ever so gently declines, he thrills to her gravelly voice. If only it could have been Bertie's.

And Bertie. *Bertie.* He has written her several scenarios about their reunion, which he fantasizes about every hour: "As soon as I hit the states I shall make a bee-line for a railroad station or airport. What I may do is to meet you in town—alone, perhaps take a room in a hotel so that I can have you all to myself first—how's that. We'll arrange later." But to his astonishment, he is having to negotiate with her about their reunion—New York? St. Louis? Alone? Or with the hordes of family? He'd much rather, though he knows it would be underhanded, meet her somewhere where it's quiet, and near St. Louis, without letting a soul know anything about it. "I'm going to take you dancing," he promises, "just you and me. You with flowers in your beautiful black hair. I shall stare at you and make love to you. I shall thrill at holding your hand."

Orders change daily, it seems, sometimes hourly—they are to move, they are to wait, they are to go to Berlin, to someplace else, to Berlin! He packs. He unpacks. And then suddenly, no, they are to move to one more goddamned field. The final order is to wait a few days—then travel to an assembly point for possible redeployment. He packs one more time.

The day before he finally heads out, he mails Bertie his diaries—first class. He's surprised to find himself delighting in the sight of the cherry tree overhanging his balcony, which is beginning to give color to its fruit, and in the fragrance of roses wafting up from the garden.

OUR VW NOSED through curtains of dust to Wolfenbüttel, just south of Braunschweig. In town Gary, Emily, and I strolled past the clock tower of the baroque castle reaching into the pastel-blue sky. I could only imagine that it looked very much the same as it did in 1945. We wandered about aimlessly on foot and then drove around in wider and wider circles, getting lost, and finding nothing recognizable. Our frustration was only a dim reflection of the frustration Bart felt here, having arrived six days after the war in Europe was concluded, when he did nothing, it seems, but dawdle and fritter away time.

We were searching for the six spacious residences the Army commandeered for the officers, Bart says from the Nazis, though I suspected not all people the Allies dislocated were Nazis. The curving cobblestone streets eventually led us to an inviting-looking gallery, where paintings of voluptuous blooms in splashes of carmine and cyan adorned austere brick walls, and a woman, radiant with artsy earrings peeking out from her silvery hair, greeted us with a smile. She scanned the details in our photographs, she listened attentively to our quotes from Bart's letters, and, in perfect English, she directed us toward several streets on which the houses we were longing to see might still be located. I dashed down her name and email address on a scrap of paper I dug out of my purse.

On the road again, as we swung around block after block and squinted at three-story houses and wrought-iron fences that just might be those pictured in Bart's photos and words, our frustration mounted. We found elements of what we were looking for, but all in fragments, all in separate buildings. We even saw cherry trees, but they looked more like saplings than decades-old trees.

We were disheartened. We had driven a long way, over several years really, and I could feel my expectations shifting. In my head I sifted and sorted. Was there evidence that the house in the photo we'd brought with us was one Bart actually ever entered? I knew I couldn't fight the invincible armies of time—its new buildings, the life cycles of its peoples and plants, its ideas changed a hundred times over in so many years. I reminded myself to focus—to focus on what we *could* do. We could imagine, for one thing. Although we did not find the house he'd lived in for those seven weeks, we could imagine the sitting room he'd claimed as his own with its piano and paintings. Although it was now autumn when we arrived, we could imagine the perfumed rose gardens. And like Bart, I could write down these imaginings and let the details tumble down to the next generations willy-nilly and make what difference they would.

I did not know it then, but my journey to Wolfenbüttel would not conclude until three months later. It wasn't until I was sitting in my office in Idaho that I got a glimpse of that house from another country and another time. My email gave me the image I'd been searching for. The message was a gift—from Inge, the woman from the art gallery. It included a photograph of the house we could not find—and a Google Earth site, which showed quite clearly the house next to the one we were searching for, a house with a balcony that would have provided Bart all the sun he longed for, and over which, surely, arched the branch of a cherry tree.

As we drove away from Wolfenbüttel, there was a sense of an almost palpable letdown. We'd been less successful this time, and I sensed a wariness creeping into this part of our journey. I said, mostly to Emily, who was new to this quest, "I always have a feeling that I'm looking for someone important. I've looked all over, and the metaphor that keeps coming back to me is two park benches, back to back, facing opposite directions. I sit on one side of the park bench and look straight ahead and to the side, but I can't find the person I am longing to see. On the other side of that bench, however, facing the other way, that other person is sitting, just staring ahead, and I walk away and never know it."

Emily's voice rang out from the front seat: "Mom," she began in her no-nonsense tone, "you have the whole story right in front of you.

You don't need in the twenty-first century to find the same field or the same house, you have pictures and diaries and letters. The story is sitting across from you on your park bench. You just have to see it for what it is." After her voice trailed off, another voice whispered inside my skull, reciting for me these words from T. S. Eliot: "We shall not cease from exploration, and the end of all our exploring will be to arrive where we started and know the place for the first time." I wondered if that knowing might bound over time, even leap over generations. I began to believe that it just might.

CHAPTER 52
THE JOURNEY BACK

I finished my painting. It's my best.

FROM WOLFENBÜTTEL BART rides in the bed of a truck for over 100 miles through the Harz mountains to spend the final days of the long wait to be admitted to Berlin—in yet another field. It's a soggy field at that, one about a mile and a half from the hamlet of Geilshausen. Instead of setting up a hospital, Bart and a few of the boys set up a volleyball net. He discovers that his air mattress leaks and the food tastes bad and is parsimoniously offered. "To begin with we are still out in the sticks, next door to no man's land. No news no love and lots of no nothin'. Most of all we have no mail. And still we are miles and miles from another American camp. I think we are definitely forgotten." They feel not only isolated but stranded. No one, not even the CO, knows what's going on.

Bart senses that there is a tense competition between their Second Armored Division and the Seventh Army about which one wins the ticket to enter Berlin. But in the last month or so he has given up thoughts of Berlin. The only thing important is going home.

All he seems to be able to do is obsess about the reunion he will have with Bertie, and, now that they're so close to being together, he's even more nervous than he was before. He wonders how they will manage to see each other alone before they're inundated with family, wonders if his parents—and hers—will forgive them if they lock themselves in a hotel room for a day. And God, how he wants to keep that door locked for more than a day, wants that time to last hundreds of thousands of days before he tells them he's home. Bertie and he have been negotiating all this in a spate of uncharacteristically tense and disturbing letters, and he's worried that he has said something wrong. He can't stand that, can't blot it out of memory. Bart arms himself with his oil paints, the only way he can think to distract himself. He borrows a hammer and saw and builds himself an easel. Easel, paints, and brushes under his arm, he strides from their camp in the field into the village.

NEARLY SEVENTY YEARS LATER, when we spiraled down into Geilshausen, I felt like I'd already seen it. I'd been staring at a photograph of the final painting Bart made overseas. We hoped the village was still small enough that we would be led by some benign force to the square in the painting with its single tree shading the church doors, with its four houses on the side, one seeming to overlap the next, dominoes style. Since the name "Geilshausen" appeared neither on our home atlas nor on our Michelin driving map, and we'd located it only by zooming far down into the minutiae of images on Google maps, I couldn't help feeling that this last stop was a Brigadoon of sorts and that those who live there appear to intruders like us only once every 100 years.

We kept driving, mechanically following the hollow voice of the GPS, boring deeper toward a site with no significance in the war, a spot just close enough to a bivouac for troops waiting to be somewhere else as soon as possible. Yet I felt a compulsion to be there largely because of the painting. For Bart, that painting, in the absence of their being allowed to march into Berlin, was his solace. We took solace in the notion that Geilshausen must certainly have a café so that we could sit outside on this mild autumn day and toast Bart's first original oil painting, by which he witnessed, and memorialized, and perhaps came to terms with the conclusion of his journey.

But when we parked the car at our journey's end, there appeared not to be a soul to witness our advent; the entire town seemed emptied out. The café I'd envisioned did indeed exist, and afforded the perfect view of the square as depicted in the painting, but the café was closed. There were four houses in the square as in the painting (though they were painted in more lively colors than Bart rendered them in), and all the window shades were down. Even the grocery store was closed. All we heard were sporadic cars zooming out of town on the narrow highway that separates the café from the square.

We meandered around the Kirkenplatz, trying to see what Bart saw, as we had done in five countries now. Gary was skeptical that this was actually the place—the tree was so tall and leafed out that it obscured the church tower, the church and attached buildings so clearly renovated, the newer buildings almost jarring, the angle from Bart's perspective so seemingly off-kilter and elusive.

We spread out: he crossed the highway, and I followed the circle of street behind the church in search of older people, people who might have seen the odd American doctor with his easel and palette and brushes, applying color to canvas in the church square in the weeks after the war. At first all the doors and windows in the semi-circular row of houses behind the church looked like vacant squares and rectangles, but then I noticed the one open door and the man standing at the entrance, peering inside. I took stock of him. Maybe just old enough, but hard to tell. As I approached, I saw that he was talking with a man sitting on a chair at a table in a room. His hair was gray, his face was webbed with wrinkles, his voice, even in German, seemed aged.

"Excuse me," Gary said in German when he reached the doorway. The men looked dumbfounded to see us there.

They both stepped outside onto the sidewalk and asked us in German, "How did you find Geilshausen?"

"GPS," Gary responded. Everyone nodded.

They seemed eager, even excited, to help these strange Americans who had invaded their ghost town. The older man ran up some neighboring steps and returned with a slightly hunched-over woman he introduced as his wife. All three of them had kind faces. Gary spoke with them in halting German; they spoke no English, and communication was taxing. Although Gary had forgotten the word for "painting" (*Really?* I thought, *Really?*), he opened his laptop and showed them Bart's work. They huddled around it, they pointed, they nodded and admired. They confirmed that this was indeed the place in the painting, the very same square. The older couple, the Schombars, were in town during the war, but did not recall the doctor-painter, and soon they shook our hands and headed back inside.

The younger man, Herr Bühmer, in an LL Bean-like khaki vest and baseball cap, lingered. When I asked my pressing question, he told us he was born in 1945. My shoulders went slack with disappointment: too young to remember the American. I was about to say good-bye when he beckoned us around the buildings. I glanced at Gary, and, shrugging in tandem, we followed his long strides past three of the houses in the painting, and we had just reached the fourth, the one that is in the foreground (though the color is no longer dingy gray but startling white and there are windows adorned in pink blooms and lace curtains) when our guide stopped. He pointed animatedly at the house, looked back to see if I was paying attention, and what he said made Gary snap his head in my direction. "This is my house," the man said, pointing. "I was born here. I live here now. *Ja?*" A smile.

What he said washed me in a wistful pleasure. I could almost see Bart looking toward where Gary, Herr Bühmer, and I stood now, dabbing azures and ambers, rusts and saffrons, and tree-leaf greens onto canvas and brushing them together to create new shades and tints. "I finished my painting. It's my best," his words from the last letter he would write Bertie echoed back. And as I pictured him painting the houses I was now staring at, I imagined a sound that soothed him, blotting out almost all else that troubled him—the happy babbling of a baby.

WHEN BART REACHES the outskirts of Geilshausen, he sees an old woman, and he turns away, tries to concentrate on the scene he will paint. Now that the war has been won, fraternizing with the Germans is a punishable offense. Offering a cigarette to a civilian costs $365, love-making (with proper evidence) can cost a soldier his life, he's told Bertie. "And that, darling, is as it should be." He's determined not to have anything to do with the enemy. But as soon as he can see the tower from the distance, children come skipping toward him. They follow him, nearly stepping on his ankles, and he finds it difficult to keep ignoring them. He doesn't want to play the Pied Piper, doesn't want to let his hollowness be filled with anything but Bertie. When he sets his easel down, they jump up and down and speak in that strange, spirited guttural. When he returns the next day, they are starting to look familiar. When he returns the third day, he expects them to be there.

"I'm a sucker about kids," he writes that evening as he listens to the swish and patter of the rain on his tent. "I hate the Germans—hate them because beneath that easy-going love-of-life surface, they carry a malignant growth of love of dominance, which is refractory to any treatment—and it always will be. Yet here I am letting these same German kids grin at me, climb over my legs and pull at my arms because they want affection and want to play."

He spends the rainless chunks of seven days applying pigment to canvas and creating something from nothing, a vision of peace from a whitewashed slab. And little by little, minute by minute, from a town populated by a nation he has learned to hate, he returns. I say "returns" because my mind swings back to all he saw, to all he heard and smelled: on the beaches and in the countryside of France, in the Netherlands and during the Battle of the Bulge—torsos with shards of skin where the legs should be, intestines drooping down the hips, faces without jaws or noses or eyes. And to Gardelegen, and to *after* Gardelegen, when he seems to have been swallowed by a place so cavernous and opaque that his wife might never have been able to find him. He *needs* to return.

The children of Geilshausen swarm around him. Little girls, mouths in little O's, spread their fingers over his palette. Little boys inch up close to his jaw and stare up curiously at his dark eyes and black hair. Perhaps it is at this moment, in this church square in the heart of Germany, that the first step in the journey of his return takes place. The journey back, most profoundly, to compassion, to humanity. And when later that day a child races up to yank the sleeve of his jacket and pull him toward a man who manages to cross the borders of language to tell him that his wife has fallen off a wagon and needs a doctor, Bart hurries to help.

THE FINAL FIELD, THE TWENTY-FIRST CENTURY

I think this is it.

GARY, EMILY, AND I find ourselves in the final field, the last we will search for in what already seems in danger of becoming a blurry series of indistinguishable fields. It is fitting that the discovery of the final field belong to Bart's granddaughter.

Our little VW has backtracked over the same road several times already. Everywhere, cornstalks stretch higher than my head. Electronic windmills line the horizon behind us. The corn and the windmills do not, of course, appear in the letters or diaries or photographs (which my researcher-daughter is now calling "data"). They block my vision and distract me from seeing this landscape through the lens of knowledge and experience: I *know* I have not been entirely successful in precisely identifying every field; I *know* I have let some of that compulsion for precision go. And now, in this landscape of fields fusing into fields, none of us has the same vision of what would have changed—and in what way—over nearly seven decades. We find helter-skelter fragments of the images the photographs and words have proffered: rolling hills, copses of trees, low buildings with flat roofs. We spy churches, a steeple, but these are not visible in the pictures we've brought with us, don't have a place in our fabricated scheme.

We pull over to explore on foot, quibble a bit about what might have been what. Tough business, this stab at seeing the past and present at the same time. Gary swerves off to scope out the other direction. Suddenly Emily darts ahead, camera in her fist, then angles left and sprints across the highway. I don't try to catch her but instead let her do the work of this part of our quest, and watch. Her legs pump over ruts and ditches. She pauses to reconnoiter, to take in the lines and curves of earth. She leaps and bounds, sometimes extending her arm in some code I'm not privy to, photographs and words and phrases and passages and entire letters and diaries all cradled in her brain. Now, literally on the same path, I suddenly see Bart in her—his sense of adventure, his loyalty to and love for family, his passion for music, his commitment to helping people, and his intolerance of the uncalled for and the unjust.

The sun has come out. I'm squinting at my backlit daughter scrambling up a boulder to get a sharper view of the hills and valleys. I imagine her considering the houses—houses with flat roofs that may very well be a renovated version of those in the photo. And beeches, which her grandfather has told us rimmed the field.

I know that millions of details from Bart's memory are missing, irretrievable, impossible to pass on. But for a moment I marvel at our rather slapdash research, the sort that yields more speculation than statistics, more fantasy than fact. The sort with the power to dispel our regrets and quell our longing. The sort that cannot, of course, resurrect a life, but that can, if we're lucky, create something new.

It is in watching Emily as she scours the earth to identify that final field, as I have done on other fields, that I witness what I now know is what I have traveled across the ocean to find. Never mind the misfiring synapses, the impossibility of precision, the isolation of the double helix, and the fact that we cannot pass on memory in our DNA. We have encoded Bart's memories, and with greater magnitude than the words and photographs he left us could alone have afforded us. And although we have transformed his memories, as every generation transforms those of its forebears, they are—and we have become—no less part of his immortal story.

Emily runs toward her expectant parents, and I open my arms for her. "I think this is it," she declares, a bit breathless, her voice vibrant. Her thinking so, I think, makes it so. Her thinking so, I *believe*, makes it so. And "so" or not, finally the decision is hers. I feel a weight lift.

The burden of memory fans out and up into the atmosphere, lingers an instant, and leaves.

Just before midnight on my last night overseas, I stepped outside into that clarified autumn air, and instead of focusing my sight on a field, or a city, or a hospital, or a grave, I looked up. I'd like to say I saw it in its entirety—that glowing band of the Milky Way, that collective light of hundreds of billions of stars arcing across the sky. But although I could see stars, and I could imagine the arch and the stardust, the only recognizable body was the moon. The same moon that Bart's steadfast artist's eye observed in its fluctuating faces: the ripening moon exposing the deck of the SS *Argentina* steaming toward Casablanca; the moon blasting the sky on a furnace-hot night in Algeria; the deep-orange moon gilding the water and silhouetting the ready ships in Tunisia; the waning full moon sneaking over the Sicilian mountain peaks as he drove away from the huts of his enemy-family; the half-moon illuminating his way to his quarters in a London blackout; the new moon signaling a temporary lull in the relentless flashes from explosions near Utah Beach; the full moons he began to count in Holland to track the months before he could see his beloved again; the three-quarters moon shrouded in clouds over Gardelegen as the lingering stench of smoldering skin made him strain to forget. And then I looked *beyond* up, to the invisible we know is there: the spiral of the double helix, perhaps, the spiral of the Milky Way.

CHAPTER 54

RESTORATION

I know when I've had enough.

IT IS STILL SUMMER 1945, and although the war in Europe has been won, the battle for the future is not quite over. Bertie is startled awake, and it takes her a few seconds to figure out why. The fan in the room she's been occupying in her parents' two-story brick house on De Giverville is whirring away, the gummy mid-June air already causing the sweat to bead on Bertie's nose. Suddenly she sits up in bed, stares beyond the fan, beyond the undulating, filmy curtains, at the sun, and begins to make plans.

By the time she's dressed and walks down the stairs into the dining room, Rosie is waiting for her. "Bart's coming home," Bertie announces. Rosie jumps up from her breakfast. She cannot wait until he returns so he can accompany her on the piano when she sings arias for him and can tell her again how much he loves her voice.

Bertie walks into the hall, picks up the receiver, and dials. Her mother hears her talking from the kitchen and comes out into the hall, wiping her hands on her cross-stitched apron, waits until Bertie hangs up, and lays the back of her still-damp hand on Bertie's forehead. She has heard enough to be confused.

"Is everything all right?" she asks. "You don't have to rent an apartment. Why can't you stay here, with us, as long as you need to?" It's more an assertion than a question.

"Bart and I are going to need our own apartment," Bertie says.

"Oh *mein Gott!*" Lena's hand flies to her heart. "Bart coming home! When did you get the letter?"

"I haven't gotten a letter in a long time," Bertie says. Lena's forehead wrinkles. "But I know he's coming home."

BART HAS FOLLOWED what scant moonlight there is back to camp from a party and wonders how late it is. He weaves back toward the tents, but Ed Hyde stops him before he can find his. He grips Bart's shoulder. "Good news," he says. And then confusion clouds Bart's brain and he thinks he hears that a decision has filtered down. Five or six from the outfit have been chosen to go home. He is to pack his bags to leave early the following morning for Paris. They'll take a plane from there. He vaguely wonders if this isn't a whiskey-induced illusion. But his mind has already snapped into gear, and he scrambles to throw everything together, dresses in officers' blouse and tie, settles his peaked cap jaunty on his head, then, heart still racing past dawn, waits for the truck.

His letters of late have been freighted with frustration and angst. A few days before, on the first day of the third consecutive July he's been separated from Bertie, he wrote that he was at a crossroads and longed for her guidance. "Did you ever want something <u>now</u>—come what may? Did you ever minimize the consequences—the price of a bit of happiness? Did you ever want something now even though you were sure to have it later?" He used outline form to make sure he was articulating the various options clearly, so both of them would understand. If he transferred to the 97th Evacuation Hospital Unit and stayed in Europe as part of the occupation, he would certainly be sent home for good—but not until after six months to a year. If he took a month's leave soon, there was a good chance he would be sent afterward to the Pacific.

On July 10, Bertie scribbles him a letter. "I love you so hard, it hurts. I love you so much, so terribly much, that I almost wish I didn't. Tomorrow I move into our apartment to wait for you. I hope so hard—

that we will be together there but if we aren't, it will be enough that you are safe and alive and will eventually come back to me." Every time she hears a noise, she runs to the door, thinking it's Bart. Even though it never is, she's happy enough that it's possible.

But a few days before she mails her letter, he has already made a decision, without her guidance.

"I know when I've had enough," he writes before he hears from her. "I've 'had it up to here,' sweetheart. I've got to see you <u>now</u> or go mad. I'm not writing again until I make up my mind—then I'm burning my bridges, come what may—" He holds off sending the letter for two days, then, around midnight, scrawls a postscript: "I'm gambling on coming home. Signing yes. I love you. See you soon." And by the time she mails her letter, he's already on his way.

In Paris he jumps out of the truck only to wait for days at a replacement depot—a "repple depple," the men call it—a dreary building with haphazard French posters. On one of the interminable days there, he sends her a telegram, a coded message—"BUY HOTEL AT BEST PRICE WITHOUT DELAY HAVE ACTED AS YOU REQUESTED MANY HAPPY RETURNS." He knows she will read each word carefully before she reads between them. But his cable gets lost in the thousands that servicemen and women are sending to herald their reunions, and Bertie does not receive it for weeks.

It's July 14—Bastille Day, he notes—by the time he boards the Blue Flight, that ugly plane used mainly for storage that would carry him and the others with its cargo, as did the SS *Argentina* those years ago, over the ocean for the last time. Bart is impatient as it touches down in the Azores and again in Newfoundland, before it finally lands in Wilmington, but then he and the others are herded into a camp, where he paces around and tries not to count every minute. When he's finally given permission to leave, he's assigned to a train to Chicago. He can feel his pulse race, wondering how long it will take the Army to figure out that Chicago is 300 miles from St. Louis. He knows he'll have to wait for godknows how long for *another* train, from there to St. Louis. While the Chicago-bound train chugs across Pennsylvania, he devises a plan.

Before the engine has fully stopped in Pittsburgh, he throws his bags out of the car and clambers down the steps, then strides, chest out, toward the MPs guarding the tracks. As he approaches the three of them, they eye him suspiciously. He faces them squarely, his Majors leaves on both shoulders front and center, and nods. They form a semi-circle around him.

"This is a mistake," Bart explains. "I was told to get on the wrong train, I'm afraid. I didn't find out until it pulled out of the station that this train doesn't go on to St. Louis, and my orders are for the Army base at Jefferson Barracks." This is only part a lie. Those *are* his orders—but not until his leave ends. When they look at him skeptically, he adds, "I have an assignment." And now that he's embarked on this fabrication, he embellishes, keeps talking and double-talking, and finally one of the guards says, "Understood. Good luck, Major," then salutes. Before they can change their minds, Bart sweeps up his bags and dashes into the station to buy a ticket home.

But as he stares at the slow clock while waiting for the train to St. Louis, a man about the age of his father appears as if from nowhere. He pats Bart just above the elbow, wants to know about his boy. He hasn't heard from his boy, who has been overseas a very long time now. Does Bart know him? As he slowly describes him, Bart tries to listen, ridiculous as Bart knows this is—there must be two million boys overseas. He recalls his own father, wondering about *him* during all these months of terror and silence.

Then Bart looks up and sees that a train is moving at the right gate, but it's moving backward. "Hey," he shouts, grabbing his bags and running toward it. "Hey!" It gathers speed and disappears into the outside world. Bart swears at himself.

It is morning when his train finally pulls into St. Louis. He shoulders his way through an ocean of people, many in uniform, pushing their way to the doors. Outside Union Station the light is hazed by humidity, but Bart hardly notices. He walks swiftly past Milles's fountain—the Wedding of the Waters, the Mississippi and Missouri in the form of bronze nudes, a man gliding toward a woman—and runs out into the street to hail a cab.

Gazing out the window and feeling the steamy breeze on his face, he passes his old life, the streets and the brick houses, and, oh, the trees—the silver maples and oaks, the hickories and elms, the scallops and star-points of their achingly green leaves. Then, from a distance, he spies the St. Regis apartment building. It is on Lindell, across from Forest Park and the waterfall where he and Bertie first kissed so many lifetimes ago. He sees its stone railings, its bay windows, and squints for a silhouette of her in a window. He pays the driver, doesn't wait for change. He grabs his bags and sprints out the car, takes the steps two at a time, all the way up. When he arrives at the door, he is panting, but he doesn't notice. His eyes catch a sliver of bright, hot light seeping from the threshold, and as he lifts his arm and curls his fingers to knock, she opens the door.

EPILOGUE
LEAVING US

My FATHER LEFT US slowly, in increments. Perhaps the first sign that he was departing was his cupping his hand over his ear when he spoke with us. But the process had begun long before, in the tiny hair cells in the snail-shaped core of his inner ear, in their infuriating refusal to send electrical signals to his auditory nerve. For decades we witnessed a series of seemingly random events we did not associate with his disappearance from our lives. But the first of these I recall is watching him lean toward sound like one of his daylilies yearning toward the sun.

Each year brought new phenomena and facts we all had to assimilate. When he could no longer hear the nurses in the OR, or see their lips and tongues form words under their surgical masks, he retired a decade earlier than he'd planned; he canceled his season tickets to operas and symphonies, and he declined to attend his granddaughter's theatre performances; he stopped listening to classical records. He couldn't hear that his piano needed tuning, and he banged out discordant chords and glissandos when the notes he was striking also eluded him. In a group, he couldn't tell if there was a break in the conversation in which he might appropriately interject an idea he was pondering while his quick-witted friends were chatting away, so he swung his head from person to person, waiting for the second when no lips were moving to jump in and make his points heard. But more times than not, his companions had already galloped toward the next subject by the time he addressed the preceding one. Whenever he strolled around the stonewalled subdivision, he was startled by the vibrations of an angry horn of an automobile that he couldn't hear when it approached him from behind. He couldn't order for himself in a restaurant, and in public places, when he did talk, his voice was shaky with insecurity and inappropriately loud.

We watched him nosedive into a depression and rail against the silence that was slowly bearing down on him. He'd pivot away from us and leave the room swearing, or push his chair back from the table with a despondent look, as if we had abandoned him. Sometimes he'd slink off into a sulk on his bed upstairs; other times, he'd stomp down the basement stairs to be alone in his study. Often he'd fall asleep in his basement hideaway for an hour or more, then trudge up the steps to ask the rest of us upstairs in the recreation room if we missed him. The truth was we hadn't; we'd become used to his absence.

Increasingly, he couldn't hear even the insistent, high-pitched ring-tone of his hearing aids, which was grating to the rest of us, and one or the other of us had to tell him to turn down the sound. When it sank in that sophisticated technology, even when he used it correctly, was not going to return the world of sound to him, we took turns try-ing to transcribe at least the highlights of the conversations he was missing during family dinners on a plethora of pocket-sized spiral notebooks and scraps of paper from Bertie's phone memo pads and leftover prescription pads. As he lurched and slid from self-conscious-ness to self-pity to moroseness, I began to wonder if he had begun to mourn his own final disappearance. Perhaps he was more prescient than I knew.

I have tried to exactly recall the chronology of what heralded his final days, as if by resurrecting my sense of the order of things, I could resurrect him. But my absence from his daily life and the vagaries of my own memory have blurred my sense of the exact, and I wonder if they have tricked me. I remember his last May. It is the first May of the new millennium. In the Midwest, the dogwoods have burst open, the redbuds' pink lace scrims the brick and stone houses. Bart has been disoriented, has trouble walking, falls on the floor after he takes a bath, again after he lies down in bed. Bertie cannot persuade him to eat or take the dietary supplements she has bought. She is tempted, she says, to take him off his other medications to see if his appetite will pick up, and I wonder if she isn't about ready to give up. It gets worse. When he wakes up at 4 a.m., Bertie does a puzzle with him. "Life is one big puzzle," Bertie says.

One morning, I scroll down to an email from my mother. My father has collapsed onto the floor an hour before, and she is about to call 911. There is a ghostly resignation in her rhetoric. The next day, I am throwing my body onto his to prevent him from ripping out his IVs and catheter. He has suffered two subdural hematomas and then had surgery to ease the blood and fluid between the skull and the brain. And in the confusion that this assault to his cranium and its tender contents, the drugs, and his own idiosyncratic dementia have given him, he thinks he is a prisoner and I am a guard in Africa during the war.

I remember his last October, when the leaves from the three oak trees in the front yard, one for each daughter he'd often say, oranged and curled, and Bart had a heart attack. Disoriented in the hospital, he tells my mother in a frantic voice that he wants to leave; he calls for his girls. I leave my home for St. Louis the next day. He is home from the hospital on his and Bertie's anniversary. My sister Jeannie, who has flown there from New York, and I make a cake for them, which she decorates with pink and yellow icing flowers and green vine leaves. We serve it with champagne. Bart turns toward his wife of sixty years and toasts: "To the most beautiful woman in the universe."

And I remember his final November. At the urging of some of her younger friends, Bertie takes him to see a new doctor, a specialist who is a member of the memory diagnosis team at Washington University, where Bart earned his medical degree a little more than six decades before. Diagnosis: some delirium superimposed on Alzheimer's disease (or vice-versa . . . ? I don't think it matters). He will also have tests for vitamin levels and metabolic activity in addition to CAT scans. He's had a bad week—he's been forgetting who his wife is. She is a stranger who has come to stay with him but whom he has not invited. On top of everything else, the doctor thinks Bart may have had a seizure or stroke. He's been eating very little, which is very unusual for him. But there is a speck of good news: the specialist says that the confusion Bart has had for the last two weeks will probably decrease as the beta blockers leave his system, which they are doing now. The confusion never does decrease.

And I remember his final December. Bart slides into total heart failure but then bounces back a bit after oxygen and medication. My mother, rather apologetically, calls in hospice. She is afraid that *we* aren't ready.

We daughters come as if summoned. When I walk into the recreation room, I have to find a seat on the sofa next to my father amid oxygen tubing and balled-up Kleenexes. My mother is sitting next to him, patting his thigh, trying to get his attention. A cardboard sign is pinned to her chest; its big block letters read: "I am your wife, Bertie." My mother has placed pairs of scissors all over the house, stuck in baskets above the fridge and on a wide fabric ribbon hanging by her desk in the kitchen. She has one pair always by her side so she can slit open his pajama legs and give his swollen feet and ankles, marbled with veins and speckled with the beginnings of blisters, room. His knees hurt, we think, possibly more than his feet. My father and I rub noses in a kind of kiss, but it looks like he is not completely sure whom he is being so intimate with.

During that winter bridging 2000 and 2001, my visits to St. Louis become odd pleasures. I love sitting quietly and alone with my father at random hours, when the earliest morning snow glitters outside the living room picture window, or when, through the bamboo shades, the moonlight stripes the floor of the recreation room. I love helping him into bed, then out again, then in again, then out again much of the night.

The downstairs has been converted to an asylum for the sick and dying. A hospital bed is set up at a right angle from where mine was nearly half a century ago. The rooms are littered with scraps from prescription pads and full sheets of paper that read: "Hear. Aid," "Chair," "I will give you a sponge bath," "Swallow pill"—all in big, black block letters, all printed as if for a third grader. In the living room next to the piano he used to play nocturnes and mazurkas on stands an aluminum table. Plastic medicine bottles and journals and notes with directions and white paper bags for drugs are scattered on it.

Outside, the cactus plants have become mottled like his skin. In the late fall, at the last moment before winter, he always dug up the cacti and carried them inside lovingly. Now I notice that no one has taken the cacti to winter in the basement. They are stiff in the snow. The lily leaves are withered and bowed over with frost.

One morning I set the table for his breakfast, just as he did every day for more than eighty years. I squeeze his shoulder to make him turn from his silent world and set down in front of him his two soft-boiled four-minute eggs, which I've peeled and broken up with a spoon. I write a note that says, "Good morning. I love you." He crumples the paper, stabs it with a fork, and stuffs it into his mouth.

One afternoon the man who took me painting and to operas before I was old enough for school, who taught me how to hit a home run and calculate a light-year, who saved thousands of lives on three continents for hundreds of days during the second world war, shaves off half his mustache, tosses his white underpants onto the carpet each time my mother hands them to him, and bends over on the bed to pull his shirt over his legs, his feet in the sleeves.

Another afternoon I rummage in the St. Louis-damp basement and find one of my dolls. She's now, technically, an antique. She's dressed in pink sheer underpants, like the kind I hid under my slip at my first prom, her arms bent back, primrose-blond curls snarled. I bring her upstairs and show her to my parents. My father reaches for her, studies her as he used to study a tear in the flesh before suturing it, and I dare to hope for a glimmer of memory. As though indeed urged toward recognition, he raises the doll toward his cheek as if to rub her against it, then moves her toward his mouth as if for a kiss. He takes a fierce bite of the curls and spits it out, the yellow strands catching in his teeth.

I'm home in Idaho again when my mother calls me and, weeping, asks me to yell into the phone at my father, to assure him that I'm still alive. He screamed himself awake at 3 a.m. His sobs rolled out in tidal waves. He is certain his three babies are dead, and nothing his wife says can convince him otherwise. I shout, but he doesn't understand. He trembles and howls all day. We are wishing the opposite of what we have been wishing for months. We are wishing for all residue of his memory to be wiped clean away.

The hospice nurse has gently offered my mother the use of morphine for her husband, the love of her life. Bertie is hesitant to give it to him, delays, says it's just a "last resort." I wonder how she defines "last."

But small pleasures weave in and out of these gloomy days. One day, he shakes off his trance on the sofa and stands up, bows slightly to me, stretches out his right arm, lifts the left in invitation for a dance, and in moments we're whirling to the living room, where he had borne me as a bedridden child with a swollen heart (I picture my small arm bent, wrist arced from clutching a doll with primrose-blond hair), somehow gracefully avoiding the corners of the unfamiliar intruding tables and all that has been changed inexorably by the imminence of death. *One* two three, *one* two three, *one* two three—we waltz by the paintings on the walls, the shelves of books with their gilt-embossed bindings, the piano on which he used to play Chopin, my mother's African violets on glass shelves lining the picture window. But it is the even older, immutable things my mind embraces most, like the stone-lined fireplace in the glow of which he read me stories from Shakespeare when I was seven or eight. And his war is here, too: the brass tray he bought his young wife in Africa; coins, mounted on velvet, from the months he pined for her in Europe; the sculpture of an alabaster woman lounging on an alabaster couch that he sent her from England the afternoon before D-Day; twin midnight blue budvases from the newly liberated Mont St. Michel; the oil portrait of him as a young Army major, painted by a then-little-known artist in the Netherlands.

He stops, still in dance position. "All this is so beautiful. Is it mine?" he asks. I nod into the tender convolutions of his neck. Oh, the joy, the awe! He doesn't notice the table with the medicines or the hospital bed.

That last day, my father leans on the kitchen sink, his eyes rolling up toward his scalp, when suddenly he proclaims, "I want you to take me with you." My face muscles twisted so that I don't cry, I kiss the smooth olive skin of his cheeks, look into his eyes, still as brown as the trunks on the pines in Forest Park, then promise I will.

BERTIE CHOSE to have a small private burial for her husband, followed by a more inclusive memorial service. The ceremony was to be under a canopy in Valhalla, the only cemetery in St. Louis they could find in their earlier years that would accommodate couples of different religions. That icy morning, just as we were backing out of the driveway, my mother suddenly asked us to stop the car. She opened the car door and walked the few steps to the magnolia tree by the front walk leading to the house. He had planted that magnolia from a sprout, and now it towered over the curving front walk up the hill from the mailbox to the green door. Bertie pinched the stem of one of its elliptical waxy leaves at its articulation at the branch and, with her other hand, smoothed the blade. When she climbed back into the car, she said not a word. She might have said, "He loved this tree so," or "He would have been happy that I took one of its leaves to his funeral," or something of that order, but we had all learned long ago what spoken words could and could not do, which sounds were necessary and which not.

We ushered my father into the earth in a plain pine box, as unpretentious as he was. Just before the coffin was inched into the ground, my mother rose and laid on the crown of the wood the leaf she had plucked from his magnolia tree.

It wasn't until half a decade later, when I returned to that St. Louis street, that house, that magnolia tree in the moonlight, when I plucked another of its waxy leaves in what was once my parents' dream house to pack it carefully in layers of tissue and to lay it in my backpack to carry it back to Idaho, that I found—not in the V's of the leaf's skeleton, nor in the elliptical curve of its pointed perimeter, not in its waxy undulations, but, perhaps, in the feel of it along my fingertip in the shadows—the vein of my father's story.